GOODNESS NOSE

Invergordon

Dalmore

Black Isle   Elgin

                    Dufftown

                    Speyside
                    Cooperage

INVERNESS

                    Glenlivet

                    Auchenblae

Dalwhinnie   Fettercairn

          Pitlochry

HIGHLANDS   *Angus*

                    DUNDEE

Tullibardine

*Loch
Lomond*   *Highland Line*

Jura   Helensburgh

                    Grangemouth   Leith

Isle of Jura   Greenock   EDINBURGH

Islay   GLASGOW   *R. Clyde*

Glen Scotia   Campbeltown

          LOWLANDS

These are the places and distilleries
that have had the greatest impact on
me in my life journey through
Scotland's whisky landscape. All of
them feature to a greater or lesser
degree in *Goodness Nose*.

Richard Paterson, August 2008.

GOODNESS
NOSE
THE PASSIONATE REVELATIONS
OF A SCOTCH WHISKY
MASTER BLENDER

RICHARD PATERSON AND GAVIN D. SMITH

www.nwp.co.uk

The Angels' Share is an imprint of
Neil Wilson Publishing Ltd
G/2 19 Netherton Avenue
GLASGOW
G13 1BQ

T: 0141 954 8007
F: 0560 150 4806
E: info@nwp.co.uk
W: www.nwp.co.uk

A catalogue record of this book is available
from the British Library.

ISBN: 978-1-906476-15-1

First published in hardback (978-1-903238-67-7) in October 2008.
This edition published in September 2010.

Designed by Mark Blackadder

Printed and bound in Poland.

CONTENTS

To Susie,
Sally, Graeme and Tom

ACKNOWLEDGEMENTS

Over the last four years many people have given Gavin and I their invaluable help towards the preparation of this book. Every effort has been made to acknowledge them but if we have inadvertently missed someone out on the list that follows, we sincerely hope we will be forgiven for this unintentional oversight. I am particularly grateful to my good friend Raymond Davidson of Glencairn Crystal who was largely instrumental in encouraging me to take on this mammoth project in the first case. Without his support we may never even have got started! We are also indebted to Jim Drysdale for his wonderful illustrations at the beginning of each chapter. To everybody concerned, our most grateful thanks.

Tom Aitken, Naeem Akhtar, Rob Allanson, Alistair Anderson, Folke Andersson, Simon Baker, Rachel Barrie, Kathleen Di Benedetto, Bill Bergius, Jim Beveridge, Knut Bie, Ian Black, Margery Browning, Rob Bruce, Ulf Buxrud, Ian Buxton, Jim Campbell, John Campbell, Maureen Campbell, George Christie, Ricky Christie, Willie Cochrane, Ashley Coombes, Douglas Cooper, Trevor Cowan, Charles Craig, Peter Currie, Bob Dalgarno, Jerry Dalton, Raymond, Paul, Scott & Andrew Davidson, Margaret Dewar, Anne Doig, David Doig, Juan Carlos Rincon Dominguez, Heidi Donelon, Lyn Doran, Jim Drysdale, Euan Duguid, Campbell Evans, William Delmé Evans, Robert Fleming, Tom Flocco, Dave Forbes, John Gaffney, Mandy Gedge, Jeannie Gladstone, Graham Goodridge-Cox, Patience Gould, Kenneth Graham, Isabel Graham-Yooll, Donnie Grant, Alan Gray, Martin Green, Chris Greig, Ian Grieve, Patrick Guedj, Paige Guzman, Jim Hanlon, Brian Harkness, Ian Harris, Alistair Hart, Ian Hart, Stuart R. Harvey, John Hatton, Margaret Heads, Michael Heads, Halvor Heuch, Charlotte Hey, Robert Hicks, Pauline Higgins, Terry Hillman, Phillip Hills, Axel Himer, Frances Horder, Teimei Horuchi, Dave Hughes, Turnbull Hutton, Vivian Imerman, Richard Joynson, Jack Kelly-Clark, Jim Kokoris, Seiichi Koshimizu, Fred H. Laing, John Lamont, Stewart Lawrie, Jackie Leck, Mike Lees, Billy Leighton, Ros Lewis, Jack Ligertwood, Graeme Lindsay, Christine Logan, Bill Lumsden, Alan Lundie, Alex Lungley, Michael Lunn, Colin MacDonald, John MacDonald, Ranald Macdonald, Lord Norman Macfarlane, Daphne Mackenzie, Donald Mackinlay, Charles MacLean, John MacLean, Ian MacMillan, Ita Macshannon,

Daljit Mahal, Craig Mair, Dr Vijay Mallya, Roddy Martine, Salve Mateus, Norman Mathison, Laurie McCall, Roderick McCall, Giles McDonagh, Jim McEwan, George McGee, Frank McHardy, Robert McIndoe, Alastair McIntosh, Dr Gary McKay, Eddie McLaughlin, Kevin McLaughlin, Ken McLean, Val McMurtrie, Brian Megson, Raymond Miquel, Ian Millar, Michael Miller, Sally Miller, Wallace Milroy, Brendan Monks, Tom Montgomery, Dr Nick Morgan, Susan Morrison, Michael Moss, Ben Mundell, Catherine Mundell, James Mundell, Douglas Murray, Jim Murray, Malcolm Murray, Adam Nice, Margaret Nicol, Willie Nielson, Martine Nouet, Paul Pacult, Prof Geoff Palmer, Ian Palmer, James Paterson, Russell Paterson, John Paul, Moyra Peffer, Fabian Pfister, Michelle Pizzi, Christian Porta, Angela Forsgren D'Orazio, John Raeside, John Ramsay, Jim Rankin, Murdo Reed, Damian Riley-Smith, Tony Riley-Smith, Ken Robertson, Maureen Robinson, John Roscrow, Christian H. Rosenberg, Dominic Roskrow, Colin Ross, Joan Ross, Stuart Ross, John Russell, Peter Russell, Dr Alan Rutherford OBE, Ken Sato, Shigeo Sato, Andrew Anderson-Scott, Andrew J. Scott, Colin Scott, Jacqui Seargeant, Ewan Shand, Charles Shaw, Joanne Simcock, Sukhinder Singh, Drew Sinclair, Helen Sinclair, Martin Skelton, Yvonne Sloan, Norman Smith, Ruth Smith, Stan Smith, Godfrey Spence, David Stewart, Jim Swan, Morag Swanson, Noel Sweeney, Christine Tait, Reg Tait, Valerie Tait, Willie Tait, Douglas Taylor, Willie Taylor, Stewart Thomson, Julia Thorold, Misado Udo, Claive Vidiz, Alistair Walker, Prof Andrew Walker, Billy Walker, Karen Walker, Stewart Walker, Paul Walsh, Tony Ward, Paul Waterson, Ian Williams, David Williamson, Neil Wilson, Alan Winchester, Julian P. Van Winkle III, Dieter H. Wirtz, Tim Wood, Margaret Wright and David Wrigley.

FOREWORD

Since Alfred Barnard first published his epic book *The Distilleries of the United Kingdom* in 1887, many other fine books about Scotch whisky have been made available to the whisky lover. Over the centuries our national drink has been inspiring writers, scholars and distillers around the world. Every whisky writer has made his own inimitable contribution to furthering the knowledge of this wonderful spirit.

Now for the first time it is the turn of a blender to share his fascinating insights into the art of whisky blending. Richard Paterson is not just any blender – he is a Master Blender with true passion for his craft, and his roots go back over three generations of whisky blenders. He began appreciating whisky with his father at the tender age of eight – whisky almost literally runs in his blood. Now with over 40 years experience, 'The Nose' as he is affectionately known in the trade, has become one of Scotland's most admired and respected blenders and his love of Scotch has taken him around the world. During his long career Richard has received a host of accolades – Blender of the Year, Industry Leader of the Year, Distiller of the Year, Diageo's Achievement of the Year award, and Master Keeper of the Quaich, to name but a few.

Although I have known Richard for many years, the first occasion I experienced his passion for whisky was back in 1993 when he was the guest speaker at our Dinner Club's 30th Anniversary dinner. Not surprisingly, Richard took the opportunity to compare this milestone to the preparation of a rare 30-year-old blend. Within minutes he had captivated and enthralled us, not only with his in-depth, historical knowledge of Scotch whisky, but in particular his fascinating insight into the art of whisky blending. It was indeed a night to remember.

Such knowledge and passion cannot be forgotten. It must be recorded and passed on. With such interest in Scotch whisky today there has never been a better time to release such a book and delve into the mysteries which surround whisky blending. For the first time Richard has unlocked his sample room door to us and thrown away the key to expose its many secrets. Secrets which have in many ways remained hidden since the mid to late 19th century when Andrew Usher first began pioneering his 'blended' whiskies.

And what better way to do it than with one of Scotland's greatest whisky writers – Gavin D. Smith. Gavin has had an illustrious career in whisky writing, regularly contributing to many publications on the subject and writing no fewer than ten whisky books.

These two whisky gurus have combined their talents to give us a unique insight into the art of blending and what it takes to become a Master Blender. It is an illuminating and memorable journey. Like a great blended Scotch I heartily recommend you sip and savour the contents of this book. Taste the passion and feel the wonderful glow of that spirit inside you.

Lord Macfarlane of Bearsden, K.T.
Hon. Life President Diageo.

Chapter One
RAW SPIRIT –
THE BIRTH OF THE BLENDER

'The noblest of drinks, it is Scotland in a bottle; invigorating and relaxing, tradition and innovation; sun and mist – and above all, a great dram!' } THE RT. HON. VISCOUNT THURSO

My father always told me, 'never stop nosing – every sample has a story to tell'.

Owww! 'What was that for?' One moment I was standing there with a glass of this mysterious golden liquid in my hand, the next minute my father was giving me a clip across the back of my head. I was only eight years old, and this was my first taste of Scotch whisky. What a start! But it was one brief moment in my life I would never forget.

To tell the truth, he didn't hit me that hard. He did it to get my full attention. He certainly succeeded. This little drama had occurred at my father's Stockwell Bond in Glasgow which was the heart of his whisky company ... WR Paterson Ltd. He had taken my twin brother Russell and I to introduce us to some of the mysteries of Scotch whisky. It was the love of his life.

During our visit to the bond, our father's infatuation became obvious from the way he cradled the glass in the palm of his hand, looking at the contents with a mixture of reverence and passion. He even closed his eyes, as he gently nosed it. It was almost as though he was mesmerised by the spirit. Needless to say, my brother and I both thought this was extraordinarily funny. It was just a question of which one of us was going to crack first and burst out laughing. Not surprisingly ... it was me. This appeared to break the spell. Suddenly my father passed me the glass.

'Right son! Since you seem to think this is so amusing, tell me what you think of this whisky?'

'What do you mean, dad?'

'Listen boy, I want you to smell this whisky and tell me how you would describe it.' Still smiling, I clumsily put my nose deep into the glass and sniffed it quickly.

'Well?' he said, impatiently as I hesitated.

I simply had no way of describing it, so my natural reply was, 'Well dad ... I don't really smell anything.' That's when I got the whack on the back of my head. As you might gather, my father was not the most patient of men.

'Listen son! You're just not thinking about this, are you? What I'm looking for is for you to tell me something about the whisky. In simple terms ... is it dry or is it sweet, is it heavy or is it light?'

'Now do you understand? ... but smell it slowly ... '

I nodded, but thought to myself why didn't he tell me that in the first place? If he had, I might have avoided this sore head. In a matter of seconds I was able to say the whisky seemed to smell sweet, and had a certain heaviness about it.

'Correct! Now you're talking! But listen ... when you say sweetness ... is it as sweet as your chocolate bar, or more like a sweet fruit? Peaches or grapes, for example. Is it as heavy in body and as fleshy and weighty as your grumpy grandfather? Always remember – take your time when you're nosing whisky, never rush it. Let the spirit reveal its identity ... its personality ... its character. Alright son, well done! Now come on and I'll show you both where we bottle it. After all, this is what pays for your education.'

And, on reflection, that day was the very start of my education into the world of whisky.

✳   ✳   ✳

I was born in Glasgow on 31st January 1949. Bonnie Prince Charlie had died in Rome on 31st January 1788 and poor Guy Fawkes was hung, drawn and quartered on the same day in

1606. Friday, at 11am, I believe. So it was quite an auspicious date even before I came along. 1949 was not only a vintage year for would-be whisky blenders, but also for Champagne and Bordeaux. The weather conditions in France were ideal for the grape harvest that season. It was a significant year, too, for the Scotch whisky industry. You could say it marked the start of the period when the first real signs of revival were seen after the dark years of the Second World War, when very little whisky distilling had taken place in Scotland. 1949 was the year in which there were the very first stirrings of new life. A new beginning. Stirrings that would lead during the next three decades to a great expansion of Scotch whisky production and an increasing global awareness of this liquid gold. The future looked bright.

Speaking of global awareness, 1949 saw the giant Canadian company Seagram acquire the old Aberdeen family firm of Chivas Brothers Ltd, going on to purchase Strathisla Distillery in Keith on Speyside. The Canadians had already established a major presence in the Scotch whisky industry before the war. The second Canadian distilling giant Hiram Walker & Sons of Ontario had bought into various Scottish distilling companies including George Ballantine & Son, and then gone a stage further by building their own grain distillery at Dumbarton in 1938.

However, the arrival of Seagram heralded the start of greater overseas investment in Scotch whisky, and much more North American, European and Far Eastern money came into the business as the years went on. Nonetheless, the vast Distillers Company Ltd, that huge, aggressive predator, remained indomitable. Nobody could touch them. After all, they were 'The DCL' and they demanded respect.

For the first time since the war ended, whisky distillers returned to their pre-war level of barley allocation in 1949, which at least meant they could in theory be making as much whisky as they had been before the war.

The country desperately needed to earn income from exports, and Scotch whisky was a key export commodity. *Harpers Wine & Spirit Gazette* noted on 25th February 1949, 'Under the agreement made last May between the Scotch Whisky Association (SWA) and the Food Ministry nearly 80% of whisky withdrawals are to be earmarked for export. It is probable that this agreement, with some modification, may be continued for some years. A valuable goodwill is, therefore, being built up for Scotch whisky in most of the world's markets.'

The Taylor family must have also felt the stirrings of fresh activity in the Scotch whisky industry when they opened their Speyside Cooperage in the years following the end of the Second World War. Casks, reliable coopered casks, would be needed for the distilleries. Blair Athol Distillery in the beautiful Perthshire town of Pitlochry re-opened, having been bought before the war by Bells of Perth. Also in Perthshire, Tullibardine Distillery started production. It had been converted from a derelict brewery by William Delmé-Evans, who was later responsible for rebuilding the Isle of Jura Distillery. Both distilleries would play an important part later in my life.

1949 was also the year in which Compton Mackenzie's great comic novel *Whisky Galore* was made into a classic movie. When I think

Naturally my father's favourite blends ... even when dispensed from a drip! (see pages 117–8)

about this marvellous Scottish film today it fills me with emotion and stirs me with nostalgic passion. It was the first time Scotch whisky was being seen on film by millions of people. What an advert! In my mind's eye I picture wonderfully labelled bottles, encased in wood, being ferried ashore by islanders in their tiny, overloaded boats. Today, bottles salvaged from the SS *Politician* (which sank off the Hebridean island of Eriskay on Wednesday 5th February 1941) are very highly prized collectors items, despite the uncertainty of their contents.

While the tranquillity of the Outer Hebrides had been disturbed by the busy antics of a cosmopolitan film crew and company of actors, back in my boyhood home of industrial Glasgow the noise and the bustle, the grime and the smell, had never really changed.

I recall as a boy, whenever I was taken into the heart of the city it seemed to be in a state of perpetual motion. Trams, black saloon cars, even horses and carts, appeared to be everywhere. Around Buchanan Street and St Vincent Street, in Glasgow's commercial centre, businessmen were dashing around in black jackets, with stiff white collars, umbrellas and bowler hats. But the skyline reminded me of another Glasgow. Smoke from a thousand chimneys never allowed me to forget this was an industrial city where poverty was part of life. For many, life was hard, but there were always consolations. The Saturday night dance halls, the chance of a 'click', pints of heavy, and, of course, the wee drams. Glasgow was very much alive with the clamour of shipbuilding and heavy engineering. But Glasgow was also very much a whisky city, with bottling halls and bonded warehouses spread along the banks of the River Clyde.

Amongst these was my father's bond in Stockwell Lane, where my brother and I made that first memorable encounter with Scotch whisky.[1] On that occasion we stood in the narrow cobbled street that was the centre of my father's working world. Our family name was proudly emblazoned above the big, heavy, black sliding doors of the bond. Was I impressed? ... not really! This was his lifeblood and I was too young to appreciate it then, but I still had a sense of pride knowing it was part of our family, our heritage.

After Russell and I had gone through our whisky initiation, and the effects of the whack across the back of my head were beginning to wear off, we were taken into the bottling hall. Immediately I was consumed by the overpowering smell of Scotch whisky. Yuck! I thought I was going to be sick, so I focused my mind on the two bottling lines which confronted me, like two giant robot arms. They were busy filling bottles of Paterson's Best Blended Scotch Whisky, and the clatter and clink of glass against glass was deafening. I thought surely the bottles must explode any minute now. It certainly took my mind off the

sickness. Suddenly, there was silence. What seemed like hundreds of girls who had been totally engrossed in working on the lines were now staring at us. What was so special about us? I didn't know. Then bursts of giggles and whispers broke the silence, and we were quickly moved on. No doubt at their tea break the visit of the boss's sons would be a topic of conversation. Needless to say, to an eight-year-old boy this was all *very* embarrassing!

From the bottling hall we were led through one of the main doors into the inner sanctum of Stockwell Bond where thousands of casks were lying. As soon as the huge sliding doors rumbled shut behind us everything went dark until my eyes adjusted to the dim light coming from the gas lamps mounted on the walls which were black with fungus. I thought it was like a prison dungeon. It was mysterious and rather frightening. What *was* going on here? I was immediately aware of the coldness and dampness that clung to the walls and even to my clothes. It sent a shiver down my spine. It seemed such an inhospitable place. Its silence reminded me of a graveyard, but the coffins here were filled with another spirit which was peacefully sleeping. Not even the hum and bustle of the nearby city streets could awaken it.

We walked between the dark stows, crammed with every shape and size of cask. Butts, hogsheads and barrels[2]. The heads of

1 The Stockwell Bond was demolished in 1986 to make way for the St Enoch's Centre, completed in May 1989.

2 A butt contains approximately 108 gallons (491 litres), and is the largest cask regularly used for whisky maturation. A hogshead holds approximately 55 gallons (250 litres), and is the most common size of cask used by distillers. A barrel is the smallest vessel used for whisky maturation, having a capacity of around 40 gallons (180 litres).

the casks were marked with mysterious letters and numbers that meant nothing to me. It was a perfect home for spiders, as I brushed away web after web from my face; not surprising, as some of these casks had been lying for as long as 25 years. I was told there were as many as 26,000 casks in the bond, and for an eight-year-old that was such an enormous number I thought the rows and rows of casks must stretch forever.

One thing you could not fail to notice was an overpowering aroma. It was a mixture of maturing spirit evaporating from the casks, blending with the rancid smell of stagnant water that lay in puddles on the pitted concrete floor. It was not just water that lay in the puddles, either. I could not help noticing a number of dead rats. I wondered how people could possibly work in this environment.

One of them was the warehouse manager, 'Papa' Kelly, a large, kindly old man, who had been given the task of showing us around. During our tour he told us all about the different kinds of casks, and how they influenced the character of the whisky. They had previously been used to hold sherry, port and even wine, which had been absorbed into the wood.

To bring this point alive for us, he removed the cork bung from a nearby butt using nothing more than one of his giant hands. Taking the valinch[3], he dropped it into the cask. There was a wonderful 'plopping' noise as the steel broke the surface of the liquid. After twice plunging it rapidly into the spirit he withdrew the 'thief', as he called it,

and poured the contents into a copper jug. He tipped some of the liquid into one of his huge, tobacco-stained hands and asked us to smell it. 'Look at the colour', he said. 'See how dark it is. That's the whisky drawing the sherry from the wood. Can you smell the nutty sweetness from it?' I quickly said 'yes, yes I can, Mr Kelly', in case I was going to get another clip. I certainly did not fancy that, having seen the size of his hands.

Even though my father and Papa Kelly thought all of this was extraordinarily interesting and exciting, *I* thought it was time to go home ... but by the same token, it was a day I would never forget. It had aroused something inside of me; something special. My *'raw spirit'* had been awakened. That wonderful smell of Scotch whisky would be with me for the rest of my life!

*   *   *

The family firm of WR Paterson Limited had been founded by my grandfather, William Roberton Paterson, in 1933, the year Prohibition ended in the USA. It was based at Stockwell Lane, which was not far from the city centre, but also close to the River Clyde. Whiskies were brought in by sea, particularly from Campbeltown, and they arrived at the Broomielaw, on the River Clyde, which was the heart and soul of Glasgow's maritime trade. Paterson's warehouses were close by, and most of the firm's whisky came in by ship, though some arrived by lorry or even horse and cart. Many of the other whisky bonds, such as Black & White in Eglinton Street and Whyte & Mackay in Midland Street, were situated close together in that area.

---

3 A long, stainless steel tube used to draw samples of whisky from casks.

Whisky runs in my blood, thanks to my grandfather William Roberton Paterson who moved from trading in coal into whisky blending.

You'll see from his photograph that my grandfather looks an archetypal Victorian *pater familias*; firmly set in his ways, self-confident, egotistical and quick to anger. But he was a man who successfully produced and sold a variety of blended whiskies, including Old Blairmhor. He was always seeking perfection for his blends, and was not afraid to experiment with sherry and port wine casks. After all, competition in the Scotch whisky industry during those early years was just as fierce as it is today – you could never be complacent. Standards had to be maintained – the customer remained KING!

Despite the damage inflicted on the Scotch whisky industry by the Second World War, my grandfather was still able to hand over his business to my father in 1956. Keen to make his own mark and improve the company's fortunes, one of the new ventures my father embarked on was to acquire the agency for Balblair Distillery in the far north of Scotland. This very traditional Highland malt distillery was located at Edderton, by the Cromarty Firth, and was owned by Bertie Cumming, a Banff solicitor and County Clerk. My father also took on the agency for Holsten beer, which he imported very successfully, and handled small brands such as Barrie's Lime Juice, which was produced and sold around Glasgow. In addition to having these agencies and producing his own Paterson's Blended

'A good deal depends on the broker,' was one of my father's many aphorisms.

Best Scotch Whisky, he also wanted to be original, and do something different. It was a competitive world, and in order to survive you had to be innovative. Since books played an important part in our family life, in particular encyclopaedias, he came up with the idea of a ceramic 'book bottle'. Instead of being filled with knowledge it was filled with spirit. For example, *The Spirit of England* naturally contained gin, *The Spirit of Portugal* was filled with port, while sherry was *The Spirit of Spain*. Those with a thirst for educating their palates could collect the whole series! The most popular volume was, of course, *The Spirit of Scotland*, which contained one of dad's favourite blends.

This new venture captured the public imagination, and was further enhanced when the BBC approached my father with a view to featuring one of the book bottles in a new television comedy series called Whacko! It starred the great comedian Jimmy Edwards as a bibulous headmaster, still remembered for his magnificent handlebar moustache. Every time the drunken, jovial headmaster went into his study, instead of taking one of the real books off the shelf, he took down this ceramic book, which looked like a normal book from its 'spine', opened it and poured himself a large whisky.

Blending and bottling obviously played a major part in my father's life, and he therefore retained a whole variety of single malts and grain whiskies at his Stockwell Bond. However, broking was really the lifeblood of the business. Whisky was in short supply in these austere, post-war years, and the role of the broker was to act as a 'middle man' between distillers, blenders and bottlers. I remember his desk being littered with notes of whisky parcels available for purchase that day, which he had scribbled hurriedly during an apparently never-ending round of frantic phone calls. A judicious purchase and a quick sale could be highly profitable.

It was all about personal contact with other whisky brokers. People like Willie Lundie, Terry and Hymie Hillman, Bobby McCall and Peter Russell. These were the broking magnates of the day. The wheelers and dealers, the 'Mister Ten Per Cent' men. They say that whisky runs in seven-year cycles of boom and bust. When the market was good they made big money, and when it was bad there was no shortage of surplus whisky in which to drown their sorrows.

Good times or bad, there was always 'The Lunch'. That was when some of the major deals took place; they could start at noon and last the whole of the day. Who said 'Lunch is for wimps?' It certainly was not then. Parcels of whisky were bought and sold to the accompaniment of clattering cutlery and the clink of glasses in Glasgow's The 101, Malmaison, Ferrari's, The Fountain and the Rogano. Given the pressures of modern business, I look back with nostalgia on those golden times. No matter the state of the market, there was never a bad lunch. When he came home in the evening with whisky on his breath at the conclusion of a particularly successful lunch

he would focus on me and say, 'Well son, a good deal depends on the broker.'

We originally grew up in Maxwell Drive, in the Glasgow suburb of Pollokshields, where my father's business was originally located at 11 Forth Street. But when the 1950's whisky boom was in full swing, we moved out to Helensburgh, on the Clyde coast. We lived in a large Victorian house called 'Northwood' in Upper Sinclair Street, near the station. One reason for its name was it had a lovely garden filled with magnificent trees. The house was later taken over by the Navy and subsequently became a retirement home. I was nine years old when we moved, and family life seemed good. One advantage of Helensburgh was that it boasted two highly regarded schools. Russell and I attended Larchfield, while my older sister Margery went to St Bride's. Perhaps more importantly, however, it gave my father access to another of his great loves, the sea. He kept his beloved boat, the *Russpat*, moored at Garelochhead, eight miles from Helensburgh. She was a white, 75-ft converted 'air-sea rescue launch', which looked magnificent in the water.

As well as providing many enjoyable family holidays, which naturally included our West Highland Terrier, Sheila, the *Russpat* also helped to entertain some of my father's most favoured clients. Northwood, too, was used for many parties and general socialising, along with orchestral rehearsals with which my mother was heavily involved.

My parents' parties were very much out of bounds for Russell, Margery and me. We were lovingly looked after by 'Wee May from Muckhart', our maid, but really our second mother, since she spoilt us rotten. She might have been small but she had a big heart for all of us – we loved her very much. The morning after one of these grand affairs Russ and I would explore the scene of devastation. Our nostrils were assailed by stale cigarette and cigar smoke, the scent of Chanel No 5, but also the scent of whisky and red wine in abandoned glasses. Slices of shrivelled lemon, cocktail sticks, maraschino cherries and olives would be scattered around the mahogany drinks cabinet and on top of the grand piano.

When we had breakfast strange accents could often be heard around the table. French, German, South African. On one occasion two of my father's clients, Louis Derksun from France and George Robertson from South Africa, were staying with us. As far as I was concerned, they could have been from the moon, the way they were speaking.

This was sociability above and beyond the call of business, but then my father was always a generous man who rewarded long and loyal service with signet rings for male employees and necklaces for the women, all bearing the family pelican crest. He liked to be surrounded by as many of his associates as possible. These included notable whisky figures like George Christie, who would eventually take control of McGavigan's Bond in Bonhill, Dumbarton, and subsequently go on to create the North of Scotland Distillery Co Ltd, with a grain distillery at Cambus near Alloa. Eventually, of course, he built the Speyside Distillery up at Kingussie. Work began on its construction in 1962, but there was not always a great urgency about it, and the first spirit did not flow until 12th December 1990. My father and George were exceptionally close, perhaps because of their shared naval backgrounds, so

when George's son, Ricky, was born, my father became his godfather. George is now in his 80s, and remains one of the great characters of the Scotch whisky industry.

Another great entrepreneur was Ian Hart, who joined my father as assistant broker when the business was based in Pollokshields. He was one of three brothers who have all made their mark in Scotch whisky. Donald and Alistair subsequently ran a successful independent bottling business focusing on limited aged single malt editions. Ian was the dynamic founder of Hart Brothers, the family business, but has now developed other successful commercial ventures. Even their father helped out by removing the whisky and wine stains from our teeth, since he ran a successful dental practice in Glasgow's Paisley Road West.

The convivial company of people like George Christie and Ian Hart meant that it was not uncommon for my father to return home well into the evening. He drank on a regular basis, and would possibly have one dram before lunch, one during the afternoon, and then a few more before he left the office to drive home. There were no breathalysers during that time, of course, and therefore people really drank quite liberally. They were not all alcoholics, they simply enjoyed their drink. It was a way of life.

Russ and I would lie awake and listen to the familiar sound of the tyres of dad's car scrunching on gravel as he arrived home. Another burnt dinner welcomed him. Later, we would hear his footsteps on the stairs, and the occasional stumble, then pretend to be asleep as he walked into our bedroom. When he kissed Russ and I goodnight, we felt the stubble of his chin against our faces, and the smell of whisky on his breath was something we became pretty familiar with. So I was not exactly enamoured of whisky during those early years, and had no real desire to go into the whisky industry. Alcoholism was a serious problem and from a personal point of view I was very much aware of the effects of whisky on my own father. Life could be tough for the young whisky executive, but on the domestic front at times it must also have been hard for my mother bringing up a young family. Yet I never heard her complain. She was a proud, determined woman.

So as a boy I was aware of whisky from my father's breath, from the socialising I saw, and from my visits to the bond, but I was also aware of it from the whisky adverts that were blazoned on street hoardings throughout the city. I remember Haig, Red Hackle, White Horse and Johnnie Walker, and in particular the Black & White adverts, featuring the black Scottie and the white West Highland terriers.

Other adverts appealed to my boyish sense of adventure – I was intrigued by the Long John Highland Chieftain, who looked so noble and distinguished. Emblems and logos appeared to be the order of the day, and my father's company was no exception. Our family crest featured an image of a pelican nobly feeding its young with the blood from its breast. Below was the Latin proverb *Dominus Providebit* – 'The Lord Will Provide'. When the lean years came later it was fervently hoped that the proverb would sincerely live up to its promise.

Unfortunately, these lean years were not far away. 1961 was one of Bordeaux's finest vintage years, but this was quickly overshadowed by the great freeze of 1963. This was also the beginning of a bleak time for whisky brokers. By this stage, most of the major companies such as DCL, Hiram Walker, Seagram and Teacher's had been able to build up their own filling stocks, and therefore the role of the broker no longer played such a prominent part in the Scotch whisky industry. The pressure was on. The golden years were slowly coming to an end. Would the broker manage to survive?

Sadly, one thing that did not survive was my parents' marriage, and as a result of this, the house in Helensburgh had to go. As you can imagine, Margery, Russell and I found this a very upsetting period of our lives. The comfortable sense of family life we had taken for granted was gone forever. Suddenly we were all adults.

Most significant for me was the split with my twin brother. This was the first time we had been parted since birth. Russell was sent to Pangbourne Nautical College, near Reading, in deepest Berkshire. This was a way of following in our father's footsteps. One of his most familiar sayings was, 'Sail the seas, my boys, and see the world'. During the war, he had done just that. Now it was Russell's turn.

As for me, at least I was not sent as far from home as Russell. I was despatched to Eshton Hall School, in the small village of Gargrave, seven miles from Skipton, in the Yorkshire Dales. There were no Wee Mays here to help me now. I was among the English! Would they accept me? No longer was it 'Richard'... it was 'Hey Jockstrap, are they all like you in Dr Finlay's Casebook? I thought we built Hadrian's Wall to keep the likes of

My father constantly reminded me it was Scotch whisky that paid for my education.

you out!' Thankfully, there were some other boys from Scotland, which helped to ease the inevitable strain of living in this foreign land.

It was essential not to remain an outsider, and sporting activities were one way to become involved, so I joined teams for cricket, rugby and cross-country running. I had the necessary ambition and drive to succeed at sport. However, this was not reflected in my academic work which was never top of my priorities, although I developed a love of foreign languages, art, geography and of course history, all of which have stayed with me to this day. I always loathed maths with a vengeance!

On leaving Eshton Hall I returned to Scotland to attend The Glasgow Tutorial College in Hillhead. Meanwhile, my brother was high on the seas with the Ben Line, and my sister was finishing her university degree. Although we were expected to achieve a high number of 'O' grades to equip us for the big business world which was supposed to be waiting for us out there, I was not in any particular hurry. I had another agenda … parties, drinking and other pleasures. After all, this was the Swinging Sixties. Mateus Rosé, Hirondel wine, Spanish Sauternes were becoming part of the scene. I was beginning to get a taste for it.

After college, and not being sure what I really wanted to do, I approached Kodak about a job, as I was very keen on photography. Perhaps sensing my lack of real commitment, they turned me down. I then considered the possibility of a career in the hotel business. At that stage the ambivalent attitude to drink which I had from my earlier years meant I certainly was not in any hurry to get into the whisky industry.

I took a job at The Atholl Palace Hotel in Pitlochry, north of Perth, where I was initially employed as a lift attendant cum hall porter. If you wanted to get decent tips, you had to treat the guests with real subservience. Apart from school, this was the first time I had been away from home on my own, and in living and working in the Atholl Palace I entered into a totally different world to anything I was used to.

Some of the wealthiest guests, especially American tourists, frequented this magnificent hotel, which boasted among its many amenities fishing, shooting and tennis. It really was almost a palace. It even had its own resident ghost, who became so troublesome during my time there that a local minister had to be called in to conduct an exorcism. I never saw the ghost myself. I was more interested in the other kind of spirit, and Blair Athol and Edradour distilleries were both nearby to satisfy that kind of spiritual need.

It may seem surprising now, but during my time in Pitlochry I never visited either of these local distilleries, but in those days nobody would ever have contemplated doing so. There was an air of mystery about them. They were closed to the general public. If you had told the manager of Blair Athol that one day more than a million people would visit Scottish distilleries each year, he would have accused you of having taken one dram too many. After all, distilleries were really just factories – and dark, dingy ones at that.

The distillery manager was an important figure in the community. In a town like Pitlochry three of the most highly respected people were the minister, the doctor, and the distillery manager. That hierarchy prevailed for many, many years. In those days, there was still a sense of 'knowing your place', and this was particularly evident in the Atholl Palace Hotel. I was taught that you had to look after the guests and cater to their every whim, always showing them respect and deference. You had to remain smart at all times. Crisply ironed shirts and shoes you could see your face in. The customer here was king ... being disrespectful to the guests or even the hotel manager was likely to lead to instant dismissal. When I first saw the film *Titanic* I was instantly reminded of that world!

I became aware for the first time that people who held the same sort of job as myself relied on this employment for their long-term livelihood, and the hotel was actually their home as well as their workplace. When I worked at The Atholl Palace Hotel, it closed down in November and it did not reopen until April the following year. It was a seasonal business, so many of the staff had to find alternative work during the long winter months. Times could be very hard for them. Being rehired was not guaranteed. For the first time this made me think life out in the big, real world is tough. If you want money you have to earn it, and being a hall porter was never going to make me a wealthy man. The question was would I make the hotel business my career? Certainly in the short term I had learnt many different aspects of the hotel trade, the one that interested me most being cellar management.

I quickly realised that as far as wine and spirits were concerned, none of the staff really knew much, apart from the wine waiter himself, and even his knowledge was limited. My natural instinct would be to find a book and learn more about the subject by reading, but the range of wine titles we take for granted today was unknown then. Copies of André Simon's books were available if you really knew where to look, but Hugh Johnson's seminal *World Atlas of Wine* was not to appear until 1971.

I quickly learned to differentiate between the shapes of the different bottles – Bordeaux, Burgundy, Alsace and Champagne – but I still knew nothing about the liquid that was inside them. Even though my family had been consumed by the drinks industry for two generations, when it came to wine it was rapidly becoming apparent to me that it was going to take years to acquire even a basic working knowledge. I was determined to overcome this shortcoming, but it was not going to be easy. However, like anything I am really interested in, I hoped my burning determination to succeed would allow my raw spirit to shine through ... only time would tell.

I was in Pitlochry for about six months and I even took a second job washing up at the nearby Glengarry Hotel, a real tourist trap for the bus parties ... though their tips were hopeless! I certainly worked hard, but this was compensated for by the many parties and boozing sessions that were never hard to find. I have never been much of a singer, and there was still a lot to discover about wine, but thankfully I learnt a great deal about women during my time in Pitlochry. I loved the place, and still do to this day. It was not just because of the women, it truly is beautiful, the 'Heart of Scotland' – situated among rivers, lochs, mountains and pine forests.

Whenever I drive north up the A9, going to Dalmore and Invergordon distilleries, as I cross the River Tay near Dunkeld, with Ben Vrackie and Beinn à Ghlo towering in the distance I always feel I am truly in the highlands. During the autumn months, passing through the Vale of Atholl, my senses are aroused by the rich, spicy, tangy scent of burning pine and the unmistakable sight of abundant purple-pink rosebay willowherb,

lining the roadside. It is a wonderful, evocative smell that fills me with nostalgia. At that time of year the copper leaves of the beech trees almost take on the colour of burnished stills. Nothing can beat Scotland in September.

I was quite content working at the Atholl Palace. The money was reasonable, the tips helped, and I had made some good friends. I was even thinking of forging an actual career in hotel management when a phone call changed everything.

'What are you doing up there, boy? Do you intend to work as a hall porter for the rest of your life?' It was a while since I had heard from my father, and he sounded just as impatient and grumpy as he had that day all those years ago back in Stockwell Bond.

'Listen son, one of the whisky companies I deal with here has just got a vacancy for an office boy. You've got an interview next Thursday morning. So start packing!'

The tranquillity of Pitlochry was suddenly shattered for me. In my mind I was back in the bustling centre of Glasgow already. I felt an instant fear and apprehension welling up inside me. This was a big step to take. Would it mean I was finally following in my father's footsteps? I wasn't sure if that was what I really wanted. My head was buzzing with unanswered questions as I boarded the train for Glasgow.

J·DRYSDALE

Chapter Two
MATURATION BEGINS

'What could be more pleasurable than the company of good friends, enjoying good food, good conversation and above all, good whisky! I'll drink to that!' JOHNNY BEATTIE, COMEDIAN AND ACTOR

The day of reckoning was suddenly upon me. I felt sick. There was no turning back now. This was the real world, where a living had to be made. Dad always said Glasgow was paved with gold … liquid gold, and this was my first chance to taste it. More importantly, it could be the start of a career. A third generation of whisky blenders. My heart was pounding as I walked up the seemingly never-ending flight of stone steps leading from Buchanan Street subway station. My mind was in utter turmoil. What kind of job would it be? Did I want this job? Did I even want to be back in Glasgow?

The interview my father had arranged was with the small whisky firm of Gillies & Co, who were based at 138 Renfield Street, located in the very heart of the city, adjacent to the Pavilion Theatre.

Even if I failed this important interview I was comforted by the fact that at least I had made an effort, having spent practically all night ironing and polishing … smart blue suit, crisp white shirt, blue silk polka dot tie, shoes you could see your face in, and, the *pièce de résistance*, a matching handkerchief. But this was Glasgow. It was September 1966. If I'd walked into the Sarry Heid[4] for my Dry Martini that evening it would not have been appreciated by the local hard men. I needed to focus on the ordeal ahead. The managing director of Gillies & Co was David Wolfe, and

he was going to be interviewing me for the position of office junior.

As I turned into Renfield Street and approached the company building I was taken aback. It looked more like a church hall than the offices of a whisky company, with its brightly-coloured stained glass windows set in heavy mahogany frames. I stopped in my tracks in front of the building. The gold lettering of 'A Gillies & Co' seemed to shine down on me intimidatingly. I gave one last nervous cough, tightened the knot in my tie and entered to the sound of a loud, clinking doorbell. I walked down the short, dark-panelled passage which led into Gillies' offices. It reminded me of something out of a Dickens novel. Was I in a time warp?

Before I could gather my thoughts I was greeted by Miss Macmillan, a well-upholstered spinster. 'Mr Wolfe will see you directly', she said, 'he's waiting for you.' I was immediately ushered into his office. David Wolfe sat behind a huge, dark oak desk, deeply absorbed in reading a report while puffing heavily on his pipe. He was a powerfully built, broad-shouldered man, immaculately dressed in a dark blue worsted pin-stripe suit. He did not look up. A dense cloud of powerful aromatic tobacco smoke hung in the air above him.

'Take a seat, I need to finish reading this, I'll be with you in a minute', he mumbled. Still he did not look up. I did as I was told, and wondered whether I should cross my legs so that I would feel more relaxed for the ordeal ahead. I was trying to be cool, but failing miserably, as I felt beads of cold sweat on my forehead. Suddenly he looked up, and smiled at me. So he is human after all, I thought.

---

4 The original Sarry Heid, or Saracen's Head, was one of Glasgow's most fashionable and best-known hostelries, established in the Gallowgate in 1755. It was patronised by such literary luminaries as Dr Samuel Johnson, James Boswell and Robert Burns, but closed down in 1792. Although the original building is long gone, the modern day Sarry Heid is still a mecca for Glasgow drinkers.

'So, Richard, your father tells me you want to get into the whisky industry', he said. 'Do you know anything about it?'

'Well', I replied, 'I've been working at the Atholl Palace Hotel in Pitlochry, where I got involved with wine and whisky.' That was certainly true. 'And of course, my dad has always tried to encourage me especially when it comes to Scotch whisky. It has been in the family for two generations, so I guess it runs in my blood too.' He nodded approvingly.

'Do you actually like whisky yourself?' he asked.

'I like the smells, but I'm still trying to develop the taste.'

If ever I needed a quick nip, now was the time! He asked me about my schooldays in Helensburgh and how I had liked boarding school in Yorkshire, being independent, and away from home. He seemed to need convincing that I had the necessary confidence, energy and ambition to succeed in life.

'Do you think you could handle this job and give us the commitment we're looking for?'

'Well I think I could, Mr Wolfe – just give me the opportunity to prove myself', I replied enthusiastically. This seemed to hit the right note because suddenly the interview was over.

'Can you start on Monday?'

This took me by surprise. As I hesitated, he reiterated, 'You can start on Monday, can't you?'

'Yes … of course, Mr Wolfe, thank you very much.'

I seemed to have made up my mind without realising it. Certainly from what he had said the role of office junior could lead to better things, if I was prepared to work and learn. It might have been a small company, but looking around his office there was every sign this was a prosperous, healthy business.

I sprang to my feet, wanting to shake his hand and thank him for giving me this opportunity, but to my surprise, when he stood up, instead of finding a giant of a man at least six-foot-six as I had expected from his position behind the desk, David Wolfe turned out to be no more than five feet tall! Those broad shoulders had been a mere bluff. But I liked him … and his company, and now *I* was part of it.

My father had already told me A Gillies & Co was an old-fashioned firm involved in broking, blending and distilling. It was owned by Sir Maurice Bloch, who had made the huge sum of £2m by selling Scapa Distillery, along with substantial whisky stocks, to Hiram Walker in October 1954. Gillies had managed to build up a successful export cased business in South America, Italy and Spain. They were also the proud owners of Glen Scotia Distillery in Campbeltown, which they had purchased in 1955.

My new job was to start on Monday 5th September 1966, and I was to be given the less than generous salary of £4 10s 6d per week. Some of my friends in similar jobs were then earning between eight and ten pounds a week. I doubted whether Securicor would be required to bring in my pay packet! It was everybody's dream to achieve that magical £1,000 a year salary, but this was clearly going to elude me for some time to come.

Bearing in mind that in 1966 an average bottle of blended whisky cost the enormous sum of £2 11s 11d, on my pathetic salary I certainly was not going to be rushing out to buy a bottle of Haig, Black & White or White Horse to celebrate my new employment. Whisky after all, and I mean *good* whisky, was a genuine luxury.

Today, most people have no conception of how lucky they really are when they can buy a bottle of supermarket whisky for as little as £8. What a bargain! No wonder distillery staff and blending and bottling workers during those former years were not averse to helping themselves when the opportunity arose. With whisky at those prices it was a very attractive bartering tool, and helped to open many doors. Technically, of course, this was theft, but the people who did it never saw it in that way. To them it was a 'freebie', a perk of the job.

By the time I joined A Gillies & Co the Scotch whisky industry was really deep into another great 'boom' period, even if the heyday of whisky broking was coming to an end. The previous whisky boom had occurred during the late 19th century, and during the 1890s alone, no fewer than 19 of the distilleries which are working today were established. These included such great Highland names as Aberfeldy, Balvenie, Dalwhinnie, Dufftown and Longmorn.

In 1965 the new distillery of Tomintoul had started production, while existing distilleries such as Glentauchers, not far from Keith, had been trebled in capacity. Caperdonich and Benriach were re-built and re-commissioned, after being silent for more than 60 years, and Inver House Distillers had begun distilling grain spirit from their Garnheath Distillery at Airdrie. As well as grain whisky it also made Killyloch vatted and Glen Flagler single malts, both now serious collectors' items.

In addition to this, construction began in 1966 on Invergordon Distillers' Tamnavulin-Glenlivet Distillery, and in September of that year Loch Lomond Distillery at Alexandria near Glasgow commenced production. It was built on the site of the old United Turkey red carpet factory, where my father's old business partner George Christie had previously had his whisky bond. Loch Lomond produced Inchmurrin and Rhosdhu Lowland single malts. The following month, Deanston Distillery at Doune in Perthshire began making whisky, having been converted from a cotton mill which dated back to 1784.

These were heady, optimistic times for Scotch whisky. There was an air of confidence about. Export markets were thirsty for our blends, and it seemed there was nothing but optimism and expansion ahead. It was the perfect time for an ambitious young man to be getting involved in the Scotch whisky industry.

My first boss at A Gillies & Co was Tom Wilson, who was responsible for the acquisition of whisky stocks, through distilling, broking and blending. Tom was a real jovial, likeable character in his 40s and wore the thickest 'jam jar' glasses I had ever seen. One of the hazards of working with him was the excessive flatulence he experienced after the lengthy lunches which were part of his working week. Being something of a well-mannered prude, I was particularly offended when he finished off a blast of flatulence right beside me with the immortal words, 'Well Richard, you won't find any bones in that one!' Thankfully the strong smell of his trademark Old Spice aftershave lotion overpowered any unpleasant odour!

My first official job was to man the brand new telephone system. To me it was like being faced with the controls of a Jumbo jet. When things went wrong it would light up like a Christmas tree. Shouts and snarls of abuse could be heard down the line, as I inadvertently cut off our customers in mid-conversation. Needless to say, my other colleagues alongside me, George Cutler and the lovely, busty Eleanor, thought this was all highly amusing. Thankfully, it did not take me too long to master the system, but there were still occasions when I got it wrong.

As I settled into the job, it was not long before George and Eleanor were playing practical jokes, which was part of their 'company policy'. For example, they would give me a number and tell me 'Mr Wilson is waiting for the call. You've to ask for Mr Lion. Now hurry up!' I feverishly dialled the number and only realised I had been conned when a voice at the other end of the line said 'Hello, Calder Park Zoo, can I help you?'! Naturally, George and Eleanor thought this was tremendously funny.

This kind of office humour inevitably helped to make mundane and even boring routine jobs more bearable. One such task for me in those early years was to log filling details from the various distilleries which were supplying us with whisky for our future blends. There were no computers, it was all down to the fountain pen, filled with Parker's black ink. Every conceivable detail of thousands of individual transactions was painstakingly recorded on the musty pages of huge, leather-bound ledgers, which dated back to Victorian times.

One particular filling I recall was a huge purchase of three-year-old grain whisky which we made in 1966 from Invergordon, the most modern grain distillery in Scotland, situated on the Cromarty firth in Ross-shire. The transaction was for 200 barrels at four shillings and nine pence per proof gallon, and it seemed to take me days to make those 200 entries. Little did I know then that Invergordon Distillery would later become such an important part of my life, after Whyte & Mackay purchased Invergordon Distillers in 1993.

Another part of my job was to deliver documents to the bank, as well as to various whisky brokers and bottlers in and around Glasgow. This included samples – usually single malts which were available for purchase but were always subject to quality approval. I particularly liked this aspect of my work as it brought me into contact with customers and our competitors. One task I particularly hated, though, was sending samples abroad. I had to make sure they were securely packaged in the famous 'Safe and Sound' boxes, and carefully complete the vital green declaration forms. Even during these early years, the Post Office demanded, what was to my mind, excessive bureaucratic documentation. Queuing up at the Hope Street post office was a constant nightmare. Some mug had to do it, and that mug was me.

When it came to visiting the bonds which undertook our bottling requirements there were no company cars and we certainly were not allowed to use taxis. It was a case of either walking or getting on a Glasgow Corporation bus, which featured the horrible clashing colours of orange and green. Glasgow Council must surely have been colour-blind when they decided on this livery! Thankfully, the tramcars were now a thing of the past, even though in some parts of the city their rails remained. Railway Bond in Bell Street, the Glasgow Bond in Duke Street, and Provanmill Bond were regularly on my itinerary. On rare occasions, I visited Castlegreen, Strathleven and Bonhill, which were situated around Dumbarton, an hour's bus ride away. This was the home ground of the famous Ballantine's and J&B blended Scotch whiskies, and the town was characterised by row upon row of blackened, whisky warehouses and smoke bellowing from Dumbarton Grain Distillery. Having been brought up in nearby Helensburgh, this environment was very much part of my life.

During the next few years while I worked for Gillies I really began to take a keen interest in the Scotch whisky industry, but I soon realised the opportunities for progressing to management status, let alone a directorship, were almost negligible. It was indeed going to be a long, hard slog. I could no longer rely on the help and influence of my father. He had done his part. At last my independent spirit was beginning to emerge, and I was well and truly on my own now.

At the opposite end of the Scotch whisky scale to A Gillies & Co was the mighty Distillers Company Ltd, which had been established on 24th April 1877. In 1966, when I joined Gillies, DCL owned no fewer than 51 out of a total of 114 Scotch whisky distilleries operational at that time. Their brands included such illustrious names as Johnnie Walker, Haig, Black & White, White Horse, Dewars, and Vat 69. They dominated the Scotch whisky market all around the world.

A Gillies & Co was, in comparison, a mere minnow … and we meant nothing to them, as I was soon to discover when I made a determined attempt to get more knowledge of the characteristics of individual whiskies. There were no books I could turn to for help with sensory evaluation – Wallace Milroy's *Malt Whisky Almanac* was still a long way off. Being a confident, eager young whipper-snapper, I wrote to all the distilleries in Scotland and asked them to send me samples of new fillings of their distillation. The majority were happy to oblige, but then one day when sitting at my desk, reading another fresh copy of *Parade*, the phone next to me rang with a tone of unusual self-importance. When I answered it, a very confident voice at the other end asked to speak to 'Paterson'. When I introduced myself, he said, 'I'm the production director for the Distillers Company Limited, and it has been brought to my attention that you have been writing to my distilleries and requesting samples. What is this all about then?'

I explained that I was anxious to have a library of the finest new fillings of single malts which I could refer to if required, and naturally this included those from the Distillers Company. 'Well', he said, 'you might want them, but we're not prepared to give them. This is the Distillers Company you're dealing with, and we do not entertain this type of request. Good morning.' And he hung up on me. So my attitude towards the Distillers Company was less than positive. I would go so far as to say I thought they were a bunch of self-important plutocrats.

DCL may have thwarted my attempts to increase my working knowledge of the drinks industry, but there were other avenues to explore. I decided to take an evening job at Macrae's off-licence in Renfrew Street, which was conveniently located a hundred yards from Gillies' offices. This attracted a very desirable clientele … mainly alcoholics and winos! They specialised in consuming some of life's greatest alcoholic luxuries such as the fine fortified wines which were so popular in the west of Scotland. These included 'Lanny' (Lanliq), 'LD' (Eldorado) and 'Buckie' (Buckfast) – the ultimate cocktail when mixed with Bulmer's cider. A half pint and you were in heaven. It was often said that one bottle of Lanliq and you could walk through walls! But then there was the last resort … a dark place from which there was no return for those unfortunate souls who consumed 'White Lightning' – also known as 'Stairheid Dynamite'. This was a potentially lethal blend of Belair hair lacquer and milk. Certainly not for the fainthearted. It was literally enough to make your hair stand on end. On the positive side, there was no hangover … but that was because your head was missing for at least a week! Some pubs in the notorious Gorbals area of Glasgow did a roaring trade in 'red biddy', a potent, fortified wine, often served straight from the cask. Not being an adventurous soul, I stuck to my pints of 'heavy'.

Some of Scotland's greatest characters came into Macrae's, and shared their exciting exploits with us, from their time in The Bar L (Barlinnie jail) to their life in 'Copper Canyon' housing scheme – so called because the pensioners would only pay their bus fares in pennies.

But there was another even more glamorous side to Macrae's, as it was situated directly opposite the Pavilion Theatre, and Scottish stars of the day such as the Alexander Brothers, Sidney Devine, Lex Maclean, Jack Milroy and Rikki Fulton would occasionally pop in for a bottle to sustain them before – and even during – their performances. Behind the Pavilion, on Hope Street, was one of Glasgow's best-known dance halls, the Majestic, or as it was affectionately known, the 'Magic Stick', for reasons probably best left unexplained. This was where the boys went chasing the 'burds' on Friday and Saturday nights.

The police used to frequent this area because there was trouble often, with excess drinking and various goings on. I remember one Saturday night when I was working in Macrae's, two sweaty policemen came in and said they had just arrested a really wild 'burd' because she had been found in the toilet of the 'Magic Stick', completely inebriated. As they pulled her to her feet her mini skirt rode up to reveal that she did not have any underwear on. Completely aghast, the younger of the two officers asked, 'What do you think your game is, love?' She grinned up at them and replied, 'What do *you* think my game is, doll? I'm here to enjoy myself. Do you want to play too? Let's see how big that truncheon really is.' Despite her generous offer, they still arrested her.

The fun did not stop at the 'Magic Stick'. Glasgow bars in those days were noisy, busy, sweaty, dark places. In the real working men's pubs there was no music, only the sound of clinking glasses, shouts, loud laughter, and the occasional cheer as a punter slid drunkenly from his stool onto the bare wooden floor. Usually you stood to drink, though there were some brown mahogany tables, and chairs with dark, distressed leather upholstery. The atmosphere was thick with smoke from many cigarettes. This was where the heart of Glasgow beat. The pub. The retreat. A home for many. After all, it was a meeting place, the social hub of the community, and drinking was just a part of that. Of course there were alcoholics, but they really were in the minority. People in Glasgow were warm, friendly, and generous, and like many Scots they wanted to share their zest for life with everyone, no matter where they came from.

And during my time with Gillies the pubs of Glasgow became part of my life too. My colleague George Cutler and I, along with some of the other lads from the office, used to frequent The Atholl Bar in Renfrew Street and Lauder's in Sauchiehall Street. Both survive to this day.

Although I occasionally drank gin and bitter lemon or Dry Martini, beer was the mainstay for me as it was for most Glasgow men. The bulk of the beer being drunk was either Tennent's or McEwan's, which we generously allowed to be imported from Edinburgh! Records show that one Robert Tennent was a brewer and maltster based near Glasgow Cathedral as long ago as 1556, and J&R Tennent purchased the nearby Wellpark brewery in 1793. Remarkably, Wellpark brewery is the only Glasgow firm listed in Tait's commercial directory of 1783 which remains in the same line of business, and trading from the same site today.

Although I was not averse to a pint or two of Tennent's, one particular favourite of mine was Fowler's Wee Heavy, a classic, very strong beer from the little brewery in Prestonpans, near Edinburgh. Like Tennent's, Fowler's brewery had a great heritage, dating back to

1720, though this did not save it from the great wave of brewing amalgamations, rationalisations and closures that swept through Scotland during the 1960s, and sadly Fowler's closed in 1969. Until that date many Friday nights were spent drinking that wonderful heavy beer.

Even though Tennent's had been brewing lager since as early as 1885, 'proper' Scottish draught beer was beginning to feel the first real threat around this time from fancy foreign lagers such as Carlsberg and Tuborg. Even my father had jumped on the bandwagon when he had taken the agency for Holsten Pilsner lager.

Traditional brewers were not the only ones to come under threat. From time immemorial, beer, like whisky, had been stored in wooden casks, but the 1950s saw the introduction of aluminium kegs. Something had to go, and it was the coopers, the practitioners of this great craft. Coopering, like whisky, is a rare art, and one for which I have the greatest respect. Even today that passion remains with me.

For many dedicated drinkers beer was only half the equation. The other half was whisky. The 'hauf an' a hauf' was a Scottish institution. A half pint of beer and a whisky chaser. There are two schools of thought as to why this combination became popular. Some say it was because of the poor quality of Scottish beer. Surely not? The theory was it helped to mask the flavour. The second school of thought was it just got you blootered more quickly!

Beer was comparatively cheap, costing around two shillings in the mid-1960s, and by comparison whisky was quite expensive. It was common to see old men having finished the whisky portion of their 'hauf an' a hauf' holding the glass upside down over their remaining beer for what seemed like an eternity, in order to capture any last precious drops.

The old Scottish music hall entertainer Will Fyffe (1885–1947) used to sing a song called Twelve an' a Tanner a Bottle, which lamented the price of whisky (62.5 pence today!) after a major rise in the level of taxation during the Second World War. It included the chorus:

'For it's twelve an' a tanner a bottle
That's what it's costing today
Twelve an' a tanner a bottle
Man, it taks a' the pleasure away.
Before ye can hae a wee drappie,
You have to spend a' that ye've got,
How can a fella be happy,
When happiness costs such a lot?'

Holding your whisky glass over the pint glass was one thing, but turning your glass upside down and placing it on the bar meant something altogether different. This signified that you were a bit of a hard man, and were ready to take on anybody for a fight!

In the early 1960s the soda siphon was still to be found in many bars throughout Scotland. From my point of view I could never understand why people wanted to drown the drink they had paid good money for in this gassy liquid. It was a relic from the Victorian era and thank goodness it was coming to an end.

We may have got rid of the soda siphon, but the lemonade bottle remained ubiquitous on bar counters throughout Scotland. Whisky and lemonade was an ideal mixture for the many Scottish drinkers famed for their sweet

tooth, and helped to seduce some of the harsh flavours often found in many of the heavily malted blends that were around during that period. More often than not the lemonade bottle bore the name of Barr's, who were also responsible for Scotland's 'other' national drink, the great Irn Bru. This distinctive, sweet, orange-coloured beverage is a Scottish icon, and is recognised in its homeland as the ultimate hangover cure. Many of my colleagues at Gillies swore by a Sunday morning fitness routine of walking to the corner shop to buy six rolls, a bottle of Irn Bru and, of course, a copy of *The Sunday Post*. Unfortunately, the smell of the previous night's curry lingered on your breath rather longer than the hangover.

When we talk about Scotch whisky we are, of course, talking about *blended* Scotch. It dominated the market almost one hundred per cent. You would never go into a bar and ask for a single malt, it simply did not happen. Whisky was blended whisky. End of story. Usually in most bars there would be Haig, Long John, Vat 69, Grants, White Horse, Teachers and of course Whyte & Mackay. In 1962 they were the first company to introduce the 40-oz bottle for the UK bar optic trade. It was an instant success and many other whisky companies soon followed their lead.

However, another entrepreneurial company was William Grant & Sons Ltd, who had the vision and foresight to market their Glenfiddich Single Malt on a global basis, beginning with a marketing drive in England during 1964. Many rival distillers must have thought they were wasting their time, but how wrong they were! Despite the increasingly fierce competition, Glenfiddich remains the best selling single malt in the world today. Nonetheless, it took decades for single malts to become recognised as a serious whisky category in their own right. What took us so long when the first reference to Scotch whisky dates from 1494?

At the same time as Grants were attempting to convert drinkers to the joys of single malts, a whole new drinking experience was emerging in Scotland. Both table and fortified wines were becoming seriously fashionable.

Harvey's Bristol Cream, Croft Original, and especially Bertola Cream Sherry were being heavily marketed in Scotland. These complemented the Spanish Sauternes, the Hirondel range, and also the famous Mateus Rosé, with its distinctive dark green bottle. Turning up at a party with a bottle of wine instead of the customary Tennent's 'kerry oot' was a mark of real sophistication. You were immediately considered a genuine connoisseur of the bevvy! The true drink for celebration was, of course, Champagne, but Asti Spumante, Babycham, and even the magnificent Pomagne, were considered to be only slightly inferior substitutes, even if they did give you one hell of a hangover.

The wine lakes were beginning to fill up, thanks to the wine-drinking phenomenon which was greatly influenced by people travelling abroad on holiday for the first time. Package tours to Majorca and the Costa Brava were suddenly within the reach of many people. They would often have their first taste of wine while abroad, and on their return wanted to maintain that holiday spirit by sourcing the same wines they had been drinking. That thirst had to be quenched, and the drinks industry eagerly responded. Off-licences and specialist wine and spirits merchants catered for their needs with a wide range of French, German and Spanish wines – even jug carafe wines from Paul Masson of California. The supermarkets with their huge choice of tempting offers were still a long way in the future. In those days it was not uncommon for queues to form along the pavement outside Macrae's off-licence, especially as Christmas approached, and we were actually open on Christmas Day, at a time when no other businesses operated then at all.

Despite the lure of foreign lands, however, holidays for many Scots were still confined to travelling 'Doon the Watter' to Rothesay, Troon and Saltcoats on board much-loved steamers such as the *Jeannie Deans*, the *Duchess of Montrose* and, of course, *Waverley*. Fun was not, of course, just confined to the Glasgow Fair Fortnight or the Edinburgh Trades holiday. Every Saturday night brought its own kind of tour. From the pub to the dance hall, and perhaps on to a party later. There was dancing at the Locarno, The Barrowland, The Plaza and The Cameo, and it was truly classless. It was a place for everybody to let their hair down and forget their troubles. But you had to be careful. Sometimes your dancing partner turned out to be already taken by a particularly menacing 'ned', who liked to dance, but preferred to fight, given the slightest provocation. Being seen on the dance floor with his 'hairy' was more than enough provocation to give you a 'Glasgow Kiss', but it certainly did not involve your lips. This was basically a head butt, or, in the vernacular, 'stickin' the heid in.' The chances were he belonged to one of the notorious Glasgow gangs. There was the 'Cumbie' from the Gorbals, the 'Wee Men' from Parkhead, the 'Shamrocks' from Townhead, and the 'Bundy' from Pollok.

There was much less chance of a 'Glasgow Kiss' in the sort of pubs where I often drank at weekends. My main haunt was the Byres Road area, where there has always been a strong student influence due to the proximity of Glasgow University. I usually drank in Curlers and Tennent's Bar in Byres Road and The Rock in Hyndland Road, where I was to meet my future wife, Susie. It really was standing room only in many of the bars, which were filled with pompous, self-opinionated students, wearing garish university scarves. They would not have stood a chance if they had strayed into somewhere like the Gorbals!

If you wanted to dance rather than drink, and dance in relative safety, there was always the Carioca Club in Bearsden, run by the fabulous Bilsland boys. One of the attractions was live music, often played by exciting new bands. When the famous Searchers arrived the place erupted, much to the annoyance of the terribly respectable residents of Glenburn Road! But who cared? These were the Swinging Sixties, and along with my great friends Alan Rankin, Nigel Gray, Hamish Gourlay and Les Frew, I made the most of those times.

To be in style meant sporting droopy moustaches, long hair, kaftans and bell-bottom trousers, with the smell of Brut after-shave hanging in the air. It was as though the album cover from *Sergeant Pepper* had come alive in respectable Bearsden. This was the time of flowers in your hair and lots of free love. I do not recall a lot of free love, however, but there was no shortage of wet dreams, hardly surprising when surrounded by girls in miniskirts and hotpants. Nancy Sinatra did not help either, when she topped the charts with, These Boots Were Made for Walking. What a pair of legs!

By Sunday evening I was exhausted, and ready for the relative tranquillity of the working week ahead. Thankfully, during my early years with Gillies, work was really quite a casual affair and could accommodate the occasional Monday morning hangover. Nobody in the whisky industry now would believe how laid-back it really was. There was no great pressure. People tended to arrive for work at half-past nine in the morning, and we usually finished at five o'clock precisely. Nobody in their right mind would ever consider working overtime ... unless they were looking for that elusive promotion, of course.

My colleagues were warm, friendly people, and office politics did not seem to play a part in our working lives. So when I look back on those times, I remember them with true affection. George Cutler and I became good friends, and he taught me a lot about the whisky business, particularly when it came to the sourcing of bottling materials, which was his area of responsibility. He took his position very seriously, particularly during the busy period before Christmas, but there was always time for a laugh, time for a bit of fun.

One example was The Cowboy Game which we used to play first thing in the morning. That's when the saloon opened. One of us would set up three shot glasses, placed carefully on his desk. Two of the glasses contained water, while the third was filled with new spirit, at a staggering strength of 68% alcohol by volume (abv). The object of the game was speed. There was no time for indecision. We drew lots to decide who would be that day's cowboy. He then had to march down the corridor, kick the office door open as though he was in a saloon in Texas, and then, without hesitation, grab the first glass he saw and knock it back in one go. It was like Russian roulette, only the shots were not bullets, but if you made the wrong choice it could be almost as lethal. You were shot to pieces by the effect. It was a dangerous game but it certainly lifted your spirits, though inevitably there were some days when work was a blur, and you had to stay well clear of Tom Wilson and Mr Wolfe.

The Cowboy Game was as close as I got to the USA, but our whiskies travelled throughout America, the ultimate land of opportunity – the number one market. Every style of Scotch was available to tempt the American palate, from light-coloured whiskies such as Cutty Sark and J&B to the more traditional Dewar's White Label. These were the leading Scotch whisky brands in the States at that time. But in this vast country there was room for everybody, and Gillies took full advantage of this lucrative opportunity.

The vibrant bars of New York, Boston, Washington, Chicago and San Francisco rang

to the sound of ice tumbling into highball[5] glasses. Scotch on the rocks. Bloody ice! It was masking the true flavour of our noble drink. There was no stopping it. But then again, who cared? For this was not only an incredibly profitable trade for many companies, but also provided much needed revenue for the British government courtesy of the high tax levels imposed on scotch.

We at Gillies spent a great deal of time and energy exporting brands not only to North America but also to South America, which was showing great potential during those years. Our portfolio included Old Court, King's Rider, Wagshaw's and many other obscure brands better known in Rio de Janeiro than Rutherglen in Glasgow. Even in Rio, however, we were only selling comparatively small quantities, no more than 500 cases in a year. It was all about building up a relationship with the agent and the customers in those markets, hoping to sell more there in the long term. But competition was never far away. You still had to contend with DCL, Hiram Walker and Seagram, who had sophisticated networks of agents in every corner of the world. We were really just picking up crumbs from the rich man's table, therefore you might imagine every effort was applied to creating a high quality, consistent blend. But in reality it came down to human contact rather than the contents of the whisky bottle. It was people who sealed the deal. The personalities of David Wolfe and Tom Wilson ensured the success of the brands.

The partnership between salesman and agent had to be developed like the marriage of the individual personalities that made a good blend. Although we were marrying our whiskies, the marrying period was somewhat

5 'A cocktail usually based on whisky, and the name given to a six-ounce or eight-ounce glass now used for serving a variety of cocktails. [Michael] Jackson explains the origins of the drink's name as follows: "It is said that some American railroads used a signal with a ball raised on a pole to indicate to the train driver that he was running late. A highball meant 'hurry'. It also came to mean a simple drink that could be fixed in a hurry".' (*Pocket Bar Book*) A-Z of *Whisky*, Gavin D. Smith.

brief. You could say it was more of a passionate affair than a true marriage. There was no great strategy to it at all. Literally, we put in whatever grain and malt whiskies were available, and let the consistency of the blend take care of itself. We needed to live for today. There was no alternative if you wanted to survive.

The same criteria applied to cask selection. The idea of any sort of formal 'wood management policy' would have been dismissed out of hand. After all, a cask was a cask. Hardly anybody thought it mattered whether it had contained sherry, wine or even a liqueur in a previous life.

By today's rigorous standards, this may all appear to have been somewhat casual, but it was the acceptable practice of many of the whisky companies of that era. Despite this laid-back attitude, the respectable malt content of our blends remained relatively high by comparison with many of today's premium blends, still around 50% of the total. It should be remembered, however, times were good. Companies were healthy and profitable, and the accountant remained a backroom figure. His influence was nothing like it is today. It was strong management that drove the business forward in those dynamic times. Redundancy, rationalisation and recession were negative factors that still lay in the future.

Like many of our counterparts we were obtaining single malts from the likes of Hiram Walker, who owned Glenburgie, Glencadam, Miltonduff, Pulteney and Scapa distilleries, and of course from the DCL who supplied us with grain whiskies such as Cameronbridge, Carsebridge, Cambus, Caledonian, and Port Dundas.

One of Gillies' roles was to hold stocks of whisky on behalf of many clients, some of whom were private investors, though the bulk was held for other whisky companies, to be traded on a 'reciprocal' basis. This method of trading ensured that blenders had consistent access to stocks of the whiskies they used most widely. These clients normally paid their rent at six-monthly or yearly intervals. To calculate this rent you multiplied the number of casks they owned by the amount of money due per cask. I believe the figure was something like tuppence per cask back in the mid-1960s. If the client failed to pay his rent then he simply was refused access to his casks. In rare situations people had invested in parcels of whisky, and subsequently died or mislaid their ownership documentation. When this occurred we were obliged to track them down through newspaper advertisements before eventually taking ownership of the casks ourselves. Even today I would not be surprised if there were a few forgotten casks lying unclaimed in warehouses scattered throughout Scotland.

Indeed, it was from warehouses scattered throughout Scotland that we acquired casks of single malt to create the range of Gillies' blends. Most of these blends were not actually assembled in Glasgow, but in the remote western outpost of Campbeltown, where they were prepared at our Glen Nevis and Ardlussa warehouses for bottling.

One day, after I had been with Gillies long enough to demonstrate my enthusiasm and competence, Tom Wilson called me into his office and closed the door behind me. 'Have a seat, Richard', he said. His serious manner took me by surprise. I wondered what I might have done wrong. Did he know about our Cowboy Game? It came as a relief when he said 'Have you ever been to Campbeltown?'

'No', I replied.

'Well, you're going now', he said. 'It's time you learnt something about what we're doing down there. You'll be staying with our warehouse manager, Euan Finlay. He's going to be looking after you.'

I thought this was at last some real progress, my first official trip from the company. I was encouraged at the prospect of getting out of Glasgow and learning something new about the whisky industry and, of course, about this famous area.

However, to me, Campbeltown was like the Siberian salt mines. It was the back of beyond, and I suppose it still is to many people today. Some even imagine it to be an island, and it very nearly is. As the crow flies it is only 65 miles from Glasgow. Unfortunately, unless you happen to be a crow, or own a boat, it takes at least three and a half hours and 140 miles to get there by road from the city. One look at a map and you will quickly realise you have to go around Loch Lomond, Long Long and Loch Fyne. It is a never-ending journey.

Through my time at Gillies I had learnt that during the last century Campbeltown had been the capital of the Scotch whisky industry, but sadly now was only a shadow of its former self. Nevertheless it was a new challenge and I wanted to taste some of that historical past for myself. One week later I was on my way to Campbeltown, which Alfred Barnard had described 80 years previously as 'the Whisky City.' Well, I came from the second city of the British Empire, and when I finally got there Campbeltown was like no city I had ever seen. But that's another story ...

Chapter Three

THE SPIRIT OF CAMPBELTOWN – GLEN SCOTIA

'The greatest pleasure of Scotch whisky is, of course, drinking it. But a close second is enjoying it with a good friend.'

}

JOHN HANSELL, FOUNDER AND PUBLISHER, *MALT ADVOCATE* MAGAZINE

Campbeltown. It seemed like an eternity away. Even though we were approaching Dumbarton I was already wondering if this bus would ever make the long journey. It was taking hours and I was beginning to feel every bump on the road.

The rickety vehicle made its leisurely progress along the shores of Loch Lomond and then headed west, out by the little village of Arrochar, round Loch Long, and with much crunching of gears it gasped its way over the 'Rest and Be Thankful', arriving exhausted at Inveraray. At last, some time to stretch out my aching limbs and get some fresh air, although a ghostly mist hung over the loch. Everything appeared still and quiet, except the bustle of the main street.

This strikingly beautiful, largely Georgian, lochside village welcomes the traveller with an array of white-painted facades. The village is dominated by its fairytale castle, with turrets which look as though they would be more at home on a French chateau than a Highland fortress. It remains home to the Duke of Argyll, head of Clan Campbell. In those days Inveraray was a quiet little village, serenely going about its business, whereas now it is a vibrant holiday centre.

Coach tours descend on it like bees to the hive, spilling out people eager to make their tartan purchases. But there are always alternatives, such as a visit to Inveraray Gaol and, of course, the Loch Fyne whisky shop. I wish the whisky shop had been there when I passed through. I could certainly have done with a large dram of something to revive my flagging spirits, especially as I had eaten all the soggy tomato sandwiches I had brought with me and long since emptied my flask of tea.

Surely it could not be much further now? The scenery was certainly dramatic, with all the beautiful lochs and rivers we passed but I was getting bored. The bus seat was hard as hell, and I was tired and grumpy. After another hour we descended on a picturesque fishing village, its harbour clogged with boats. Campbeltown at last, I thought. My heart sank with disappointment when the driver told me this was Tarbert. 'Tarbert!' I gasped. 'How much longer will it take to get to Campbeltown?'. The driver looked at me in a condescending manner. 'Dinna fash yersel, sonny, it'll take as long as it takes. Away back to yer seat.'

I do not know which annoyed me most, being called 'sonny' or the driver's irritating lack of precision. I swore under my breath with exasperation, but nevertheless did as I was told. The bus rumbled on, stopping in every tiny village, stopping even where there did not appear to be a village at all. How much further? But just as the light began to fade, I saw the flicker of some dim lights of a town ahead, but did not dare to hope this really might be my destination. A few minutes later, however, we pulled up beside a harbour, and as I looked inquisitively out of the window I saw my suitcase had already been unceremoniously dumped onto the street. 'Come on sonny, this is Campbeltown. Your stop.'

As I descended from the bus to retrieve my cast-off case a young, stocky man with thick blond hair brushed back with Brylcreem stepped forward and greeted me in a boisterous manner. He shook my hand like a long-lost friend. 'Hello, you must be Richard, I'm Euan Finlay', he said. 'Let's get your luggage home, then we'll go for a few pints and you can meet some of my mates.'

'Are the warehouses far from here?' I asked.

'What! Bluidy relax, man. I'll show you them tomorrow.'

As we walked to Euan's car I was immediately aware of the plaintive crying of herring gulls and great blackbacks swarming around the fishing boats which lined the harbour. But most overwhelming was the smell. The smell of fish, thousands of fish, which seemed to have seeped into every crevice of that old harbour over centuries of plundering the seas. It was the very lifeblood of Campbeltown. But behind the overpowering stench of fish I began to detect other smells. Diesel, tar, rotting seaweed and, in the background, the faint scent of whisky making.

'How can you live with this constant stink?' I asked, screwing up my nose in disgust, as we got into Euan's car. He burst out laughing as he drove away from the pier. 'Och, you get used to it. Stop fretting. You obviously need a drink.'

On arriving at Euan's house I was welcomed by Mr and Mrs Finlay. They were warm, friendly, hospitable people, and they were there to meet me on the doorstep. 'Come away in', said Mrs Finlay. 'You've had a long journey, Richard, you must be hungry. Can I get you something to eat?'

'Stop fussing, mum' said Euan impatiently 'we're going to get something to eat down the White Hart'.

'But remember Euan', she said, waving her finger at him, almost hitting him on the nose, 'there'll be no drinking now.'

Euan did not seem to be paying much attention as he pulled on his heavy, black donkey jacket. After all, he must have heard this sort of thing from his mother many times before.

'We may be back late, mum. Leave the door on the latch.'

With that, he grabbed me by the shoulder and literally pulled me out of the house. 'Bluidy women, they're always nagging! Now let's get a drink inside you. We'll start at the Royal.'

Everybody in the pub seemed to know each other, which came as a bit of a surprise to someone like me, who was used to the comparative anonymity of Glasgow bars. I could feel a real community spirit, a genuine warmth. Some of the regulars appeared never to have left the place. They were obviously fishermen, by the looks of their leathery, tanned faces and black roll-neck sweaters. Roll-up cigarettes clung to their lips.

Immediately we were surrounded by Euan's pals, and it soon felt as though I had known them for years, as we began exchanging jokes and sordid details of our female conquests, real and imagined.

By closing time I was totally out of the game, but as you might have guessed, I was beginning to like Campbeltown, especially its people. Euan looked me up and down with a stupid grin on his face. 'You don't appear to be holding your drink too well, Richard. You are truly pissed.'

'No I'm not', I replied, slurring my words, 'I've had nothing to eat since lunchtime.'

'Neither you have, I forgot all about the food. Well we'd better get you sobered up before we go home or mum's going to kill us both.'

I managed to focus on the face of my watch. 'But it's after one in the morning', I said. 'Where the hell are we going to get food at this time of night?'

'Just shut up and follow me', Euan rasped.

As we turned the corner off the main street the smell of freshly-baked bread hit my nostrils, reminding me just how hungry I really was. Euan went up to a side door in the lane and hit it with his fist. Almost immediately the door opened. A sweaty figure with flour on his hands and face appeared.

'How's it going, Donnie? What's baking tonight? I've a friend from Glasgow here who's badly in need of food, or else he's going to have one hell of a hangover in the morning. How about some of your magic pies?'

Within seconds we were gorging ourselves as though we had never seen food in our lives. After the third one, the pies were indeed magic, as they were casting spells in my rebelling stomach. Greasy pies and five pints of heavy do not always mix. However, the icy cold wind coming over the loch seemed to be helping sober me up as we neared Euan's house.

'Right Richard, keep the noise down. It's action stations. Mum may be on guard at the top of the stairs. I'll see you in the morning. Don't be sleeping in.'

I ascended the stairs like an arthritic puppet and was just congratulating myself on making it to the top, when my foot slipped clumsily on the last step. I collapsed in a heap like a dead weight.

'Who's that?' an angry voice growled. Oh bugger! It was Mrs Finlay, and she certainly did not sound as warm and hospitable as she had earlier in the evening.

'It'sh Richard, Mrsh Finlay. Shorry if I woke you.'

'You've been drinking, haven't you? I'll see you in morning. Now get to your bed.'

Like a scolded schoolboy I crept into my revolving room. And that's the last thing I remember.

The next morning I woke up to the smell of toast and frying bacon. I was half afraid to go downstairs after the occurrences of the previous night. My head was still fuzzy. As I entered the kitchen Euan was already getting stuck into an enormous plate of porridge. Thankfully, Mrs Finlay seemed to have forgiven me, as she pulled a chair out for me at the table. 'This'll be your place from now on, Richard.' Euan was not in the mood for talking and barely acknowledged my presence.

'Don't be wasting too much time', he muttered. 'We've got a bluidy blend on for Glasgow today.'

'What he needs is a skalk', he said, turning to his mother.[6]

'There will be no more drinking', she declared, firmly, and Euan returned to his meal. The magic pies were still taking their toll on me, and I could not even manage a small bowl of porridge. Mrs Finlay obviously recognised my symptoms.

'Take this glass of warm milk, it'll put a lining on your stomach.'

6 Skalk: 'Anglicisation of the Gaelic *sgailc*, which has the meaning of a smart knock or blow, and also formerly "a full draught of any liquid", and specifically "a bumper of spirits taken before breakfast ... a morning dram", according to Edward Dwelly (*Illustrated Gaelic-English Dictionary*). Samuel Johnson (*A Journey to the Western Isles of Scotland*, 1775) records that " ... no man is so abstemious as to refuse the morning dram which they call a skalk".' *A–Z of Whisky*, Gavin D. Smith.

With breakfast over, Euan took me down to the Glen Nevis and Ardlussa warehouses to start our working day. It was only ten minutes' walk from Euan's house, and the fresh, damp air helped to clear my head.

Glen Nevis and Ardlussa had both been distilleries at one time, and were situated in the shadow of the Gallow Hill. Ardlussa was the last Campbeltown Distillery to be established, in 1879, and at one time held in excess of 18,000 casks. Glen Nevis had been founded two years earlier. Unfortunately they had both closed in 1923, and now only their warehouses remained. Gillies had subsequently acquired them as a base for their blending and maturing operations.

During my short time in Campbeltown I had already seen many buildings which had obviously once been whisky warehouses. Although mostly derelict, their blackened, fungus-stained walls were a clear reminder of a thriving distilling community. They looked neglected and forgotten, and I could not help but feel slightly sad about their predicament.

Euan obviously sensed my mood. 'What's wrong with you?'

'Look at all these old buildings', I replied. 'What's happened to them, does nobody care?'

'Listen Richard, Campbeltown has changed a lot over the years, and whisky is just one part of it. I suppose before we start I'd better fill you in, especially as you were boring us all to death with your passion for dates last night!'

I listened intently. I learnt that Campbeltown had been established as a burgh in 1609 by Archibald Campbell, 9th Earl of Argyll, and received its Royal Burgh Charter on 19th April 1700. However, there had been

a tiny settlement called Ceann-Loch-Chille-Ciaran (the head of the loch of the church of Ciaran) on the site for many years previously. Despite the grand sounding old Gaelic name and the formal one linking the place with the most powerful family in the west of Scotland, Campbeltown is referred to by many of its residents as 'the Wee Toon', just as Auchterarder is known colloquially as the 'Lang Toon' and Peterhead as 'the Blue Toon'.

The Kintyre peninsula, on which Campbeltown stands, was a notorious hotbed of illicit distilling, and when Thomas Pennant visited in the summer of 1772 he was obviously far from impressed by this part of the 'black economy.' In *A Tour in Scotland and Voyage to the Hebrides* he wrote 'not withstanding the quantity of bear [bere, a primitive barley variety] raised, there is often a dearth, the inhabitants being mad enough to convert their bread into poison, distilling annually six thousand bolls of grain into whisky.'

When the *Old Statistical Account of Scotland* was published in 1794, the Revd John Smith wrote in the entry on Campbeltown that 'next to the fishing of herrings, the business most attended to in Campbeltown is the distilling of whisky … '

In total, distilling is documented as having taken place in no fewer than 34 locations within the burgh of Campbeltown, and from the mid-19th century until the early 1920s around 20 distilleries operated. The figures for overall output are impressive, as in 1885 the 21 working distilleries turned out 1,938,000 gallons of spirit, and more than 250 men were directly employed in distilling. The distilleries working in that year were Hazelburn,

The view over Glebe Street, Campbeltown, from Gallow Hill. *Courtesy of Neil Wilson.*

Springbank, Dalintober, Benmore, Ardlussa, Dalaruan, Lochhead, Glen Nevis, Kinloch, Burnside, Glengyle, Lochruan, Albyn, Scotia, Rieclachan, Glenside, Longrow, Kintyre, Campbeltown, Argyll and Springside.

An idea of the Campbeltown distilleries that have passed into history, and the prevailing style of whisky they made, can be gained from a verse of Aeneas MacDonald's rhymed guide to Scottish distilleries, which appeared in his 1930 book, *Whisky*.

Last port seen by westering sail
'Twixt the tempest and the Gael,
Campbeltown in long Kintyre
Mothers there a son of fire,
Deepest voiced of all the choir.
Solemnly we name this Hector
Of the west, this giant nectar:
Benmore, Scotia, and Rieclachan,

Kinloch, Springside, Hazelburn,
Glenside, Springbank and Lochruan,
Lochhead. Finally to spurn
Weaklings drunk and cowards sober,
Summon we great Dalintober.

Campbeltown boasts a number of fine mansion houses, many of which were built for successful distillery owners, and you cannot help but notice the number of churches, too. Big Victorian churches with confident, high towers. When that indefatigable chronicler of Victorian distilling Alfred Barnard visited Campbeltown in 1885 he observed that, '... it is said that there are nearly as many places of worship as distilleries in the town.' Many of them were endowed by wealthy distillery owners. Barnard wrote of 'the United Presbyterian Church, possessing a lofty tower, surmounted by a handsome and massive

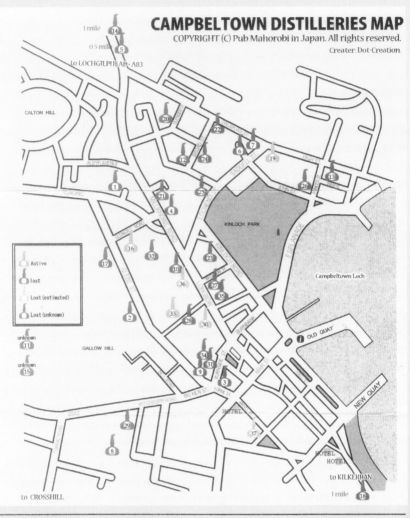

CAMPBELTOWN DISTILLERIES MAP

1 mile

0.5 mile

To LOCHGILPHEAD · A83

CALTON HILL

AUBYN AVENUE

KINLOCH PARK

Campbeltown Loch

Active

lost

Lost (estimated)

Lost (unknown)

unknown

GALLOW HILL

unknown

OLD QUAY

NEW QUAY

HOTEL

HOTEL
HOTEL

to KILKERRAN

1 mile

to CROSSHILL

01 Albyn (1830-1927)	11 Campbeltown (1798-1852)	21 Hazelburn (1825-1925)	31 Mountain Dew/Thistle (1834-1837)
02 Ardlussa (1879-1923)	12 Dalaruan (1824-1922)	22 Highland (1827-1852)	32 Rieclachan (1825-1934)
03 Argyll/McKinnon's Argyll (1827-1844)	13 Dalintober (1832-1925)	23 Kinloch (1823-1926)	33 Springbank (1828-)
04 Argyll (1844-1923)	14 Drumore (1834-1837)	24 Kintyre (1825-1887)	34 Springside (1830-1926)
05 Ballegreggan (1790-97)	15 Drumore (????-1847)	25 Lochhead/Lochead (1824-1928)	35 Toberanrigh (1834-1860)
06 Benmore (1868-1927)	16 Glengyle (1873-1925)	26 Lochruan (1835-1925)	36 Union (1826-1850)
07 Broombrae (1833-4).	17 Glen Nevis (1877-1923)	27 Lochside (1830-1852)	37 West Higland (1830-1860)
08 Burnside (1825-1924)	18 Glenramskill (1828-1852)	28 Longrow 1824-1896)	
09 Caledonian (1823-1851)	19 Glen Scotia (1832-)	29 Meadowburn (1824-1886)	
10 Campbeltown (1815-1924)	20 Glenside (1830-1926)	30 Mossfield (1834-7)	

cupola, which was built mostly at the expense of Mr Ross.'

At the time of Barnard's visit John Ross was 85 and was described by the author as ' ... the oldest living Distiller in Scotland'. He had founded Longrow Distillery in 1824, and his distinctive church in Longrow, now re-named the Lorne and Lowland Parish Church, remains one of Campbeltown's most significant landmarks. Perhaps the distillers endowed churches partly as insurance, as a way of improving the chances of getting into Heaven after making their fortunes out of such an evil commodity as whisky! Despite all the prosperity which whisky had created, however, by 1925 the number of distilleries in Campbeltown had fallen to 12, and in 1934 just Rieclachan, Springbank and Glen Scotia remained, with Rieclachan falling silent that year.

Campbeltown single malts were traditionally heavy and oily in character and, indeed, David Daiches (*Scotch Whisky*) wrote that 'Campbeltowns have in the past had something of the strength and body of Islays, and indeed are traditionally regarded as the most manly of whiskies.' Yet in the 1880s Barnard was apt to dismiss the Campbeltown malts as 'generally thin, useful at the price'. He meant useful to blenders. By that time some of them must have begun to cut back on quality for the sake of quantity, it seems. The importance of these malts to the blenders was reflected in the number of ships discharging the spirit of Campbeltown both at the Broomielaw in Glasgow and Leith docks in Edinburgh. Campbeltowns certainly helped to satisfy the demand for blended Scotch whisky during its great Victorian boom period.

The distilleries of Campbeltown are almost as near to Bushmills in Northern Ireland as they are to any of the Islay distilleries, with the Northern Ireland coast only a few miles away. The medium-bodied style originally found in the Campbeltowns by many drinkers is probably not dissimilar to that of certain Irish whiskeys. It was quite obvious from the way he spoke about it that Euan had a genuine warmth for the town, with its strong traditions and colourful heritage.

'Right. Enough talking. Let's get on with some work. Come and meet the men.'

The 'men' were a motley crew, dressed in the black dungarees and black caps that were typical of distillery workers in those days. Many bore thick, handlebar moustaches which would not have looked out of place a hundred years previously. They seemed to be quite a grumpy lot, and eyed me with some disdain. However, Wee Wullie, the warehouse foreman, shook my hand vigorously.

'So you're the young un from Glasgow? I hear your father was a whisky blender, and you're following in his footsteps. Well now, you've come to the right place, because as far as we are concerned this is the whisky capital of Scotland. Not bluidy Speyside! So if you want to know anything about whisky, ask us. They know nothing up in bluidy Glasgow.' I liked him immediately.

'The first thing we do here before we start work is we have our tea.'

'Great. I take mine with two sugars and some milk, please.'

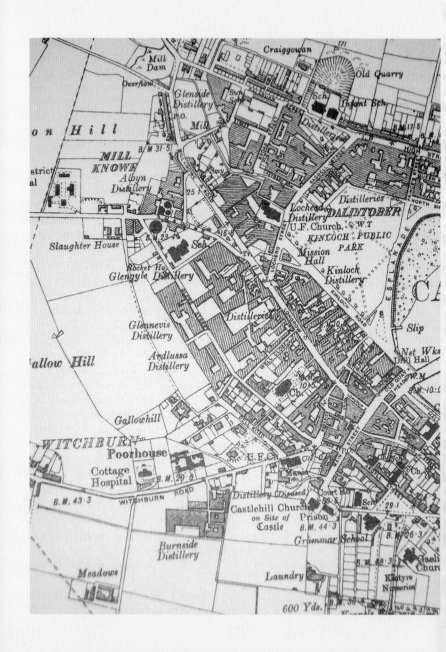

'No, no, no it doesn't work like that here', Wullie replied, shaking his head at the pernickety ways of someone from the city.

'Listen, there are nine men working here, and they all take their tea or coffee differently. We've no time for messing about, you get what you're given. We just put everything in one pot, with Carnation milk. Now sup that up.'

It was the worst cup of tea I had ever tasted but, to be honest, after two or three days I really started to like it. That may have had something to do with Wullie's habit of adding a large splash of raw whisky to the magic brew.

I certainly needed some Dutch courage when it came to using the toilet. This was an old working warehouse and the only place to relieve yourself was an outside lavatory, which smelled disgusting, and was a sanctuary for a variety of wildlife. Spiders and beetles welcomed me as I gingerly sat on the seat for the first time. One visit was enough.

After the tea break was over we went to work, and my first job involved following Wullie into the warehouses, where he took hold of a small hammer and said 'come on young un, we're going to waken the spirit.'

'Waken the spirit?' I queried.

'Don't look so confused, you'll see what I mean in a minute.'

He took a large bunch of keys out of his overall pocket and unlocked the heavy, rusted padlock that secured the bar on the warehouse

Opposite. Part of the 1924 Ordnance Survey map of the town. Glen Scotia Distillery is actually in Dalintober on the other side of Kinloch Park at the junction of Saddell Street and the High Street. Ardlussa Distillery is on Glebe Street beneath the Gallow Hill. *Courtesy of Neil Wilson.*

door. He jiggered the bar forcefully and slid it back. Using both hands and a considerable amount of strength he opened the heavy, sliding wooden doors. It was almost as though I was back in Glasgow again, eight years old, and with dad at his Stockwell Bond.

The smell of whisky immediately consumed me, as it still does today when I walk into a warehouse. I love it. The difference here was the air was much heavier, damper, and had a briny tang to it. Once again, rows and rows of casks stacked three high lay silently in a dark and dingy warehouse. Another graveyard, I thought, although the souls here seemed even more depressed. The silence was haunting. Wullie, almost like a musical conductor, took his 'tap-stick' and began to drum a rhythmic beat on the ends of the casks as he strode up and down the stows.

'Wullie, what are you doing?' I asked in a puzzled voice.

'I'm checking for criers and leakers. Just watch and listen. You'll see what I mean.'

Wullie must have tapped a hundred casks without any change in the sound. The monotony was beginning to test my patience. Suddenly a deeper, hollow note echoed around the warehouse. Donggg!

'A bluidy leaker!' shouted Wullie. 'Now do you see what I mean? We'd better check this cask and find what's caused the problem.'

With the use of his torch, Wullie shone a light on the head of the cask. 'No sign of crying there. The head joints are tight. Let's feel its arse.'

His hand disappeared underneath the cask and came back wet and dusty.

'Here's the problem. A bluidy weevil! The

greedy bugger has eaten through the wood at the worst possible place. The only good thing is it must have died with a smile on its face.' The entire contents of the cask had been lost through one tiny hole.

'We need to record this quickly or the bluidy Customs will be down on us like a ton of bricks.' Wullie wrote down the cask details on the back of an empty Capstan Full Strength cigarette packet, and we returned to his office immediately. The loss was then more formally recorded in one of a series of huge ledgers.

The rogue cask was then taken away to the cooperage at Glen Scotia distillery for repair, but not before the men had drained the dregs from it, ready to filter and drink later. They did not seem unduly bothered about what the weevil had done inside the cask, and this free dram or two was one of their unofficial perks.

Wullie handed his tap-stick to me and said, 'Away and lose yourself in the warehouse and let us know if you come across any more buggers like that. I'm up to my eyes, I've got a bluidy blend to vat. See you later.'

Back in the 1960s, particularly in Campbeltown, preparing a blend was a somewhat low-key affair compared to today. Wullie's sense of pressure was certainly not felt by his men. To them it was just another day. They continued to work at the same steady pace as always. Slow and methodical, only speeding up if there was a dram offered at the end of their break.

That afternoon Wullie explained there was an urgent need to prepare a four-year-old blend for Glasgow. 'Them' up in the city wanted it in a hurry, and it was up to him to deliver. The last thing he wanted to hear was their moans and groans. He liked his sense of independence, and the responsibility that went with it.

The specification he had received from Glasgow required him to vat up to 33 single malts, aged between four and eight years. There were even some 12-year-old parcels amongst the recipe, which suggested they were either short of stock or they wanted to introduce a more mature, mellow feel to the blend. The majority of the component whiskies were delivered by road. It seems astonishing in our security-conscious times that they were transported on 'open' lorries, simply blocked and roped in place. Considering how vulnerable the whisky was, thefts were remarkably rare. Casks were also transported by rail, and in the case of Campbeltown, even by sea.

However, one of the whiskies we regularly used did not have far to travel at all. It came from just around the corner. As we owned Glen Scotia Distillery, only a few streets away, it was quite natural that we would draw a significant proportion of this for our blends, along with the great Springbank. Back then, its outstanding qualities were still to be appreciated by discerning whisky connoisseurs. Blending with these Campbeltown whiskies was almost a throwback to a previous era, because during the 19th century they dominated the market and provided the main structure and backbone to many prominent blends. These characterful whiskies added genuine body and muscle, imparting almost an oily, pungent influence to the blends. But to the man in the street they were rough and ready. Whiskies to be knocked back like a parched cowboy in a smoky Wild West saloon.

One of Mundell's 'open' vehicle fleet leaving Tarbert in 1972.

These Campbeltown malts were manly whiskies and needed to be tamed, kept under control. The soft, feminine tones of the grain whiskies were readily available to seduce them, and grains from the DCL distilleries of Cameronbridge, Cambus, Caledonian and Port Dundas in particular were used in the Gillies blend. However, some of the lighter grains made their own inimitable contribution. Strathclyde, Dumbarton, Garnheath and Girvan were prime examples.

No wonder Wullie was feeling the pressure, he had a lot of whiskies to contend with. He was required to meet Tom Wilson's exact blending specification. The formulation was sacrosanct. Every variety of the spirit was here, in every variety of cask. Butts, hogsheads, barrels, and even some small quarter-casks had been lined up and were waiting to be 'dumped' into the blending troughs. Only on Wullie's approval could the business of blending begin, and he had already nosed the casks, with everything appearing to be in good order.

Just like in Glasgow, huge, dusty, leather-bound ledgers were kept to record every detail of the blends. At the end of each day they were locked away in a safe, as they were the one and only record of the company's transactions. The risk of fire was never far away. It was a very real threat when you had warehouses full of thousands of gallons of flammable spirit and cooper's using live flames to shape and char the cask staves. Over the years, many a distillery in Scotland has been lost beneath the flames, along with its irreplaceable documentation.

During my time in Campbeltown, I sometimes explored the venerable pages of these historic ledgers at Glebe Street and at Glen Scotia Distillery. They were literally works of art. Magnificent memorials to times long past. The painstaking old clerks had spent their working lives taking days to do what a computer can now do in seconds. Unlike today's computer print-outs, however, any one page could have been removed and framed with pride. The indelible ink and the foxed pages would remain a testament to almost forgotten days. I would never forget them.

After dumping had taken place the rich aroma of whisky seemed to have steeped into every crack and crevice between the cobblestones of Glebe Street, temporarily blotting out the perpetual smell of fish. Once the vast oak blending vat had been filled, the whisky was gently 'roused', using mechanical wooden paddles. More modern blending halls were already utilising air rousing, but in Campbeltown such innovation was still a long way off. After the whisky had been thoroughly mixed for approximately 40 minutes the strength was tested several times, using a Sikes hydrometer, and as soon as the spirit had become stable, the blend was run off into casks. The heads of these casks had already been painted white in preparation for the obligatory details of the blend's name, cask number and, of course, the rotation, to be stencilled onto them. This particular rotation was 69/4, which showed this was the fourth blending operation to have taken place in Glebe Street during 1969.

Then came the laborious, almost painful, repetitive job of weighing the casks and recording these details under the watchful eye of an HM Customs & Excise officer. The local officer for Glen Nevis was a stickler for detail. You could never pull the wool over his watchful eyes. He was 'Mr' Black to everybody. He drank alone. The job of filling the casks from the blending vat went on for the next two days, before the final 'out run' was taken. It was a long, drawn-out, labour-intensive process, but there were no alternatives in those days. Thankfully, the tediousness of the work was rewarded with a sly dram or two, unseen by Mr Black.

After the rigorous ordeal to which the blend had been subjected it was time for a rest. A long sleep, a marrying period, but this very much depended on demand. Tradition dictated that six months was the optimum marrying time, but on many occasions the international thirst for whisky meant it had to be prematurely awakened from its slumbers. Nevertheless, whenever possible, time would be allowed to weave its magic spell before the blend was finally despatched from Campbeltown up to Glasgow or even Grangemouth for bottling. Little did I know the bottling plant in Grangemouth would one day become the main bottling facility for Whyte & Mackay.

During my time in Campbeltown we prepared many different styles of blends. The age varied from four up to majestic 21-year-old expressions. These were the nobility, the royal family of de-luxe whiskies, distinguished and dignified by age. When the men were not working on these blends in Glebe Street they were either initiating the removal of casks for despatch or were employed in the warehouses over at Glen Scotia Distillery, assisting in cask filling of new spirit and helping out generally in the warehouses. One week later it was my turn – a new insight into the wonders of Scotch whisky. For the first time I was to be introduced to the 'art' of distillation; the very lifeblood of the Scotch whisky industry. No wonder I was excited at the thought of visiting Glen Scotia – one of the last survivors from Campbeltown's great distilling era.

Glen Scotia Distillery was situated at 12 High Street. The address was quite a puzzle to me. It certainly was not the 'High Street' in terms of its importance to the town, and it did not seem to be situated at any particular altitude. Nevertheless, I was looking forward to seeing inside Glen Scotia. Despite my family history and the fact I was working in the whisky industry, I had never been in a distillery before. Naturally I was eager to see it and feel the real spirit of my life.

The distillery had been founded as 'Scotia' in 1832, by Stewart, Galbraith & Co, and was apparently built near to Campbeltown's ancient Parliament Square, where Fergus, first king of Scotland, constructed a parliament house in 503. For the next 340 years Scotland was governed from this location, and it has been suggested the Stone of Destiny on which Scottish monarchs were traditionally crowned came from here. Not a lot people know that!

Scotia was owned by Duncan MacCallum from 1924 to 1928, when it fell silent. The story goes that MacCallum was defrauded of the enormous sum of £40,000 by a group of con men. This would seem to have caused him to become deeply depressed, because on 23rd

December 1930 he drowned himself in Crosshill Loch, from which the distillery takes its process water. However, another version of the story is that he hanged himself in the distillery mill room. I have been told one stillman hated going up to the mill room alone at night because, not surprisingly, he sensed an eerie presence there.

Subsequently, Glen Scotia was owned by Hiram Walker & Sons (Scotland) Ltd, before being acquired by A Gillies & Co in 1955. In 1970 Gillies became part of Amalgamated Distilled Products Ltd, Glasgow, and the licence was held by A Gillies & Co until its closure in 1984. Gibson International bought Glen Scotia and reopened it in 1989, but Gibson went bankrupt in 1994. I hope you are paying attention to all these dates now! The distillery was then purchased by the Glen Catrine Bonded Warehouse Ltd, which now trades as Loch Lomond Distillery Co Ltd.

I must confess when I approached the distillery it was not quite what I was anticipating. Although I had never been inside them, Edradour and Blair Athol distilleries at Pitlochry always appeared well maintained, and all the photographs I had seen of distilleries featured smart stone buildings equipped with proudly polished stills. From the outside, Glen Scotia looked more like an American penitentiary prison than a Scottish distillery. The place clearly had not been painted since before the War, and upstairs rows of windows were boarded over. It was not a good start. My heart sank with disappointment. Once inside the distillery office I was rapidly reminded of the warehouses in Glebe Street. Glen Scotia was also dark, dingy and somewhat depressing. Obviously I hoped

The Glen Scotia stillroom today. Very little has changed for over a hundred years. *Courtesy of Gavin D. Smith.*

things would improve. The warm, welcoming smile from Michael Smith certainly went some way towards lifting my spirits. Michael was the manager, and he had taken over the role from his father.

'Richard Paterson, I presume', he said. 'Welcome to the true spirit of Campbeltown. Forget about the others, this is the real stuff.'

Because it was not the done thing to visit rival distilleries, it would be decades later before I would have the pleasure of seeing the 'others' in action. It was obvious from the way he spoke Michael was passionate about his distillery, but he was also clearly frustrated by the lack of funds made available to him. It was not long before he was telling me as far as

Glasgow was concerned, he might as well have been on another planet, since the directors rarely made any genuine effort to visit his pride and joy.

Michael appeared to be in a hurry, as no sooner was I in his office, than I was entering into the inner sanctum of his distillery. As we walked into the stillhouse I expected to see big, beautiful, gleaming pot stills. This was not the case. They were big, or at least they were bulbous, with very thick necks, but they were dark and sad, almost lifeless.

They reminded me in a way of a riveted hull of a ghostly ship. They were cold and sinister, you could barely see the gleam of copper through their blackened overcoats.

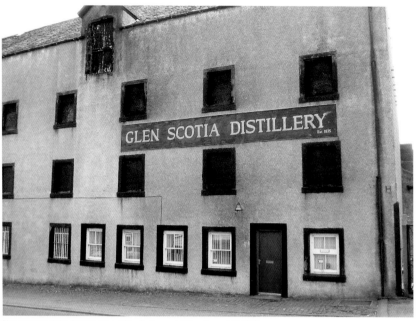

Not a pretty sight. But it's the whisky that counts! *Courtesy of Neil Wilson.*

These were not the gleaming stills of my imagination, all polished up in their finery for an elegant evening out. These were stills you would not want to meet in a dark alley ...

It was obvious they were just regarded as functional tools, nothing more than a means of producing spirit.

It was not just the stills, either. I could not help but notice that some of the barley spread around the malting floor looked decidedly black and unhealthy. Almost burnt. Now, I was no chemist, but that surely had to be a bad sign. It was only many years later I learnt this discolouration was caused by 'ergot'. Ergot is a fungal organism which had caused the deaths of many a Scotsman during the

famine years of the 19th century. Thankfully, today, with improved cereal analysis, ergot is a thing of the past, though it was used to develop medicines that enhance sexuality, and the hallucinogenic drug LSD is an ergot derivative. So the old fungal organism did have its positive side.

I am not saying the Smiths and their staff were not dedicated, that was the accepted level of professionalism during the 1960s. There were no tourists to please. No need to have shiny stills and polished spirit safes for them to photograph. This was essentially a factory devoted to producing whisky for blending. Nothing else.

Michael must have detected my lack of

enthusiasm for the distillery. 'Remember, it's the actual spirit that's important, along with the casks. Forget what you see. Always remember that.' To this day I still try never to be deceived by appearances. Some of the ugliest distilleries with the ugliest of casks, on occasion can produce the most beautiful whiskies.

'This is called a spirit safe', said Michael. For a second I was mesmerised. I was transported back to boyhood adventure stories. It reminded me of a golden chest which had been stolen by pirates from some faraway land. But the treasures it contained were pure liquid, soon to be transformed into liquid gold.

The spirit safe was introduced by Septimus Fox at Port Ellen Distillery on Islay in the early 1820s, and in 1825 became a compulsory requirement as a result of the 1823 Excise Act. The spirit safe is the stillman's crystal ball. He can see the spirit running. He alone decides when the spirit is right. When the middle cut can be finally drawn off, to become his stillman's dram.[7]

But if you are thinking of having a wee drink, forget it. A heavy padlock quickly reminds you that HM Customs & Excise control its destiny, and woe betide any distiller who abuses the regulations.

This great treasure chest was almost like a mother's womb. At last it was revealing new life. Aqua vitae, 'the water of life'. These dark, dingy, riveted stills were at last showing me their worth. I immediately wanted to smell it, but Michael said 'you'll have to wait till we're back in the office. You can sample some of the new spirit then. But you must remember the spirit is upset. It's 'angry'. It needs to be tamed, nurtured and comforted, by one of Mother Nature's greatest blessings ... wood. Now come along and see the final stage.'

As we came out of the stillhouse I could hear the 'thud thud' of bungs being driven home into casks, and the echoes of men shouting out things like '55 and three-quarters, did you get that?' While this weighing was going on, another team of men was already rolling casks out of the filling store towards the warehouses where their long slumber would commence.

As the casks rolled over the courtyard the scrunch of wood on gravel and rough cement echoed out like cap guns. I was truly amazed by the dexterity and expertise with which the men controlled these heavy, unwieldy characters. I was surprised, too, by the speed at which they moved the casks, making them change direction by the mere touch of a finger against the rim. What a bunch of performing artists they were. They made it look so easy, but I later found out that certainly was not the case. It took many hours and blisters to master the 'buggers' as they were often referred to by the men.

As they approached the warehouse door the men unceremoniously gave each cask one final kick. 'Away to bed', they would cry out

7 Dram: 'Defined by *The Dictionary of Drink* as a Scottish slang term for "a measure of spirits (usually whisky)." Usage is principally Scottish, but has now become synonymous with a *nip* of whisky in any geographical location. [David] Daiches, like most commentators, considers the word *dram* to be of Greek derivation, coming from *drachma*, one-eighth of an ounce or sixty grains in apothecaries' weights. In the sense of liquid it was originally one-eighth of a fluid ounce of medicine, and ultimately "a small draught of cordial, stimulant, or spirituous liquor". (*Oxford English Dictionary*).' *A–Z of Whisky*, Gavin D. Smith.

disrespectfully. Inside the warehouse another group of men were beginning to build up a stow in the far corner. This would now become the spirit's home. For many casks, there was to be a long, uninterrupted sleep, although the cold, rough spirit would breathe gently through the pores of the wood, relaxing its aggressive temperament.

'As you can see, Richard, everything's traditional down here', Michael said. 'We've none of this metal racking that seems to be the order of the day. Do you smell it? It's damp, it's dark, with a minimum of concrete on the floor. The rest is compressed soil covered by cinders. You must let the elements work their magical spell.'

'Every shape and size is in here. Butts, hogsheads, barrels – we've got the lot! But my preference is for hogsheads. These big bastards, butts or puncheons, are the devil to handle, and they always give me inconsistencies. They're never the same, despite what people tell me. The trouble is I have to make use of what I'm given, and judging by the number of leakers we get, head office in Glasgow don't know much about wood. Their attitude is "distil it, fill it, and mature it". But given good wood, we can transform this aggressive spirit into something really special. Come on back to my office, and we'll see what you think of the new make.'

Michael poured out the innocent-looking white spirit from a 20-oz 'dock' sample bottle. It immediately reminded me of our Cowboy Game back in Glasgow, only this time there were no games, this was for real and now I was treating the watery spirit with respect. The glasses were the same as my father's – small copitas, short-stemmed, awkward and thin at the top. I never liked them! I much prefer the large, more bulbous, long-stemmed style which I use in my sample room today. (You can't blame me when you see the size of my nose!). I swirled the spirit around the glass and eagerly drew it to my nose. BANG! The high strength hit me immediately, but I managed to control my visible emotions; the last thing I wanted was for Michael to think I was a complete amateur ... which I really was.

As the raw spirit started to settle down its true character began to be revealed. Complex, rich, aromatic, with hints of sardine oil, damp leather, hot milk, subtle tones of baby sick, but that inevitable whisper of briny sea salt. But not just any salt. Damp salt, which gracefully lingered in the background. The spirit was demanding to be filled into good wood, to take it through its various stages of development. It needed tender love.

'Compare it to this five-year-old, which we're now bottling', instructed Michael. Certainly the burn of the strength had been removed, and the spirit had a gentler, more attractive side to it. I was not very impressed. To my mind its boisterous character had not been truly tamed. It was still immature. Simple as that. I looked at Michael, and he nodded in unspoken agreement.

'Yes Richard, five years ... it is too young. And look at the bottle and its label, no great thought has been put into that either – they are obviously not expecting great sales.'

It was rather curious. Small, dumpy, and reflecting the old style of whisky bottles which would have been made of black glass, only this one was well cut and green. The label carried the age statement of five years, and I seem to recall it had a swarthy highlander standing in the middle. It truly lacked appeal.

In my opinion, Glen Scotia needs age; between 15 and 25 years, matured in both American white oak, and also specially selected sherry butts. At its best it can be quite magnificent … charming, elegant and refined. However, these 'babies' are rare, which is not surprising, as the distillery has had so many owners and periods of closure over the years. Glen Scotia had really made an impact on me, and in particular those tarnished, unloved stills. This visit would be the first of many I was to make to distilleries the length and breadth of Scotland during the years to come.

Sadly, it came to a sudden end, when Michael stood up and said abruptly, 'Sorry, but you'll have to excuse me now, as I've got a speech to make tonight at our local Rotary Club in the White Hart Hotel, and I haven't even prepared for it. If there's anything else you want to see, don't hesitate to come back, but I hope this afternoon has been of some interest to you. Goodbye.'

I barely had time to thank him before I was out on the street again. Thirty-five years later I was back on that very same street, and nothing much seemed to have changed. I am afraid Glen Scotia Distillery is just as depressing today as when I saw it for the first time all those years ago. If it has been painted since, I did not notice, and the windows are still boarded up. It continues to look like the outside of a prison. Inside, the stills remain dark and sinister, weeds grow through a gap in the corner of the roof, and the blue-painted washbacks are badly rusted and corroded. Today, Glen Scotia still appears to be regarded as nothing more than a 'whisky factory', but I remembered Michael's words of wisdom: 'It's

the actual spirit that's important. Forget what you see.' But it is difficult.

What I will never forget is Campbeltown itself. After that eventful afternoon, with an hour to spare before I knocked off work for the day, I decided to follow my nose down to the harbour, the heart of this historic town. There was a brisk, fresh breeze blowing, the usual dampness was in the air, and the smell of fish was very apparent, which was not surprising, because between 60 to 70 fishing boats were unloading their precious cargoes to an audience of screaming herring gulls and the usual assortment of bus trippers and old men at a loose end.

There was a real buzz about the place, with the fishermen coming and going, shouting and whistling, winding in nets, and boxes of fish being hauled in and out of the fish market. As I walked along the beach, the aromas of fish gave way to the prickly, medicinal scent of seaweed, and that indefinable smell of things decomposing you experience at all harbours, wherever in the world you travel. However, Campbeltown harbour is steeped in history. Its busy past has left an indelible mark not only on the town but also on myself.

On my way back towards Euan's house, I passed the entrance to Springbank Distillery. A visit was out of the question, of course, even if the distillery sign was inviting. I was determined one day I would return. Little did I know that, like Glen Scotia, it would only take 35 years to fulfil my burning ambition! Today, Springbank is one of the most highly regarded and sought-after single malts, with a devoted following all over the world. It truly is an outstanding single malt.

It is thanks to Springbank that 'Campbeltown' is still recognised at all as a single malt whisky region, though many people now disrespectfully include Campbeltown whiskies within the Highland region. Bollocks! It is an independent region as far as I am concerned, and always will be. People say, 'oh well there's only three distilleries there, how can that justify a region?' The simple answer is there are only three Lowland distilleries working, too, but nobody suggests scrapping *that* classification!

Springbank Distillery was founded in 1828, and its survival is due principally to dedicated family ownership, which has kept it alive through many lean times, when the rest of the distilling industry in Campbeltown was crumbling all around it. The continuing global success of Springbank, and the revival of Glengyle Distillery, the first new distillery in Campbeltown for over a century, makes me optimistic there is a viable and even vibrant future for Campbeltown single malts. After such a precarious past, Glen Scotia is also doing well, currently making three or four mashes per day, working five days a week, and turning out 100,000 litres of spirit per annum.

Frank McHardy is general manager at Springbank, and also oversees Glengyle Distillery, where the 'Frank McHardy Production Building' has been named in his honour. Frank arrived at Springbank in 1977, and worked there for a decade, before taking up the manager's role at Bushmills in Northern Ireland. He returned to Springbank in 1996. I was delighted to meet up with Frank when I went back to Campbeltown so many years after my initial visit. The genial Frank was more than pleased to give his version of the development of Scotch whisky, and of Campbeltown as a centre for distilling.

'Whisky, as the old story goes, came from Ireland, where they used it as horse liniment, and the Scots perfected it, and made it fit for drinking. But the natural stepping off place from Ireland was the Mull of Kintyre, then up to Iona, and on to mainland Scotland. But really, at the end of the day, if you go back to the mid-1800s there were 34 distilleries here. Now some of them were so small they would fit in this room, I mean it was your farmer who grew some barley and wanted added income, so he had a distillation process.

'Licensing laws then came along and killed all that, so it fell to around 24 distilleries in Campbeltown. The main reason there were so many here was the good access. You have great access by ship into Campbeltown. If you go away back in the mid-1800s there was no road system in Scotland, so you went places by sea. Now you had a ready, obvious supply of peat in this area, massive stocks of peat, you even had a coal mine. Also the climate. There's a lot of rain here. Also lots of farmers came from Ayrshire and settled in this area; they brought some whisky-making expertise from there. So all these things combined to make Campbeltown basically the whisky capital of Scotland at one time.

'So, you have all these distilleries operating here, 24, around about the turn of the century, booming, because they were feeding the blending market in Glasgow. I hope you're taking all this in, Richard?'

'Yes, I am, but give me more dates.'

'Well, you had all this whisky going across to Glasgow, going into the blends and being exported and one of the most important destinations was America. Prohibition [the

Volstead Act, 28th October 1919 to 20th February 1933] came along in America and that basically killed one of the main markets for Campbeltown distilleries. But before that, Campbeltown distillery owners couldn't see any end to this sort of boom, people were making more and more whisky, but they were not investing heavily in new equipment so they were beginning to take short cuts. Really the start of the demise of Campbeltown was the poor product that they produced.

'Prohibition basically finished them off, but in between times, remember, you had all these Speyside distilleries coming on stream as well, and Speyside produced a much lighter, fruitier, more estery spirit which was more palatable to the blenders and the public than the heavy, oily Campbeltown malts. Springbank was an exception, of course. We produce a much lighter spirit.

'So all these things, Prohibition, Speyside, and a poor spirit, meant that lots of distilleries closed down, so about 1930 you had only three left working. People then stripped out their buildings, took away the plant, knocked them down, found other uses for them, so basically there's nothing left except Springbank, Glen Scotia and now we have Glengyle which closed in 1925 and has re-opened again. It was built in 1873.

'The actual town of Campbeltown is beginning to take off again, not due to the whisky industry in any way, but due to Vestas of Machrihanish who are a Danish company. They build windmills and employ around 240 people locally in the town.

'When I came here about six years ago the town was basically down and out. The shipyard closed, the Jaeger clothes factory closed, and a lot of civilian jobs went when the RAF pulled out of their Machrihanish base. Shops were shutting, things like that, but you don't see too much of that now, there's a new sort of optimism and enthusiasm. It carries forward, even to the fact that they've formed a school pipe band, a junior pipe band, who are sweeping all before them throughout Scotland, things like that. So employment is good. If you want a job here, you'll get a job.

'We don't tamper with things at Springbank. Not for the sake of efficiency. My remit here is to make Springbank the way it's always been made and so what, if it costs a little more. What's most important is making it the same way.

'And we are the only distillery in Scotland that does 100% of the whole process; we don't buy malted barley, we buy barley and we malt it. 100% of the malting is carried out in our malting floors and if you buy a bottle of the product with our label, it's all bottled here, everything is bottled here.

'Springbank has something in it which is salty-like in taste, and that comes during maturation. It's only three and a half miles to the Atlantic out there, you've got the prevailing winds coming in. I mean, all our buildings are full of salt, the windows get grimy and have to be cleaned. It's all salt.

'One of the reasons why we decided to start up Glengyle was we did think we might want to sell a little bit more whisky but we don't want to expand Springbank, so having another distillery helps the sales a bit. Hedley Wright, our Managing Director, was always very keen to have another distillery in Campbeltown, due to his long family connections with the place.

'We walked along that road one day, where Glengyle is, and the buildings used to belong to the Kintyre Farmers, who were a farmers' co-operative. They went, and it was taken over by BOCM who sell animal feeds, barley and all sorts of things. Then they decided to get rid of it, and as we walked past it we saw a 'For Sale' sign. Hedley said 'Mmm, for sale. My great-great-uncle founded that place, I think I'll put in an offer for it', which he duly did. He bought the buildings with no intentions of putting a distillery in them. And it was only later on that he thought, 'well I've always fancied having a distillery in it, we'll have a go at it, let's put in a small distillery.' So we did, and the small distillery can produce about 750,000 litres of alcohol a year. You wanted dates, Richard. Well, it opened on Friday 26th March 2004, and we made 60,000 litres of alcohol. We plan to do the same next year, but no more.'

Just listening to Frank and the passion he still has for Campbeltown and its people bodes well for the future, though the fishing industry there, as in all of Scotland, remains a precarious occupation.

If you look at photographs of the quayside in Campbeltown a century ago, all you can see are enormous stacks of barrels. People have sometimes thought these were whisky barrels, but they were actually for storing and transporting herring. If they had been filled with whisky I doubt they would have stayed on the quayside long enough for the photographer to get his picture!

One hundred years ago around 80 Campbeltown boats would be at the herring fishing, and Campbeltown was home to a vigorous fishing fleet until quite recent times.

Today less than 20 white fish boats regularly work out of Campbeltown. Herring fishing declined at the same time as distilling, and now mainly shellfish are landed. The harbour is actually Campbeltown Loch, immortalised in song by the late Andy Stewart. 'Campbeltown Loch I wish you were whisky, Campbeltown Loch, och aye!' Everyone thinks that it was an old music hall song, but Andy Stewart actually wrote it himself in the early 1960s.

A multitude of distilleries sprang up throughout the 'wee toon'. As the distilleries multiplied over the years, Campbeltown's golden cargo flooded into the ports of Glasgow and Edinburgh. The taste of Campbeltown malt during these industrial years was very much in vogue but as the demand increased, the quality began to suffer. Many complained, particularly in England, that the spirit was too rugged and gutsy for their delicate Sassenach palates. Some say that the emerging Highland malt distillers put a story about calling Campbeltown malt 'stinking fish' to deride it and divert demand to Speyside. Whatever the truth, this was certainly a golden opportunity for the competing Speyside and Lowland distillers. Geographically, the Lowlanders were ideally placed to service the English thirst for Scotch whisky. The Lowland Ladies[8] were enthusiastically embraced by the blenders at the expense of the heavy, oily, fishy Campbeltown malts.

The demand for Campbeltown whiskies rapidly declined and it was not long before

8 Lowland malts, in view of their light, elegant, feminine style, were affectionately christened the 'Lowland Ladies'.

many of the famous distillery names of that great 'Whisky City' became relics of the past.

Meanwhile in North America, descendents of the ingenious Scots and Irish who had emigrated to the States, taking with them the tradition of whisky-making, demonstrated their resourcefulness by charring the inside of used bourbon barrels to impart greater flavour. These charred casks gave the spirit that was filled into them a notably distinctive, attractive character with notes of vanilla, cinnamon, caramel and light citrus. This charred character became synonymous with bourbon, so much so that an act of 1964 stipulated that all bourbon by law must be 'matured in charred, fresh barrels'. Once the bourbon distillers had used them the casks were dismantled and shipped to Scotland where they were rebuilt in the cooperages, creating an historic and enduring link between Scotch and American distilling. More than 90% of the 18.4 million casks currently in use for Scotch whisky maturation held bourbon in a previous life.

Walking around Campbeltown today, the heritage of Scotch whisky distilling lingers in lots of unexpected places. You only have to look at West Coast Motor Services bus depot in Saddell Street to discover the former Benmore Distillery, which operated from 1868 until 1927. Incidentally, during his visit to this distillery in July 1886, Alfred Barnard made a remarkably rare comment on the new spirit of Benmore, which he described it as 'clean, bright, and sparkling'.

When Barnard toured Burnside Distillery he noted, 'it is the only distillery in Campbeltown that is actually in the country, being planted on the grassy slopes of Bengullien, and about half a mile from the centre of the town.' Today Burnside is engulfed by the Campbeltown Creamery Ltd, which took over the site when the distillery closed in 1924, although the old distillery buildings still stand at the heart of the extended plant.

The spirit of Campbeltown is also to be found in the derelict warehouses of Glebe Street where once I worked, and in Lochend Street, where a Tesco supermarket replaced much of the remains of Lochhead Distillery during the 1990s. Today, only a bold, stone warehouse frontage remains between two adjoining buildings, a faded sign above the blue door announcing to an uncaring public its former status as a bonded warehouse for Lochhead Distillery.

Happily, one historic building with whisky industry connections that survives today in Campbeltown is the famous White Hart Hotel, at the top of Main Street, where Michael Smith of Glen Scotia and the rest of the Rotary Club were meeting that evening almost 40 long years ago. The White Hart dates from Georgian times, and was also where Alfred Barnard stayed for a fortnight in July 1886.

Barnard's time in Campeltown was comparatively brief, and so was mine. My days working in the warehouses and Glen Scotia Distillery, were soon over. It was time to return to the city. Only now it would be different. Things had changed. I had a newfound confidence, having worked with the spirit itself, and experienced, however briefly, the realities of whisky-making at the sharp end.

The people of Campbeltown had taken me into their hearts, and I had come to value their generosity of spirit and their respect for mother nature. Behind their hospitable smiles one sensed a hidden sadness, the sadness known all too well to fishing communities throughout Scotland. The sadness of loss. The sea could be devastatingly cruel, and over the generations had taken its toll on the community of Campbeltown. But the sea had also brought prosperity, playing a significant part in the town's whisky trade. I was sad to leave.

Like the whisky in the Ardlussa and Glen Nevis warehouses, I felt I had matured during my short time in Kintyre. The spirit of Campbeltown had taught me more than I could ever have imagined. It had certainly been a horrendous bus journey to Campbeltown, but looking back, the trip had been well worth it. I now thought I was ready for new challenges, beyond the confines of A Gillies & Co.

A new beginning. And that beginning was to be with the distillers Whyte & Mackay.

Chapter Four
A BLENDER IN THE MAKING

'Scotch whisky is the true spirit of Scotland. It has a timeless mystery and romance which is enjoyed and appreciated by people throughout the world.' } ALASTAIR MCINTOSH, MD, THE SCOTCH WHISKY EXPERIENCE, EDINBURGH

Whyte & Mackay was difficult to ignore in Glasgow during the late 1960s. The company had a high profile in its home city, so I was already well aware of its whiskies. Travelling on the Glasgow underground was one prime example. Every station I passed through carried an eye-catching advert for Major Hartley Whyte's 'Whiskycisms'.

The main theme of these 'Whiskycisms' was drawing the consumers' attention to the light character of the Whyte & Mackay blend. One advert proudly stated 'It is the lightest, cleanest-tasting whisky obtainable today.' The major looked every inch the retired army officer, with his curled moustache and dignified manner. He was not only the company chairman but also its master blender.

You could not fail to be drawn to the brand by his obvious respectability and commitment, which seemed to guarantee quality. Bearing in mind that although these were the 'swinging sixties' the Second World War were still a very recent memory for a large part of the British population. If a major endorsed a product in those days it carried weight. People took notice. If you tried the same marketing campaign today they would just laugh.

The Whyte & Mackay adverts were not confined to the Underground by any means. At Glasgow Central Station a giant Whyte & Mackay bottle had been displayed in 1967, when the *Evening Times* had offered a case of whisky to the person who correctly estimated the number of standard bottles it might contain.

I was captivated by the originality of this form of marketing, and also by the firm's daring attitude in its adverts. One sequence which demonstrated this was 'Beware Sassenach!' The message was forget 'heavy' whiskies. 'It is the lightest Scotch your customers can buy.' This cheeky campaign was directed at establishing the Whyte & Mackay brand in England during the early 1960s.

They obviously knew their market and where and how they wanted it to develop. I wanted to be part of that. So when I heard they were looking for an assistant blender I was eager to apply for the position. The chief blender was Alistair Hart, whose older brother, Ian, had worked for my father back in the late 1950s. This at least meant my name would be familiar to the man interviewing me for the job. I hadn't forgotton either that his father had looked after the Paterson family teeth. I just hoped I would not be as nervous during my interview with Alistair as I was when visiting his father's surgery!

I duly applied for the job, and a few days later Alistair himself phoned to say Jack Ligertwood, one of Whyte & Mackay's directors, wanted to see me. It was great news. I was in with a chance. The interview took place at Whyte & Mackay's head office in Baltic Chambers, 50 Wellington Street. It seemed to go well, because three days later I was asked to go back for a second meeting at 9.15am.

I distinctly remember Jack Ligertwood was somewhat irritated because Alistair was not present, particularly as he would be my direct boss if I was lucky enough to be appointed. Drawing on my 'apprenticeship' with Gillies, and in particular my time spent in Campbeltown, I must have been able to convince Jack Ligertwood that I already had a sound working knowledge of distilling and blending, as at the end of our conversation he offered me the job. £750 a year. Not a fortune, but at least I was getting closer to that magic figure of £1,000.

I sprinted down the staircase, elated with my success. As I reached the bottom I almost knocked over Alistair Hart as he hurried, breathlessly, into the building.

'How did it go then?' he panted.

The smell of his breath was fearsome. Garlic, curry and beer seemed to be oozing from every pore of him.

'I should have been there', he said. 'Big Jack'll kill me, but I had a bit of a heavy night with the lads last night, and I slept in … like most mornings. I've got to go, I'm late enough already. See you next month.'

And with that he was gone.

Looking backwards as I walked up Wellington Street, I became aware for the first time of the sheer size of Baltic Chambers. It was a huge, confident red-sandstone Victorian building. It had been generating wealth for the best part of a century. Not only was it the home of Whyte & Mackay, but also many other companies and organisations, including, ironically, Alcoholics Anonymous, which was handily located on the same floor.

To my mind it was the perfect place for such a prestigious whisky firm with a long and distinguished heritage to be based. For, despite its willingness to be fresh and innovative, Whyte & Mackay was no Johnny-come-lately on the Scotch whisky scene. Today, the firm claims to have been established in 1844, but this was not strictly true. It would be more accurate to say it was founded in 1881.

In 1875 James Whyte and Charles Mackay joined the thriving company of Allan & Poynter, whose roots went back to 1844. The founders had both died some years previously, and the company was now under the stewardship of the energetic and entrepreneurial William Hunter Scott. The firm was based at 83 Jamaica Street, close to the River Clyde, and had warehouses in nearby Eglington Street. It specialised in agricultural products, chemicals, and warehousing, including wine, sherry, brandy, rum, and Scotch whisky.

In the early 19th century the River Clyde had been deepened, and as a result, warehouse space was increasingly in demand, as larger ships were able to dock close to the city centre. During the 1830s, Glasgow became a key centre for the import of tobacco and tea, and 80 general warehouses were listed in the Glasgow Post Office Directory. Ten of these offered bonding facilities.

By the late 1880s Scotch whisky had become a significant part of the firm's business. The decimation of so many vineyards due to the phylloxera aphid greatly increased the popularity of Scotch whisky in preference to cognac, particularly in England, and Allan & Poynter was well placed to take full advantage of this golden opportunity.

The company expanded its whisky business by warehousing for a number of major companies, such as J&W Harvey of Dundashill Distillery in Glasgow, J Ferguson & Son, proprietors of Jura Distillery, W&J Mutter of Bowmore Distillery on Islay, Thomas Stewart & Co of Glenturret Distillery in Perthshire, and William Gillies of Oban Distillery over on the west coast.

Allan & Poynter did more than just

Our founding fathers – James Whyte and Charles Mackay – who both died of cirrhosis of the liver.

warehouse whisky, however. The firm advanced money to the owners of Strathclyde Distillery, Talisker on Skye and Tobermory Distillery on Mull to help fund business expansion.

William Scott died on 24th March 1881, and James Whyte and Charles Mackay took the opportunity to secure their own futures by purchasing the wines and spirits part of the business from Scott's widow Rachel Morrison Scott. Denied the use of the familiar title Allan & Poynter, they named their joint venture Whyte & Mackay, set themselves up at 35 Ann Street (now Midland Street), and rather cheekily claimed the company had been founded in 1844.

Unfortunately, there is no surviving record of when Whyte & Mackay first started blending whiskies, but when they acquired large, new premises at 26 Robertson Lane in 1882 blending was certainly an important part of their overall business.

A visitor to Robertson Lane described the blending vats as ' ... huge specimens of the cooper's art where thousands upon thousands of gallons can be blended at the one operation'. Significantly, provision had been made on the other three 'flats' in the vaults for blended whiskies to mature and marry. Warehouse capacity exceeded 10,000 casks, and the majority of whisky being filled into this warehouse was brought by sea from Campbeltown. This was soon to change, however, as Speyside and Lowland whiskies increasingly became attractive to blenders, at the expense of Campbeltown malts.

The staff of Whyte & Mackay in Robertson Lane, Glasgow in 1887. Our first Managing Director was John McIlraith (third from the right), who was to spend a remarkable 70 years with the company.

In 1896 it would appear that Whyte & Mackay began to blend and sell whiskies under their own name. Overseas markets were important for the company from this early date, and the first issue of the *West Australian Sunday Times* of 19th December 1897 exhorted readers to 'Drink only Whyte & Mackay whisky.' Business was prospering, and the company moved into the brand new and fashionable Baltic Chambers, which had been completed in 1900.[9]

Records show that while the company warehouses took in 955 casks of whisky in 1898, that figure had risen to 2,561 casks per year in 1904. Whiskies used by Whyte & Mackay included grain whisky from Dundashill, Cameronbridge and Glenochil, and single malts from Auchtermuchty in Fife, Speyside Distillery at Kingussie, Glen Garioch in Oldmeldrum, and Linkwood near Elgin. By this time both James Whyte and Charles Mackay had become wealthy men. Whyte lived at Tudor House in Skermorlie, Ayrshire, while Mackay liked to be nearer to the heart of his business and owned a large villa, called Bellevue, in the desirable Glasgow suburb of Pollokshields.

Another sign of their prosperity and confidence in the blended Scotch whisky

9 The estimated cost of building Baltic Chambers was £38,500 and in August 2004 Clerical & Medical Managed Fund purchased it for £6m.

market was James Whyte's purchase of shares in the DCL and the North British Distillery. The 'North British' was a grain distillery in Edinburgh's Gorgie district, established in 1885 by a consortium of whisky blenders and merchants, headed by Andrew Usher. The distillery was set up to guarantee supplies of grain spirit for independent operators in the face of a growing DCL monopoly.

During the next three decades, the whisky industry experienced periods of both boom and bust, but despite its varying fortunes James Whyte and Charles Mackay left substantial estates when they died. Charles Mackay died at 4.10am on the 5th September 1919, leaving £182,998 (worth approximately £5.5 million today), of which £65,000 was held in cash at his bank. He was 69 years old, and was buried at Craigton Cemetery, Glasgow. James Whyte died at 10pm on 27th August 1921, leaving an estate valued at £66,091. He was 77, and was buried at Largs Cemetery, Ayrshire. Both men died of cirrhosis of the liver, but that was an occupational hazard of working in the whisky industry at that time.

By 1921, the company was effectively being run by John McIlraith, Whyte & Mackay's first managing director, who had already put in more than 40 years service with the company. Following the death of James Whyte, his middle son Hartley Waddington Whyte, aged 23, became a director of the company under the watchful eye of the veteran John McIlraith. Although it is the high-profile Whytes and Mackays whose names are principally remembered, it is important not to underestimate the enormous contribution of people like John McIlraith. Aged just 23, Hartley Whyte must surely have relied heavily on his vast experience of the Scotch whisky industry.

During the following three years the company enjoyed its greatest prosperity of the inter-war years, thanks in part to a clandestine trade with 'dry' America, via the firm's established Canadian markets. The situation was also aided by a slowly recovering world economy, which featured particularly strong trading with the Empire.

However, by 1926 things were far from rosy, and not just for Whyte & Mackay and the whisky industry. It was a time of great industrial unrest in Britain, and between early May and mid-October the country was in the grip of the 'General Strike'. In that year a number of notable distilleries fell silent. These included Auchenblae, near Fettercairn, Auchtermuchty in Fife, Ben Wyvis and Glenskiach in Ross-shire, Isla in Perth and the Campbeltown trio of Glenside, Kinloch and Springside.

High stock levels and low profits were the focus of Whyte & Mackay's problems. The company was hanging on by its fingernails, and to avoid takeover it had to be restructured, but trading difficulties persisted for the next decade. In 1934 a loss of £5,091 was posted, the worst financial result in the firm's history. Two years later, however, the situation was improving and a profit of £5,411 was recorded.

As the Second World War loomed, Scotch whisky distillers were determined to avoid the problems experienced during the previous conflict, and began to stockpile large volumes of whisky. Remarkably, Whyte & Mackay managed to make a profit during each of the war years, with the indefatigable John McIlraith still at the helm.

The evolution of the Whyte & Mackay brand. From left to right: 1887, 1911, 1920, 1960, 1980, 1985, 1990, 1998, 2000, 2006 and the Rare and Prestige bottling of 2007 mirroring the 1887 original.

With peace declared, Hartley Whyte and his brother Alex, who also worked for the company, returned from army service to 'Civvy Street', and the ageing John McIlraith began to take a back seat. He died on 24th October 1950, after an incredible, and almost unprecedented, 70 years of devoted service.

Someone else who would devote a major part of his life to Whyte & Mackay was Jack Ligertwood, who joined as company secretary in 1946, aged just 21. Despite the daunting competition which the comparatively small company was facing, he soon recognised its enormous potential. Nevertheless, Whyte & Mackay was only selling a paltry 3,000 cases a year in the Scottish market in those post-war years.

The war had taken its toll on Britain's industrial might and economic wellbeing, and Scotch whisky was just one commodity coping with its effects. Jack must have realised it was going to be an uphill struggle, but if one man could turn things around it was 'Big Jack' Ligertwood. Even today, in his 80s, he retains all the passion and drive that propelled him to the highest office in the organisation.

One way in which Whyte & Mackay tried to compete was by enthusiastically embracing advertising. In 1951, a mere £296 was spent on promotion, but the following year, that figure leapt to £2,300. That was nothing, however, as in 1958 the firm's advertising budget stood at an extraordinary £20,000. The message was clear. Whyte & Mackay meant business.

Jack Ligertwood gathered a young,

dynamic team around him, and set about consolidating Whyte & Mackay's position as a leading whisky brand in its native Scotland. He was also keen to conquer the English market, and in 1955 appointed Jarvis Halliday & Co as sole distributors for England and Wales. This wine-based company was located in Aylesbury, Buckinghamshire. A few years later, Whyte & Mackay strengthened its position south of the border when it opened a London office at 62 Pall Mall.

Jack recognised that if you wanted to build a brand you had to have a large-scale distribution network in place. Also you had to have reliable blending and bottling plants. During the 1950s, Whyte & Mackay was spoilt for choice in terms of bottlers, mainly employing the Clyde Bonding Co Ltd;

Glasgow Bonding Co; Arbuckle, Smith & Co and Leith-based William Muir (Bond 9) Ltd.

By 1960, Whyte & Mackay was sufficiently successful to require guaranteed stocks of malt whisky, but was also concerned about its vulnerability to takeover, in particular from the mighty DCL or the increasingly powerful American-owned whisky conglomerates.

The month of May saw two marriages. One involved HRH Princess Margaret and Anthony Armstrong-Jones, the other was Whyte & Mackay Ltd and Mackenzie Brothers (Dalmore) Ltd. A new holding company, Dalmore, Whyte & Mackay Ltd, was formed.

There was a long-standing relationship between Whyte & Mackay and Dalmore

Distillery on the Cromarty Firth in Ross-shire, as the company had first purchased nine casks of whisky from Dalmore in 1895. The merger with Whyte & Mackay was attractive to the Mackenzies, as it removed the prospect of a potential hostile takeover bid, just as it did for their new Glasgow partners (see chapter 5).

Although safe from DCL's expansionist policies, Whyte & Mackay nevertheless still had to fight the giant for its share of the market. This necessitated increasingly innovative and exciting developments. Something different was required. Something to capture the imagination.

In the same year that the Dalmore merger was established, Jack Ligertwood introduced his famous plastic 'jigger'[10] cap to the Whyte & Mackay Special Blend. This was a golden-coloured, moulded plastic screw top, which could be used to measure ¼, ⅕ or ⅙ of a gill shots, the standard measures used in Scotland and England at the time. This new approach found immediate success. A success due in no small part to an inventive marketing campaign which declared, 'Free! With our 41/6d measure cap, one bottle of Whyte & Mackay!'[11]

The innovations continued. In June 1963 the 'Imperial Quart' (40-floz) bottle was unveiled to the on-trade. It contained half as much again as the standard bottle, yet would fit into the same shelf space. Because it was cheaper to produce, an estimated 12 shillings [60 pence] saving was passed directly to the trade. Such was the success of the venture that within a matter of months all of Whyte & Mackay's major competitors had adopted the Imperial Quart, and it was soon standard in the licensed trade.

Wishing to capitalise on what they boasted of as 'the lightest, most delicately blended … Scotch whisky you can buy', Whyte & Mackay embarked on an advertising campaign in late 1964 aimed directly at the female market. This was a radical departure, as whisky advertising had previously always been directed at men. If women appeared in whisky adverts at all, it was either to pour their 'masters' an adoring dram, or simply to be decorative.

The strapline for the new campaign was 'Once a good woman has tasted Whyte & Mackay, no man's dram is ever safe again.' The intention was to soften the image of the brand, while also being careful not to alienate male consumers. The Scotch whisky industry had finally recognised that female drinkers represented a vast, untapped market. This was in the same year that three women in London were found guilty of indecency in August for wearing the new trend in topless dresses. I doubt very much if they would have been prepared to pour their 'masters' an adoring dram. A year later they would be wearing Mary Quant's mini skirts. There was no end to it.

Perhaps in order to offset such outrageous feminism, Whyte & Mackay kept 'the lads' happy by running a major competition in association with *Playboy* magazine during

10 'The name given to a measure of spirits, specifically for use in cocktails, and also to the measuring vessel itself … the word "jigger" is first recorded in 1824 as a slang term for an illicit distillery … the modern cocktail-related use of jigger probably evolves from the occurrence of the word as an American synonym for "dram" in 1899 …' *A–Z of Whisky*, Gavin D. Smith.

11 £2.075 in today's money.

September 1965 which offered barmen a free trip to New York as first prize. The company's energy and imagination was soon rewarded in hard sales terms, and by late 1965 Whyte & Mackay Special Blended Scotch had risen to become the fifth most popular brand in Scotland.

This was the situation when I became part of the company in September 1970. Concorde had landed at Heathrow for the first time on 12th of the month, and I felt I had landed on my feet, having joined this dynamic, 'young' organisation. In terms of the Scotch whisky industry, 1970 marked something of a 'breathing space' between two frantic periods of distillery expansion and increasing output. The mid-1960s had seen new distilleries created and existing ones expanded and rebuilt, and the 1970s were to see the energetic continuation of that trend.

1970 itself was a 'quieter' year, no doubt due to the effects of a minor slump, but there were a number of distillery acquisitions, including Stanley P. Morrison Ltd's purchase of Glen Garioch Distillery in Aberdeenshire for £100,000 from the DCL subsidiary Scottish Malt Distillers (SMD). Morrison already owned Bowmore Distillery on Islay, and was to add the Lowland distillery of Auchentoshan to its portfolio in 1984. 1970 also saw Auchentoshan, at Dalmuir, near Glasgow, bought from Bass brewers by Eadie Cairns for a similar sum as Morrison had paid for Glen Garioch.

The process of industry consolidation which had begun in the late 1940s continued in 1970 when Hill, Thomson & Co Ltd merged with The Glenlivet and Glen Grant Distilleries Ltd and Longmorn Distilleries Ltd,

forming The Glenlivet Distillers Ltd. Similarly, October 1970 saw Highland Distilleries Ltd acquire the Perth-based Famous Grouse producer Matthew Gloag & Son Ltd. Chivas Brothers opened a major blending and warehousing operation not far from Auchentoshan Distillery, while International Distillers & Vintners Ltd (IDV) officially opened their new Blythswood warehousing site at Inchinnan, near Renfrew. The first phase of this project cost £2.5 million alone, and saw maturation capacity for 18 million gallons of spirit fully operational by the end of the year. Capacity was later extended to 25 million gallons. IDV operated the Speyside trio of Glen Spey, Knockando and Strathmill distilleries and were best known for their popular J&B blended whisky brand.

On my first day in my new job I was eager to make a good impression, and so arrived 20 minutes early, at ten past nine. I had taken just as much trouble in my preparation as on that first day at Gillies & Co back in 1966. Only this time the polka dots on my tie were bigger, and the tie itself was wider in order to accommodate them – though the matching silk handkerchief was still there!

I was pleased to see my name was on the 'signing in list' at reception, and I duly initialled it, but happened to notice that beside Alistair Hart's name was a multitude of red crosses, signifying his perpetual lateness. I was soon to discover the original starting time had been 9.15am, but because Alistair never made that, it was amended to 9.30. He very rarely made 9.30 either. And my first day was no exception.

When Alistair did eventually appear, nothing seemed to have changed since I met him after being offered the assistant blender's job. The smell of curry still lingered on his breath and clothes. He offered me a firm handshake. 'Hi, man', he said, bearing his teeth in his trademark grin. 'First thing, let's show you some of the talent we've got here.'

With only around 35 staff, the tour of the offices did not take long, and soon Alistair and I were sitting drinking coffee while he outlined what my areas of responsibility would be. These included preparing the specification of blends, ordering stocks of the component parcels of whisky from various distilleries, arranging transport for the casks, and scheduling the actual blending with either the Glasgow Bond or William Muir (Bond 9) Ltd at Leith. The assembled blends would then be exported in bulk by sea to markets such as the USA and the Far East, or bottled for the home trade and export markets.

Had Alistair made it to my job interview with 'Big Jack' I might already have known this. As it was, it all sounded interesting and challenging, and much more promising than my work with Gillies. It might not have been DCL or Hiram Walker, but it was big time to me.

My first-day nerves, coupled with the coffee, meant that I soon needed to use the gents. 'So where's the toilet, Alistair', I asked, 'I don't remember seeing it on our tour.'

'You wouldn't have, man', he replied. 'There isn't one. It's around the other side of the building, and you have to share it with the whole floor.'

Memories of my Glen Scotia constipation quickly came to mind. 'Here's the key', said Alistair, with his toothy grin.

'But surely our customers don't have to use that too?' I asked.

'Got it in one, son', he replied. 'Even "Big Jack" and the guys from Alcoholics Anonymous have to use it. If there's anybody in there swigging from a bottle make sure it's Whyte & Mackay!'

During the next few weeks as I settled into my new role I quickly came to realise that there was a lot more to Alistair Hart than met the eye. Behind the rumpled image of curry, bad breath and bad timekeeping lurked a well organised figure with a shrewd professional mind. He may have played the clown at times, but Alistair was really nobody's fool. Once he had set an agenda he rigorously maintained it. And nobody was going to stop him.

One thing that soon became apparent to me was that unlike Gillies, Whyte & Mackay had access to a large inventory of stocks. One way in which these stocks were acquired was through a filling programme which embraced not only all the major whisky producers in the industry, but also the many small independents who were still operating at that time. DCL, Hiram Walker, Highland Distillers, William Grant, Chivas, Inver House, IDV, Long John Distillers, Arthur Bell, Seager Evans, Eadie Cairns and Stanley P. Morrison. What a fantastic line up!

In 1970, amalgamations and consolidation still largely lay in the future, though there was a widespread feeling in the industry that there were just too many players out there and something would have to give. The 'Old School' said it would never happen, but the reality was that change was inevitable. After all, nothing stands still.

Another way in which we obtained stocks was through 'reciprocal trading'. Basically, this meant that instead of purchasing new spirit, we filled casks of our own new make at Dalmore for other producers in exchange for theirs. Part of the deal was that we would supply our own wood and transport if required. In those days, the majority of distillers filled and stored the whisky in their own warehouses. Today, in view of the financial constraints operators face, many new fillings are removed directly to the customer's bonds, sometimes in casks, but often in large bulk tankers. This cuts rental, manpower and handling charges, gives easy access to stocks for blending, and allows full control over the storage process, whether the casks are stored on metal racks or on wooden pallets in the warehouses.

The third way in which we obtained spirit was through the surviving brokers, who included Willie Lundie, Hay & MacLeod, and Andrew Wilson. This was always a last resort, as it inevitably meant we incurred additional costs. At this time, my father was still in the broking business, but it was harder than ever to make a living. His 'House of Paterson Broking Co Ltd' made a sad comparison with the heady days of the now closed Stockwell Bond.

One of my principal tasks was to prepare sufficient blends to meet our bottling programme at the Glasgow Bond and William Muir (Bond 9) Ltd. Although we had a basic formulation for Whyte & Mackay, in reality the volume of stocks and length of the marrying period were largely dictated by demand, particularly over Christmas and New Year, and therefore some minor variations were inevitable. On occasions the success of a particular marketing campaign could catch us unawares. This was one area where Alistair and I tried to improve the efficiency of the operation by increasing stocks and initiating more dialogue with Jack Ligertwood and the sales force.

I first became aware of the need for more dialogue when one Friday afternoon, bursting with naive enthusiasm, I sought out our top Scottish sales rep, Tom Macauley. Tom was a true Glaswegian salesman, with 30 years experience behind him. He knew everything there was to know about the on-trade, from the dirtiest, seediest pubs of Govan Cross and Bridgeton to the rarefied atmosphere of the Central Hotel. Along with other salesmen he was preparing his weekly sales report in the canteen, eating a bacon roll, deeply engrossed in figures, when I approached him.

'Hi Tom, how were your sales this week?' I asked. He stopped chewing, looked me up and down with total disdain and rasped, 'Whit?' splattering me with bread and bacon in the process. 'It's got fuck all to do with you!'

I was shell-shocked by his answer, but luckily Alistair Hart had overheard his reply and came to my rescue.

'Look Tom, there's no need to take that attitude. Richard's just interested in how things are. It does affect us as well, you know.'

'Okay, I hear what you're saying, but just not now, okay, I've got to get these figures in.'

I soon realised Tom's bark was worse than his bite, and after that unfortunate encounter he was always willing to help me, even taking me on several occasions to meet his customers. The salesmen, particularly long-term, dedicated salesmen who had a real relationship with their customers, were worth their weight in gold. All our ingenious advertising and promotional campaigns were really only as good as the men on the ground getting the product onto bar optics and off-licence shelves.

The Whyte & Mackay sales team was devoted to the brand, and this devotion was spearheaded not only through Jack Ligertwood, but also our sales manager Ken Maclean. He was arrogant and energetic, and used to march down the office corridors, full of bustle and purpose. He was clearly out to establish Whyte & Mackay in the market-place, and woe betides any member of his team who did not live up to expectations. They had to have fire in their bellies. It was exactly what the company needed at that time. He certainly had my respect.

The sales team provided us with the infor-mation we needed to gauge the trends of the market, which enabled us to blend accord-ingly. My motto was always 'stock it or cock it.' From a sales perspective, if you cannot supply the goods when the customer demands them, then there is rarely a second chance. The sale is lost. From the point of view of quality, 'over-stocking' means the spirit gets to spend more time in the wood, which is an added benefit to the consumer, though perhaps not to the accountant. But then pleasing accountants can sometimes be harder than blending good whisky.

The firm was small enough that I could get involved with most departments, including marketing, which was really 'Big Jack' Ligertwood's domain. I spent many long hours at home with white boards, Letraset and multi-coloured felt pens, working on my own Whyte & Mackay advertising campaigns. Even though many ended up in the bucket

when I presented them to Jack, they at least proved my enthusiasm and commitment.

During my first year with the company my principal role as assistant blender, however, was to 'nose' a sample of every cask arriving in the warehouse for use in the Whyte & Mackay Special blend. Usually the Glasgow Bonding Co at 80 Duke Street carried out the blending operation for us. It was a very old bond, situated not far from Tennent's Brewery. It amazed me how such a compara-tively small company managed to turn over millions of gallons of whisky a year, particu-larly as every time a lorry arrived it had to reverse laboriously through the narrow main gates of the bond, holding up the traffic on Duke Street.

The managing director of the Glasgow Bond was Tom Montgomery. To my mind, he carried out his work meticulously on Whyte & Mackay's behalf. Not only had he our blends to contend with, but additionally those of the House of Campbell, which owned the bond.

House of Campbell also owned Aberlour Distillery in the heart of Speyside, having acquired both businesses at the end of the Second World War. The firm was best known for its Clan Campbell and White Heather brands, and in 1974 became part of the Pernod Ricard Group, which has subsequently expanded its Scotch whisky interests consid-erably, becoming the industry's third-largest player in the process.

Once the casks from as many as 35 to 40 different distilleries for Whyte & Mackay Special blend had been unloaded from the 'open' lorries, samples were drawn, crated up, and despatched to 50 Wellington Street for my evaluation. The whole process was very time-consuming and laborious, as it involved at least 300 casks on every occasion. That meant 300 samples every time, and not surprisingly, my room was soon clogged with crates and bottles.

This inefficient system became a nightmare for me. Something had to change. The obvious solution was that rather than the whisky coming to me, I should go to the whisky. Bob Anderson, blends manager at the bond, would phone to confirm that the stocks had arrived, and I would duly make my way to Duke Street to nose the whiskies straight from the cask. This excited me, because I now felt much more physically involved with the spirit. I was accompanied in the warehouse by Betty Toal, the charge hand. She carried a stainless steel valinch, and moving up and down the rows of casks, with one sweep of her hand she plunged it deep into the cask, drawing out just enough whisky for me to evaluate. She would pour a measure into my nosing glass, I would look at it, add water, swirl it, nose it twice and return it to the cask. During the winter months the whisky was so cold that only the addition of hot water would persuade it to reveal its identity.

Eventually, Betty and I built up a warm working relationship, and with her invaluable assistance I could usually nose samples from six casks in less than a minute. One thing that impressed me was Betty's dexterity with the bung-starter – which was really just a cane-handled mallet, used for removing bungs from casks. Her apparent strength was incredible for such a petite woman. She would flex the cane mallet and bring it down with such force onto either side of the bung that within seconds it was soaring into the air. It was a sight to be seen, and thanks to copious amounts of lacquer, her black, beehived hair remained undisturbed.

Nosing the whisky was essential, but the first impression came from its colour. This was vitally important, as it determined the health of the spirit in the casks. If it was too pale, almost white, perhaps, that would suggest an exhausted cask, and I would expect the nose to reflect this with sharp, fiery and very immature notes. Such a cask would immediately be rejected, having an 'X' or 'R' chalked onto it. At the opposite extreme, the sample might be totally black in colour, which would indicate iron contamination. This was usually from a nail, and again, the cask would be withdrawn. Tinges of orange or yellow would identify casks that had at one stage contained liqueurs, such as Glayva. This could seriously affect the character of the blend, and these casks, too, would be rejected.

Something that would not be reflected in the colour of the spirit, however, was 'sourness'. This is when the whisky has taken on connotations of sour milk, baby sick or vinegar wine, often derived from casks that have been badly stored and have perhaps been contaminated by rancid water. It was very rare that casks of malt whisky were prone to contamination. It mainly affected the grain whiskies. In view of the large volumes being filled, it was inevitable that sometimes wood quality was of secondary importance.

Essentially, I was there to safeguard the consistency of the blend, to maintain its style, its character. When I spotted one of these rogue casks I always felt I had done my job effectively. After all, just one of them could ruin the whole blend, and even damage the reputation of the company. This was one part of my job I really did love, and I took great pride in it. I enjoyed the independence and sense of responsibility, and every cask brought its own excitement. It was like meeting a person for the first time. I always worked on my father's theory that 96% of what you need to know about whisky is based on the colour and the nose. Only when you are not sure of these two indicators do you then taste it.

As soon my inspection was complete, the casks were dumped into the troughs, the whisky was vatted, and then run off back into its original wood for a period of four months. On completion of this marrying period, the whisky was reduced in strength with pure water, coloured and filtered prior to bottling.

Whyte & Mackay's blending and bottling business was not just confined to the Glasgow Bond. As I mentioned previously we also used William Muir (Bond 9) Ltd in Leith and Cumbernauld in order to encourage a little healthy competition for our business. In May 1972 William Muir introduced chill-filtration, which removed the problems of cloudiness in whisky. Chill-filtration was not a new development, as DCL had pioneered the process as far back as 1933, but it was the early 1970s before it was widely embraced by the Scotch whisky industry.

In the days when most whisky was sold in dark brown or green bottles this problem, and others, could easily be masked. The trend towards widespread use of clear glass, however, meant that discerning customers could quickly spot this apparent imperfection, and a remedy was required. The reality is that the consumer must be presented with a product which appears to be totally flawless. Sometimes, looks are everything.

Traditionalists like my father were rather dismissive of chill-filtration, and complained that it removed a significant element of the whisky's character. Its inner body had been reduced, and he took great exception to this. Today, however, my father might gain some comfort from the fact that a number of independent bottlers currently make a virtue of not chill-filtering their single malts.

When the Glasgow Bond failed to follow William Muir's lead regarding chill-filtering, Whyte & Mackay were already considering increasing their business with William Muir, and made the decision to end their agreement with the Glasgow Bond in 1976. It had been a long, warm association, and I for one was sad to see it end. I had gained a great deal of knowledge and experience with them.

Before we moved all our blending and bottling to Leith and Cumbernauld, one of the emerging markets for our bulk vatted malt business was Japan. The principal companies that we, and many other Scottish distillers, dealt with were Suntory and Nikka. Thanks to the efforts of Jack Ligertwood this was going to be a long and lasting relationship, though the venture was not without its critics. There was a fear that the Japanese might copy Scotch so well that they would not want or need the real thing in the future. What a lot of people did not realise was that this trade helped to maintain distillery output, cooperages, export departments and shipping lines. More importantly, however, the profit that Whyte & Mackay made was reinvested in our many advertising campaigns.

The Japanese distillers were purchasing bulk malt Scotch whisky to enhance their own blends, almost all of which were drunk in

Japan itself. Our critics naively thought that we should only be exporting *bottled* whisky to countries like Japan, but what they failed to realise was that this was simply not what the Japanese wanted.

Unfortunately, to the older generation in Britain there was still a degree of antipathy towards the Japanese during the early 1970s as a result of the Second World War. I am sure this must have influenced much of the criticism that was directed towards the bulk malt whisky exporters. Suntory demanded quality and consistency. The master blender at that time, Ken Sato, made annual visits to Scotland to ensure his requirements were fully met. The relationship I built up with him endures to this day.

The bulk malt side of our business was carried out in William Muir's bond at Condorrat, Cumbernauld, some 15 miles from central Glasgow. I frequently visited the bond in order to nose the component malts. Around 20 single malts were used, principally drawn from the Highlands and Speyside, with a small percentage from Islay. The whisky varied from four to eight years old, and was normally shipped to Japan in containers, each of which held 66 barrels or 48 hogsheads. It was a thriving business for everybody involved, particularly the coopers. Along with the increase in work from new and expanded distilleries, this made the 1970s a boom time for the coopers of Scotland which has never been repeated since.

Bulk exports to Japan were obviously increasing in popularity, but so too were aged blends. One of these was Harrods, which we launched in 1972 on behalf of the exclusive London store, both for the North American and Japanese markets. The component malts for the Harrods blend were rare, as they varied from 21 to 25 years old. I particularly enjoyed working with these distinguished whiskies, in view of their rare, complex attributes.

I was experiencing exceptional whiskies at their very best for the first time, and on occasions some of them were beyond my wildest dreams. I simply could not let them go. I would remove them from the formulation and hold them for future use in prestige blends that were destined to carry the Whyte & Mackay banner. Much to the annoyance of Alistair Hart this became a habit of mine, and remains so to this day. Little did I know it was part of the making of a master blender. If he wants to truly make his mark with high quality blends and single malts, his obsessions and passions must include preserving, nurturing and maturing outstanding whiskies.

At the same that we began to market the Harrods blend, we also introduced the Whyte & Mackay Special blend pvc half-bottle. This followed the favourable launch the previous year of the pvc miniature bottle, developed by the Rockware Group.

It was a great success with British Airways, particularly as it was 45% lighter than the glass equivalent. Along with Whyte & Mackay, Teachers had plans to introduce similar packaging, and both companies had undertaken stringent testing to ensure that the blend's taste was not tainted by the pvc. It was puzzling, therefore, when the SWA intervened, forcing the two companies to restrict pvc bottle sales to the airline trade. Did some of our more conservative competitors on the SWA board bring pressure to bear?

Nineteen-seventy-two was certainly an

Jack Ligertwood (right) launching the PVC miniature drinks' pack with British Airways in 1972.

eventful year for Whyte & Mackay, with the most significant development being the ending of family ownership after almost a century. This process had started the previous year when the company began seeking a capital injection to fund future growth. Talks were held with another famous family-owned Glaswegian distiller, William Teacher & Sons Ltd, but ultimately it was Scottish & Universal Investments Trust Ltd (SUITS) which took control in April 1972. They paid almost £3 million for the company.

SUITS had been formed in 1948 with a capital of £500,000 by Lord Fraser of Allander, who went on to embrace many diverse business ventures, and energetically developed his Scottish portfolio. One of the most immediate effects of the takeover was the replacement of the chairman Major Hartley Whyte by Sir Hugh Fraser. The major became honorary president, but an era was over. Sadly, he was not to enjoy a long retirement, dying in December 1976. For me, his departure represented the ending of something very special. After all, he was the last tangible link with the firm's founding fathers. Times were changing across the industry: a new generation of less 'gentlemanly' businessmen was in the ascendancy.

As they had promised, SUITS soon proved willing to invest capital in the company's development, with the first evidence being a

The end of an era – Chairman Major Hartley Whyte receiving a retirement gift from Sir Hugh Fraser in 1972.

£100,000 programme of warehouse construction and upgrading at Dalmore Distillery. There was more money to spend, and in November 1973 the Glasgow whisky-broking firms of Hay & MacLeod Ltd and W&S Strong were acquired for a total cost of £5.5 million. This brought Whyte & Mackay large and diverse stocks of whisky along with two new distilleries in the shape of Fettercairn and Tomintoul.

We were no longer a vulnerable family company, but part of a major Scottish commercial enterprise. We now owned three distilleries. Tomintoul was in the heart of Speyside, in the parish of Glenlivet, no less. It was a comparative newcomer in the most

famous glen in Scottish distilling. Fettercairn, by contrast, was established the same year as Glenlivet Distillery. And of course there was Dalmore, for so long at the heart of many of our blends. I would develop lasting relationships with the new distilleries, just as I had with Dalmore, absorbing their heritage and personalities, and working with their spirit. Glen Scotia had shown me the importance of getting out of the blending room and into the distilleries where the spirit itself is born. If I ever hoped to be a master blender, I needed to be heavily involved with the distilleries themselves in order to understand what lies behind the whisky's personality, what shapes its character. The Highlands beckoned me!

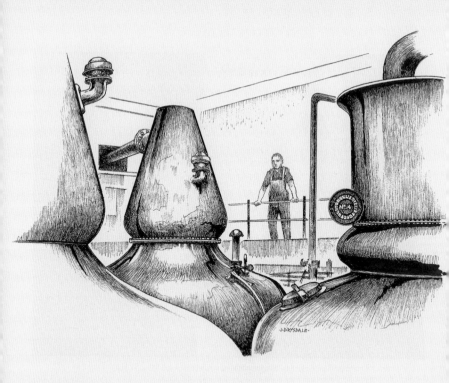

Chapter Five

THE SPIRIT OF THE HIGHLAND
– DALMORE AND FETTERCAIRN

'In its nobility, its profundity, its bigness, its complexity,
whisky of either spelling is a pleasure meant for men and
women who enjoy drink, and probably food. It is not
suitable for people who are afraid of their own shadow.'

THE LATE MICHAEL JACKSON,
WORLD GUIDE TO WHISKY

You cannot help being captivated by the Highlands of Scotland, with their extraordinary physical grandeur, colourful, turbulent past and present day reputation for excellent hospitality. But 20,000 years ago a warm welcome to the Highlands would have been out of the question, for Scotland was covered in ice. But over the centuries this great Eurasian glacier, which covered northern Europe and was more than a mile thick in places, began to recede as temperatures rose. The melting ice acted as a giant sculptor, changing forever the land beneath. When this process was complete, the Highlands were a barren place of endless valleys and lochs, vast expanses of rock, with little fertile soil. It would take hundreds of years before man made his mark on the new landscape.

As you travel north of Pitlochry, the very heart of Scotland, the skyline of the Highlands with their countless, jagged peaks opens up before you and bears testament to that bygone ice age. For me, the north of Scotland is a place where past and present sometimes seem very close together. It is steeped in clan history, with ruined castles, battlefield sites, and at the heart of it all is the romantic story of Charles Edward Stuart (Bonnie Prince Charlie) and the Jacobites' attempts to restore a Catholic Stuart monarch to the throne of Britain. Bonnie Prince Charlie's dream ended in defeat at the battle of Culloden, near Inverness, in April 1746, and this ultimately led to the demise of the clan system and depopulation of the Highlands, as the clan chiefs lost their power and influence, and began to replace tenants with more profitable sheep. Highland emigrants found their way to every corner of the world in order to make a living, enriching the culture of their chosen lands right up to the present day.

Over hundreds of years the roads leading into the Highlands have carried many travellers, and today they annually transport thousands of tourists, keen to explore the beauty and heritage of the Highlands for themselves. Many of these modern day visitors are descendents of Scots emigrants, making their way to the 'old country' to experience the land of their forebears at first hand. But when I travelled the roads into the Highlands back in 1972 I was in search not of history but of knowledge.

During my comparatively short time in the whisky industry I had already become familiar with single malts from most of the distilleries of Scotland. Although I was beginning to understand and appreciate their characteristics, I always feel that until you have actually been to a distillery and witnessed the birth of its spirit, the association is not complete. Until now, I had never been north of Inverness, so when the opportunity arose that year to spend some time at Whyte & Mackay's flagship Dalmore Distillery I was naturally excited at the prospect of getting to know it intimately and also having the opportunity to visit some of the other distilleries in the area, such as Teaninich, Balblair, Glenmorangie and Ord. Dalmore Distillery lies on the shores of the Cromarty Firth, north of Inverness, and to get there I had to pass through the village of Tomatin. This was an ideal opportunity for me to sample a parcel of whisky which we had recently bought from the local distillery.

In 1972 Tomatin was already a large distillery, operating eleven stills, but two years later a second stillhouse was added, taking its annual capacity to an amazing five million proof gallons of spirit. At that point it became Scotland's biggest distillery, with no fewer than 23 stills! Tomatin was located close to the main A9 Perth-Inverness road, but in winter this was a very bleak and isolated place, and snow often cut it off from the outside world. However, a visit to Tomatin was always warmed up by the genial presence of John McDonald, the distillery manager, and one of Scotland's true whisky characters. A dying breed.

His greatest claim to fame was his involvement in a fracas with the late Billy Bremner, Scottish football's legendary hard man and captain of the FA Cup winning Leeds United team of 1972. This was one redheaded firebrand you didn't mess with – on or off the field. John had once played for Inverness Thistle and acted as a Scottish Football Association official. During an overseas tour with the Scottish national side he had confronted Bremner about some horseplay that got out of hand, and ended up decking the player. Even to this day, he is quietly proud of that event. Bremner may have had a reputation as a hard man, but there were clearly harder men in the Scotch whisky industry too.

As usual, the welcome from John was very warm, but it was not so warm in the warehouses, where I was forced to clamber up the racks like a monkey in order to find the relevant casks and nose them. Usually, I would have expected the casks to be laid out ready for me to sample, but on this particular day John's warehouse team had been too busy. In retrospect, having to locate the casks for

myself was a very valuable experience, although I was not particularly pleased at the time. The warehouses in question were comparatively new, and unlike the cold, damp, traditional 'dunnage' warehouses where casks were stored three high on wooden rails, with an earth or cinder floor, these were 'racked' in the latest fashion. This meant that casks could be stored eight to ten high; using forklift trucks to handle them saved on manpower and was a more efficient use of space.

However, when I scrambled around in my increasingly dirty white lab coat, I discovered there were marked differences between whisky from casks in the bottom stows and those at the top of the racking, despite the fact that all these casks had been filled with the same spirit at the same time. The principal difference was that the casks at the bottom, particularly those on the cement floor, contained milder, mellower whisky, which was generally softer in character. Although the middle body of whisky from casks at the top was good, the edges were rather sharp and raw. It had probably retained more of its strength than that maturing at the bottom of the racks, due to the dampness lingering around ground level, whereas the air circulating near the roof was drier and warmer. Had these casks been laid out in a row ready for me to nose, I would never have related the differences in spirit so clearly to the storage. It had been another valuable lesson.

Freezing cold, and covered in cobwebs and rust marks from the cask hoops, I returned to John's office. He looked me up and down, as though I was something the distillery cat had dragged in. 'You'll take a dram before ye go?' he declared. It was not so much a question as a statement. He proceeded to pour an enormous glass of cask-strength aged Tomatin and handed it to me. Three drams later and with a stupid grin on my face I was driving at top speed into Inverness in my white Ford Cortina. I might have been in the Highlands but I was really in heaven. The chances of being breathalysed were few and far between, but when I felt more sober I realised that I had been totally irresponsible. The fact was, however, during the early 1970s drinking and driving did not carry the same stigma it does now, particularly in the north. A dram was an integral part of Highland hospitality, and to refuse it could easily have caused offence.

Today, the A9 north of Inverness carries the traveller over the Kessock Bridge on to the Black Isle, which is not really an island at all, but a peninsula famed for its fertility. The term 'black' derives from the rich, dark, fertile soil of the promontory. It then crosses the Cromarty Firth bridge and runs along the northern shores of the firth to the village of Alness and the nearby Dalmore Distillery. The journey to Dalmore from Inverness takes little more than half an hour, but back in the 1970s, before the firths were bridged, the road wound laboriously inland through Muir of Ord, Beauly and Dingwall. Especially in summer, when the road was clogged with caravans and lorries, the journey was very long.

Nowadays, Inverness is bypassed, but in those days the A9 went right through the centre of the old Highland capital, and I passed the great trinity of Inverness distilleries, Millburn, Glen Albyn and Glen Mhor. All three were working busily in those days, but

now Millburn is the Auld Distillery Slice restaurant and bar, while Glen Albyn and Glen Mhor have been totally obliterated, making way for the Telford Retail Park. I was particularly interested to see Glen Mhor and Glen Albyn, which stood beside the Caledonian Canal, since one of my grandfather's early business ventures had involved selling coal to many distilleries, including these two. Through this connection he came to realise there was more money to be made from whisky than coal, and thus the whisky company of WR Paterson Ltd of Glasgow was born.

Despite the rigours of the old A9, getting to Dalmore was nothing like as exhausting as getting to Campbeltown had been, and I arrived eager to explore. But, as I drove along the shoreline of the Cromarty Firth, I could not help sensing the peacefulness of the place. It was different. The water of the firth was still, seals were basking on rocks not far from the road, herons stood motionless, waiting for elusive fish. Only the screech of oystercatchers overhead interrupted the tranquillity of the scene. Even the barley seemed to sway lazily in the gentle breeze. I felt I was entering another part of Scotland. These were the Northern Highlands, a region that produced whiskies as varied and individual as the landscape.

One feature of that landscape was the amount of barley being grown. Indeed, barley seemed to be everywhere, and looking around it was not difficult to see why the name Dalmore was derived from the Gaelic for 'big meadowland'. Even after all these years, I still have a sense of wonderment that a crop in a field can ultimately be transformed into a beautiful, complex malt whisky. However, in

Dalmore Distillery overlooking the Cromarty Firth.

contrast to the golden fields of barley, I suddenly saw blackened distillery warehouses which almost appeared to be in the sea. A pair of wrought-iron gates with 'Dalmore' emblazoned on them welcomed me. A narrow, wooded lane led down into the heart of the distillery, and within a matter of seconds the whole of the Cromarty Firth opened up to me, with the Black Isle beyond. It was a spectacular sight. A long, narrow pier seemed to dominate the waterline, but was overshadowed by a large, elegant yacht anchored just off shore.[12] A vast flock of swans swam around the mouth of the distillery outfall pipe. Something there was keeping them happy.

Turning to the distillery itself, smoke was lazily drifting from the pagoda head. The maltings were clearly in production, and the smell of mash hung in the air. In the background I could see a white flagpole. The Mackenzie clan crest, featuring a gold stag's

12 The yacht was the *Jaluroch*, named after HAC Mackenzie's four children, James, Lucilla, Roderick and Christopher.

head on a black background, hung proudly from it. The flag proclaimed this was Mackenzie territory. After all, the distillery had been in their hands for more than a hundred years. I was soon to meet the distillery director, Colonel Hector Andrew Courtney Mackenzie, affectionately known as 'HAC' to his friends.

The colonel was the very epitome of a senior army officer. He stood tall and erect, with a handlebar moustache. He wore a Mackenzie tartan kilt, with a very battered badger sporran that looked like it had seen some active service. The effect was slightly spoilt, however, by a pair of not particularly muscular legs. Despite his rather formal, military appearance, Colonel Mackenzie turned out to be a charming, likeable man. He had served with distinction in the Seaforth Highlanders during the war, and was a greatly respected figure, both within the Scotch whisky industry and the local community. He was immensely proud to serve as chieftain of Invergordon Highland Games for many years.

His family had distilled at Dalmore for

more than a century, but the distillery had actually been founded by Alexander Matheson, nephew of the colourful and controversial Sir James Matheson who had been born at Lairg, Sutherland in 1796 and who became a trader in the Far East. Along with his business partner William Jardine, he formed Jardine Matheson & Co in 1832, smuggling opium into China in exchange for tea and silks, with the tacit support of the British Government. Chinese opposition to this trade was ultimately to lead to the Opium Wars between Britain and China between 1839 to 1842. Their successful trading made Jardine and Matheson very rich men, but it also brought great wealth to young Alexander, who had been taken into the firm by his uncle.

Some of Alexander Matheson's money was subsequently spent acquiring large estates in Easter Ross, including that of Dalmore, purchased for £24,700. In total, he laid out the vast amount of £773,020 buying 220,000 acres in the county of Ross.

However, the restless energy which had propelled him to commercial success would not allow him simply to sit back and watch the crops grow. He proceeded to 'improve' his estates, following the example of many estate owners in Scotland. Additionally, he constructed a distillery next to Dalmore Mill, on the Alness Water. It is now universally thought that the distillery built by Matheson dates from 1839, but there are old advertisements and bottle labels in existence which also give 1841 as the year of establishment.

Thanks to Alexander Matheson, two very different worlds were linked. Intriguingly, the distillery that he built in a peaceful, rural part of the eastern Highlands, was indirectly financed by money acquired from the humid, tumultuous arena of the Chinese opium trade on the opposite side of the world. Today, Jardine Matheson Holdings is a highly profitable, Asian-based conglomerate, with a broad portfolio of commercial interests. Dalmore turned out to be a shrewd business development for Matheson, as Scotch whisky was thriving in the years after the 1823 Excise Act, which had stimulated legal distilling. In 1823 there were 125 licensed distilleries in

The Dalmore Distillery Staff July 1971. Fourth row, left to right: John Longbotham, Danny McGruer, Jimmy Urquhart, Denis Sinclair, Ricky Whythe, Charlie Ferguson. Third row: Gordon Wilson, Willie Pirie, Alan Morrison, Andy Rose, Wilf Wilson, Jimmy Sinclair, Bill Brockie, Stuart McPhillips, Bob Robertson, Davy McLeod, Jim Wilson, Willie Elder. Second row: George Ross, Harold Gordon, Willie Daniel, John McGinn, Willie McLeod, Jimmy Wilson, Ron Palmer, Bobo Gunn, Drew Sinclair, Jackie Sutherland, Jimmy Mackay, Dave Sinclair, Front row: Joan McNicol, Arthur Anderson, John P. MacDonald, Frank Martin, George Watt, Colonel HAC Mackenzie, Donald J McLeod, Alec Henderson, Tom Fulton, Ian McKenzie, Charlie Wood, Walter McLeod.

Scotland, but this figure had risen to a staggering 329 just two years later. This was clearly a boom time for Scottish distilling.

Teaninich Distillery, close to Dalmore, had been established in 1817 by Captain Hugh Munro, and in 1835 he declared that 'An extraordinary change was soon perceived; smuggling was greatly suppressed, and for one gallon that was permitted in the country from my distillery previous to 1823 there were,

from that time till 1830, an increase of from thirty to forty times.'

Easter Ross was a great location for distilleries, with large quantities of barley being grown locally, while abundant supplies of peat were also available. Coal could be brought in by sea, as in 1838 a regular steamer service between Leith, Inverness and Invergordon had been established. Once the Highland Railway line opened in 1865, coal was transported from the Fife coalfield to Alness station, and some 14 years later, Alexander Matheson commissioned the creation of a branch line from Alness directly into Dalmore Distillery. By now the Scottish railway network was extensive, and connected many remote distilleries with the urban, Lowland centres where much blending and bottling took place.

Most celebrated of the local distilleries was undoubtedly Ferintosh, run by the Forbes family. According to the Japanese whisky researcher Teimei Horiuchi, 'Ferintosh used to be the name for a parish, situated east of Conan Bridge in the Black Isle. It was said that the estate of the family of Forbes was 6,500 acres.' Duncan Forbes was a staunch supporter of the Protestant King William III, who deposed the Catholic James II in 1688, and his estates were ransacked during the Jacobite rising in favour of James the following year. Forbes claimed compensation of £54,000 from the government for fire damage caused to Ferintosh Distillery, and by way of settlement, the Scottish Parliament granted him the highly lucrative right to distil at Ferintosh free of duty in perpetuity on payment of 400 Scots marks per year.

During the 1760s, Ferintosh was enlarged, and a further three distilleries were built on the estate. More land was also acquired on which to grow barley in order to qualify for the continuing exemption from duty payments. By the late 1760s the Forbes were making the vast profit of £18,000 per year from their whisky, and a few years later were reported to be distilling almost 90,000 gallons per year.

When new excise legislation was introduced in 1784 the exemption ended, and the Forbes family was awarded £21,580 in compensation. Robert Burns, for one, was outraged by the ending of the Ferintosh privilege, and included these two verses in his poem, Scotch Drink:

Thee, Ferintosh! O sadly lost!
Scotland lament frae coast to coast!
Now colic grips, an' barkin hoast
May kill us a';
For loyal Forbes' charter'd boast
Is ta'en awa?

Thae curst horse-leeches o' the' Excise,
Wha mak the whisky stills their prize!
Haud up thy han', Deil! ance, twice, thrice!
There, seize the blinkers!
An' bake them up in brunstane pies
For poor damn'd drinkers.

During the early 19th century there were no fewer than 29 distilleries operating in the Black Isle area, according to Teimei Horiuchi, and later there were also distilleries at Evanton, where Glenskiach operated from 1896 to 1926, and Dingwall, where Ben Wyvis worked from 1879 until its demise in the same year. However, the Diageo-owned Teaninich is still proudly turning out single malt today, as is Inver House's nearby Balblair Distillery in Edderton, while the world-renowned Glenmorangie is located at Tain.

By the 1850s, Alexander Matheson had extended his Ardross estate to more than 120,000 acres, and his Dalmore Distillery had been run by a number of tenants. These included several members of the Sutherland family and Robert Pattison. Then, in 1867, Andrew Mackenzie, 24-year-old son of

Matheson's land agent, was granted the tenancy. Thus began almost a century of involvement in Dalmore by the Mackenzies. Matheson hoped his new tenant would expand the business and Andrew Mackenzie certainly rose to the challenge. Mackenzie was a meticulous man who maintained detailed diaries of his distilling and farming activities. A key diary entry for 26th October 1867 reads, 'Arranged today that Charlie [his younger brother] and I were to have Dalmore Distillery and Farm and to enter at Martinmas next.'

Their father, William, who had been instrumental in making a commercial success of the Matheson estates, encouraged his sons to take on the leases of a number of local farms. These provided a source of barley for the distillery, while the farm cattle were fed on the distillery waste and provided manure to fertilise the crops of barley. By all accounts, Andrew Mackenzie was a natural farmer and skilled stockman, who became renowned as a leading breeder of Aberdeen Angus cattle, producing many champions. Indeed, reading his diaries for the 1870s, it is easy to believe he was a farmer rather than a distiller, as most of the entries relate to agricultural activities. This is not surprising, as Mackenzie farmed a total of around 400 acres.

Some 28 years had now passed since Alexander Matheson had constructed Dalmore Distillery, and it was therefore not surprising that investment was required. On 26th November 1867 a new filling store was commissioned, and a week later an Edinburgh coppersmith made the journey to Dalmore in order to repair the low wines still and worms. The first consignment of malting barley arrived at the distillery on Wednesday 11th

December, and the following day, Robert Ross of Balblair, took up his new appointment as brewer. By then, the bachelor brothers Andrew and Charlie had settled into Dalmore House, a large baronial property which enjoyed spectacular views across the Cromarty Firth to the fertile lands of the Black Isle to the east.

Andrew Mackenzie immediately realised that if his new distilling enterprise was to be as successful as his farming ventures he would need to become something of a salesman. With this in mind, he set out to establish markets for the spirit they would soon be making, gaining customers from as far south as Grantown-on-Spey. This was quite an achievement, considering that Dalmore would have to compete not only with a number of well-established local distilleries, but also those in the Speyside area.

On 1st January 1868 the first malted barley was ready for distilling to begin, but the initial processes of whisky-making had to be interrupted for New Year celebrations. As Andrew Mackenzie noted in his diary for 12th January, 'The work people held their new year today.' It was common practice in rural Scotland at that time to observe the 'old' Julian calendar, rather than the Gregorian calendar, adopted in 1752. Celebrating New Year on 12th January persisted in remote parts of the country until comparatively recent times. Indeed, to this day 200 inhabitants of the Gwaun Valley in a remote area of Pembrokeshire in Wales continue to adhere to the Julian calendar for their New Year *Hen Galan* celebrations.

In the aftermath of their New Year festivities, the Dalmore staff ground the first malt on Wednesday 22nd January, and the following day mashing began. Thursday also saw a visit from the excise officer, who had to ensure that Dalmore complied with all the excise regulations. Even in those days, the watchful eyes of the 'gauger' were ever present. Over the cold winter weekend fermentation was completed, and the wash was ready for distillation on Monday 27th. It must have been a momentous occasion for the Mackenzies when spirit flowed for the first time, but in typical restrained Victorian style, Andrew Mackenzie simply recorded the following day, 'We had the first whisky into the charges and receiver today, and tasted it. It was fine quality and very pure. Sent out several casks of the fresh whisky today.'

The Immature Spirits Act of 1915, which imposed a legal minimum maturation period of two years, was a long way off, and much whisky was sold, and consumed, as new make. The pure spirit had to be of a high quality to ensure the survival of any distilling venture, and Dalmore certainly met with public approval. Andrew Mackenzie sold 1,800 gallons of new-make spirit, and as he wrote in his diary, it 'pleased well' in Invergordon and gave 'general satisfaction' in Dingwall. By the end of Mackenzie's first, short distilling season in March 1868 almost 16,380 gallons had been produced.

The new distilling season did not begin until Monday 9th November, and the long silent season allowed the Mackenzies to undertake the multitude of agricultural activities necessary to maintain a thriving estate. As many other Scottish farmers knew, agricultural and distilling activities dovetailed very neatly, with whisky-making often taking place during the long winter months when there

Marshall Wane   EDINBURGH

Andrew Mackenzie (1841–1923), distiller and farmer.

were few farming tasks to undertake. Despite being a very busy man, Mackenzie had found time to meet and court Annie Martin of Edinburgh, becoming engaged to her on Valentine's Day in 1872. It was a comparatively short engagement, as on 8th August Mackenzie noted, 'Was married today to Annie E. Martin at 49 Castle Street by the Revd Wm Arnot at 3 o'clock pm. Everything went off well.' Perhaps this was just typical Victorian, Presbyterian reticence, but Mackenzie does seem to show more emotion in diary entries relating to his prize cattle!

Nevertheless, these were happy times for

the Mackenzies, but also for Alexander Matheson, who had no cause to regret his choice of distillery tenant. By 1874 Dalmore was turning out an impressive 44,214 gallons a year, and this continuing success meant that Andrew Mackenzie added a second stillhouse to double capacity in that year. Remarkably, the upper part of one of those 1874 spirit stills made by Henderson & Dickson of Edinburgh survives to this day.

Around this date, the Mackenzies were selling Dalmore 'self' or single whiskies in several expressions. Some whisky went into new barrels, known as 'distillery wood', while other whisky was filled into sherry wood. For the true connoisseur, some stocks of Dalmore were matured for between five and six years, and then both styles of these aged whiskies were vatted together. Nonethless, there was still a great demand for younger whiskies as well.

By this time, however, the great 'self' whiskies like Dalmore were increasingly coming under pressure from blends, as pioneered by Andrew Usher of Edinburgh (see chapter seven). To compete in this crowded market the packaging had to be right, even in those less image-conscious days. The younger expressions of Dalmore were offered in bottles with eye-catching tartan labels, while the older whisky was sold in bottles with white labels. The Mackenzies were proud of their clan heritage and this was the perfect opportunity for them to display their stag's head motif, which has remained at the heart of Dalmore's packaging ever since.

The clan crest features a stag as the Mackenzies trace their origins back to Colin Fitzgerald, reputedly an Irish exile who saved the life of King Alexander III (1241–86) when he was attacked by a charging stag in 1263. In recognition of this feat, the king is said to have granted Fitzgerald the lands of Kintail in Wester Ross and allowed his family to use the stag emblem as its crest. In 1786 Benjamin West, historical artist to King George III, commemorated Mackenzie's encounter with the stag in a vast painting, commissioned by Francis Humberston Mackenzie. The painting remained in the Mackenzie family seat of Brahan Castle until 1952, and now hangs in the Scottish National Gallery in Edinburgh.

Over the years, some of the interpretations of the stag's head on Dalmore labels – even referred to at times as the 'deer's head' – have been less than convincing, and sometimes positively comical. Even in those early years, when marketing was almost an unconscious art, a label featuring traditional Scottish iconography, such as castles, lochs, mountains, tranquil glens and noble stags certainly aided the promotion of whisky.

The Mackenzies were well aware of this as they set about expanding their business not only in Scotland, but around the world. One way in which they managed to do this was through their close connection with Alexander Matheson, who had commercial interests as far afield as Australia and the Far East. Accordingly, Dalmore became the first malt whisky to be exported to Australia, in the early 1870s, and Far Eastern markets were also reached at what was a very early stage for malt whisky. When the Australian and New Zealand trade slumped in 1877 the Mackenzies looked to other new markets, employing agents in Shanghai, Karachi, Otago and Yokohama.

The Mackenzies were also keen to tap into the burgeoning English market, and in 1882 the Dalmore agent Alexander Murdoch & Co was supplied with several thousand gallons of Dalmore single malt, up to 12 years old, in order to try to increase sales south of the border. Efforts were hampered by the fact that Dalmore was considered too distinctive, and the Mackenzies responded by changing the style to have 'more body and Highland flavour or character.'

In my opinion that distinctiveness may have related to peatiness, but is more likely to have taken the form of peppery, burnt notes, caused perhaps by driving the stills too hard. Clearly, something had to be done, adjustments had to be made, if southern customers were to be won over.

Presumably, whatever changes were made proved successful, because shortly afterwards Andrew Mackenzie wrote to Alexander Murdoch, having tasting the revised spirit. 'We are very much impressed with its quality and think it should hold its own against the best Highland whiskies, it comes out so rich, sweet, fine flavoured ... '

Sales in Scotland were encouraging, but overall the trade was sluggish, however, principally due to overstocking of colonial markets, and various slumps affected the whisky industry. These hard times were reflected on a personal level by the demise of the Mackenzie patriarch, William, who died in January 1882, aged 73. After his death the lease of his estates passed to his three sons and Andrew carried on his father's passion for breeding Aberdeen Angus Black Polled cattle and Clydesdale horses. Even in 1883, good stock was at a premium, and he paid 238

guineas for the prize-winning cow Lady Ida and one calf. While Andrew was preoccupied with his farming activities, his younger brother William was entrusted with undertaking a campaign in England to market Dalmore single malt. Despite these efforts, however, the next two years were to be extremely difficult, not just for Dalmore, but for the whole of the Scotch whisky industry.

Production was cut by 20,000 gallons between 1884 and 1886, and in an effort to stimulate business, agents were appointed in Liverpool and Bristol. Then, in 1887 the Mackenzies stopped selling new make for immediate retail completely, and advised their agents to try to press sales of five-year-old whisky at 18 shillings per case, only selling the two-year-old alternative at 14 shillings if really pushed. During these challenging times, the Mackenzies were given a golden opportunity to secure their long-term future. Dalmore's founder Sir Alexander Matheson – who had

A Dalmore label from around 1890 showing 1841 as the year the distillery was founded.

been created a baronet in 1882 – died in July 1886, and his eldest son Sir Kenneth offered the Dalmore Distillery, associated farms and the Belleport Pier to the Mackenzies for £14,500 in 1891 – a bargain even in those days.

Despite poor trading conditions generally, even in far off markets such as Australia, the Mackenzies must have felt that the business was a sound long-term investment, particularly at such an attractive price. Nevertheless, in order to help fund the purchase and future development of Dalmore, Andrew decided reluctantly to sell all his pedigree cattle and horses. This must have been a very difficult decision for such as proud and successful stockman, but clearly the distillery was his guiding passion. He truly believed in the spirit of Dalmore. Work on doubling the distillery in size began during 1892, and lasted almost eight years. Andrew Mackenzie took a keen personal interest in the design of these improvements, but the actual architect commissioned was Andrew Maitland of Tain, who had an intimate knowledge of distilling, being managing partner of Glenmorangie Distillery.

During the 1892–3 season output exceeded 100,000 gallons for the first time, and the mood of confidence continued. In 1895 this figure climbed to a massive 271,694 gallons, and this period of great activity saw 32 people working at the distillery. It was not just Dalmore that was riding the crest of a whisky wave, however. With blended whisky having become established all over the world, no fewer than 33 new malt distilleries were constructed during the last decade of the 19th century.

The erudite whisky author, Alfred Barnard, writing to Andrew Mackenzie regarding the script for the new Dalmore brochure in 1900.

Speyside, with its good rail connections, was at the heart of this boom, with an extraordinary 21 distilleries being built during the 1890s, including Aultmore, Benriach, Craigellachie, Dufftown, Glendullan, Glen Elgin, and Longmorn. The Mackenzies appear to have been justified in their faith in Dalmore's future, and with more money and time at his disposal Andrew Mackenzie was even able to re-establish his herd of Aberdeen

Angus cattle with stock directly descended from Lady Ida. The Mackenzies were far from alone in combining farming and distilling, and as the *Wine & Spirit Gazette* for 13th January 1894 remarked, 'Cattle rearing amongst distillers in the Highlands of Scotland seems to be a congenial and successful pursuit. Clynelish Distillery in Brora took first prize in the Highland Oxen class at Smithfield Show.'

The good times for distilling were not to last into the new century, however. Inevitably, a whisky loch was filling up, with so many new distilleries pumping out vast quantities of spirit, the perils of over-production were about to decimate the industry. In 1891–2 the quantity of warehoused whisky in Scotland amounted to two million gallons, but by 1898–9 that figure had risen to an extraordinary 13.5 million gallons, and the bubble was soon to burst (see page 135). In the aftermath of the economic crisis that hit the distilling industry around the turn of the century, the trade came to be dominated by large blenders, who bottled blended whisky under their own labels or sold it in bulk to English brewers as 'house' whisky. Inevitably, distillers of single malts like the Mackenzies felt threatened by the might of the blending interests.

Along with many of their fellow pot still distillers, they campaigned to restrict the term 'whisky' to malt whisky alone. In April 1903 Andrew Mackenzie wrote to his customers stating, 'Once one gets initiated to a "Pure Highland Malt" or "Self" whisky that is the product of one Distillery it is invariably preferred to the *best* of blends, but it requires a little education at first with people who have never taken it before.'

The matter came to a head two years later, in the unlikely location of the London borough of Islington, when in November 1905 magistrates declared that 'Whisky should consist of spirit distilled in a pot still, derived from malted barley.' Sensing victory, Mackenzie wrote to his London agent HM Roose stating, 'It is generally thought that the blenders through excessive greed have brought the trouble on themselves by passing off comparatively new patent spirit as pure old Scotch whisky and the general feeling and sympathy in the country is against them.' This was by no means the end of the matter, though, as a Royal Commission was set up in 1908 to investigate what became popularly known as the, 'What is Whisky?' case, as a result of pressure from the blenders, who were not content to abide by the Islington verdict (see pages 135–6).

While the Commission deliberated, Dalmore was forced to cut back its production to the lowest level since 1867, and these sluggish times for whisky trading were reflected in Dalmore's maturing stocks, which included whisky dating back to 1886. The distillery staff was reduced to as few as four workers who were paid on a daily basis. Other workers, surplus to requirements, were employed by the Mackenzies as salmon fishermen.

The Royal Commission issued an interim report in June 1909 which declared that grain whisky was just as much whisky as malt. Distillers like Andrew Mackenzie were shocked and dismayed, and Dalmore remained closed during the 1909–10 distilling season. A deal with Perth blenders John Dewar & Sons, who had long used Dalmore in their blends, effectively saved the business, as Dewar's bought a large quantity of mature whisky and guaranteed not to release it onto the wholesale market.

Just when it seemed the corner was being turned, a fire on Saturday 1st July 1911 destroyed two acres of bonded warehouses, and a total of 63,874 gallons of whisky was lost. This was just another blow to the 70-year-old Andrew Mackenzie, who, two years later, sold the Dalmore estate to his neighbour Charles William Dyson Perrins, of Lee & Perrins sauce fame, while retaining the distillery. Lee & Perrins' Worcestershire Sauce was first commercially produced in 1837, so the Perrins family dynasty very much mirrored that of the Mackenzies.

Single malt sales had been at the heart of the Dalmore operation before the turn of the century, but in the years leading up to the First World War, the bulk of whisky distilled was sold to blenders, notably the Glasgow firm of Bulloch, Lade & Co and Whyte & Mackay.

Dalmore distilled until 1917, when all pot still distillation was stopped due to the shortage of barley. The war years were taking their toll even on the home front. The Admiralty subsequently took over the Dalmore site and converted it into a mine factory for the US Navy – a fate which also befell Glen Albyn Distillery in Inverness. The Cromarty Firth was strategically important because it had been decided early in the war that the deep water anchorage of Scapa Flow in Orkney was vulnerable to attack by German submarines, and therefore large numbers of vessels were deployed off Invergordon.

Dalmore's extensive whisky stocks – valued at more than £1million – were removed to nearby Balblair, Glenskiach and even Brora, further north on the Sutherland coast. When the casks were transferred back to Dalmore after the war, not one had been lost!

Building materials and equipment were transported from the USA into Kyle of Lochalsh on the west coast, and then carried by the Highland Railway to Invergordon. Mines made at Dalmore were laid between Orkney and Norway, forming part of what was known as the Northern Barrage, intended to curtail the activities of German submarines operating in the area.

In 1920 the site was returned to the Mackenzies, including a large deepwater pier which had been constructed for the US Navy, and to this day it is still affectionately known as the 'Yankee Pier'. I remember one glorious, calm day walking along the solid stone pier, out into the glittering waters of the Cromarty Firth and looking across at the fine dark soil of the Black Isle opposite, patch-worked with fields of green and golden crops. It was easy to imagine the intense and feverish activity of the wartime years.

The war may have been over, but its implications lingered on for the Mackenzie family. In view of the severe disruption caused to the business by the US Navy's wartime activities, the Mackenzies considered £30,000 to be a reasonable amount of compensation. The Admiralty, however, disagreed, and in the words of one of the Mackenzies, 'the damned swine' offered a meagre £8,000. This dispute was to drag on for many years to come.

Major WF Mackenzie (William, son of Andrew, who was running Dalmore by this time after his war service with the 3rd Seaforth Highlanders) set about creating a unified stillhouse, with two new stills being constructed by Archibald McMillan & Co of Prestonpans, near Edinburgh. McMillan had worked with Andrew Mackenzie on upgrading the distillery 40 years previously. During the 1923–4 distilling season 192,000 gallons were produced, the largest amount since the great days of the 1890s. By then, Andrew Mackenzie was an old man, but he must surely have taken great comfort in the knowledge that his son was running the family firm with such passion and vision for the future. The same distilling spirit clearly ran through his veins.

On 12th September 1923 Andrew Mackenzie died, aged 81, leaving £50,000 to be divided among his children. His agricultural achievements had been immense, rearing some of the finest stock in Scotland, and pictures of his prize-winning animals are displayed today in the Dalmore visitor centre. At the time of his death he had been at the helm of Dalmore Distillery for more than half a century, through good times and bad, becoming president of the Pot Still Malt Distillers Association along the way. Under his guidance the firm remained proudly independent. In my opinion, his contribution to the Scotch whisky industry ranks alongside that of the likes of James Whyte, Charles Mackay, Andrew Usher and Charles Doig; unsung heroes, who have been so instrumental in shaping distilling and blending in Scotland. I salute them all.

One of the provisions of Andrew Mackenzie's will was that a new limited company should be formed to run Dalmore, and this was subsequently registered in January 1927. By now the situation for Scotch whisky distilling was bleak, partly due to US prohibition, and many small, independent companies foundered in these troubled times, falling easy prey to the might of the Distillers Company Ltd, who picked them up at bargain prices. Dalmore was not immune to this downturn, and the firm posted a loss of £1,010 in its first year of trading. The Mackenzies must have been seriously worried. It needed energy and commitment if it was going to survive, and Major Mackenzie proved to have both.

In 1928 he undertook an exhaustive sales drive which reached as far south as Jersey, attempting to revive the demand for mature Dalmore single malt. A circular issued in the hope of stimulating trade in 1929–30 advertised both new make and mature Dalmore. Interestingly, one of the virtues stressed was the whisky's early maturity, and the circular went on to state that 'Dalmore is clean, sweet, and full-bodied, with a medium malty flavour … useful as a top dressing and for combining other whiskies in making up a perfect blend.'

Reading this statement today, I wholeheartedly agree with these sentiments. Whether used as a single malt or for blending purposes, Dalmore remains a key tool of my trade. If I am seeking softness and elegance in a blend, Dalmore is one of the first malts I reach for. Happily, Major Mackenzie's efforts to revive Dalmore whisky were to pay off, with the repeal of US Prohibition in December 1933 being a significant factor in the improvement of the Scotch whisky industry's fortunes. As the prospect of another world war became increasingly likely, there was a rush for whisky stocks, and Dalmore worked at almost full capacity. When war broke out in 1939, Major William Mackenzie's son,

Hector, joined the Seaforths, his father's old regiment. He had clearly inherited William's leadership abilities and courage in times of peril, for he also rose to the rank of major, winning the Military Cross along the way. The distillery worked until 1942, when, in common with most Highland distilleries, it shut down until peace came in 1945.

After the war, on 14th April 1946 Hector 'HAC' Mackenzie joined the family firm, taking over at Dalmore when his father became ill and subsequently died later that year. Morris Crichton was then elected chairman, and Hector Mackenzie became managing director. He had really been thrown in at the deep end. Showing the same sort of vitality that his father had 25 years previously, Mackenzie set about modernising the distillery. Production rose to record levels, reaching more than 440,000 gallons in 1946–7. Improvements included the replacement of floor maltings with mechanised Saladin Box maltings in October 1956, and these remained in use until 1982.

The Saladin malting system had been developed by Frenchman Charles Saladin in the 1890s, and consisted of a long, concrete or metal box, in which revolving metal forks moved slowly from end to end, turning and aerating the grain. However, it took the Scotch whisky industry half a century to embrace this innovation, and the first Saladin boxes were installed at Edinburgh's North British Grain Distillery in 1948. A year later Glen Mhor in Inverness followed suit, with Tamdhu adopting them in 1950.

In 1957 the Dalmore stills were converted to mechanical stoking, and a Hydram Cask Stacker was acquired to remove some of the hard labour in the warehouses. Three new warehouses with a total capacity of around one million gallons were constructed between 1955–8 to house the extra spirit now being produced.

Mackenzie was keen to maintain a balance of modern innovation and traditional practice, writing, 'Our aim has been not to tamper with the old traditional methods of making whisky, yet to employ wherever possible modern electrical labour saving devices. We have now gone a long way towards achieving maximum efficiency and economy from the plant which was originally installed by my grandfather.'

By the late 1950s a number of family shareholders were keen to realise some of their investment in the company, and the possibility of an amalgamation with Whyte & Mackay, a long standing customer, was investigated. The Whyte family and the Mackenzies had been friends since the days of Andrew Mackenzie.

In May 1960 the two firms combined to form a new public company Dalmore, Whyte & Mackay Ltd, and shares were subsequently offered to the public. Almost a century of family ownership through three generations of the Mackenzie family was at an end. It was thanks to the merger between Dalmore and Whyte & Mackay that I came to be standing in the distillery courtyard that summer's afternoon in 1972, eager to learn all about Dalmore. During the next few weeks, I would follow in the footsteps of Andrew, Charles and William Mackenzie, and at times I could almost sense their presence, especially in the old dunnage warehouses. Little did I know that some of the whisky distilled during their lifetimes would play a significant part in my

The Dalmore Distillery staff, 1993. Back row, left to right: J MacLorey, B Dunnett, D Dunnett, J Dunnett, D Fraser, C McIntosh. Middle row, left to right: R Robertson, R Stewart, R Tait, R O'Brien, S Horner, J Sutherland, R MacDougall. Seated, left to right: A Sinclair, H Hune, JP MacDonald, J Francis and CR Wood.

own future role as master blender.

When I first visited Dalmore, there were no fewer than 53 people working at the distillery, which was managed by George Watt. The staff included John MacDonald and Drew Sinclair, both of whom went on to become distillery managers there. Many distilleries were notable for employing several generations of the same family, and this old tradition certainly continued at Dalmore, where three successive generations of the Dunnetts were eventually to be employed. People such as these were the true backbone of

Dalmore; to them it was much more than just a workplace, it was almost a home. Woe betide anyone who said anything disparaging about their distillery, or worse still, their whisky. After all, it was their life.

Over the years I spent many long hours with John MacDonald, a lovely man about whom I never heard a bad word spoken. I like to remember him sitting in his wood-panelled office overlooking the Cromarty Firth, smoking his pipe and regaling us with stories of Dalmore in days gone by. He eventually retired in 1995 after no less than 44 years of service at the distillery. Another long-serving giant of the Dalmore distilling scene was the late Drew Sinclair, who had been at Dalmore since joining the company on 3rd February 1966. He was a warm, jovial character, fit and full of energy, with thick black hair, and in the best Dalmore tradition, his father, Dave, also worked there, while his brother David used to work on the floor maltings.

Even when I visited in the 1970s, he was full of enthusiasm for Dalmore and was a mine of information on the place. Reminiscing on his time at the distillery, Drew said, 'I mind like yesterday my first day at Dalmore. It was 3rd February 1966, and I was 19 years old. My first job was in the old malt barns, and then I moved quickly to the Saladin boxes. I worked there for two and a half years maybe. Golden Promise barley was coming in then, along with French and Australian barley from time to time.

'One old way we would test the barley, checking on germination, was to take 100 grains and count them. We used to spread them out and split them open with a fingernail. If that spur was three-quarters of the way up the seed, that was just about right, you know. If you got 87 grains out of the 100, that was pretty good, and it was time to dry the grain.'

Later, Drew graduated to working as a tun room man, which was his position when I first met him. He recalled that on occasions, especially during the summer months, the fermentation would be over-active, frothing and spitting all over the tun room. It had to be controlled, and quickly. The answer, according to Drew, was to add soap to the washback!

'It was curd soap, obviously not scented soap that we used. You'd pick up a handful of wee chips of it, and just throw them into the washback. It just knocked it back, the head would go down.'

One thing that interested me during my visit to Dalmore was that during the summer months when the silent season was in progress, Drew and other workers would collect peat from the peat bogs of Baldoon, but also, to my surprise, they would collect heather, too.

'We used to attach it to a big long pole, dip it into hot lime, and swish it all round the washback. We'd have a wee bit of a competition to see who did the best job.'

Thankfully, such laborious jobs are a thing of the past. Apart from anything else, modern health and safety legislation would not permit such practices. Equally unacceptable today is the much lamented practice of 'dramming.' According to Drew, 'We were given three drams a day. At seven o'clock in the morning you'd queue up at the brewer's office to get your first dram. I kid you not! You'd get drams again at midday and at three o'clock, before you went home. It was new spirit, at 63 to 68% alcohol, and it was served in a big glass.' Even this amount of spirit was not enough for some of the workers, as Drew explained. 'Some of the boys would rub dirt onto their faces and go and tell the brewer they'd just done a dirty job and needed a 'dirty dram'!'

Many of the distillery workers came to prefer the new make, or 'clearic', but I remember distinctly talking to the lads in the warehouse about dramming during my first visit to Dalmore. 'New spirit? Forget that! We've got the real stuff here. Fully matured, as soft as milk. Goes down a treat.' One look at their cloudy eyes told me they might be too fond of the real stuff, but I have to say that during my time at Dalmore I never saw anyone inebriated and unfit for work. Maybe they were totally immune. After all, whisky was very much part of their lives.

As my two weeks of work experience at Dalmore in 1972 came to an end I was instructed to write a report on my time there for Whyte & Mackay's managing director, Jack Ligertwood, highlighting the principal factors that influenced the character of Dalmore spirit. Obviously, factors such as the distillery water supply from the River Alness and the maritime location and climate made their contributions to the final spirit. The damp warehouses, especially warehouse number four, were very significant, and to this day I use it to mature the most precious casks destined for prestige, aged bottlings. Perhaps most crucial of all is the types of cask used for maturation. In addition to these elements, however, it was the design of the Dalmore stills which I realised as soon as I saw them, must surely play a major part in determining the spirit's style.

There were four pairs of these idiosyncratic, bulbous beasts. I affectionately refer to them as the 'big bastards'. They represented a real link with Dalmore's past, with Andrew Mackenzie's era, as the upper part of spirit still number two dated from 1874, and even today, remarkably, it remains in use. Unlike the dark, depressing stills of Glen Scotia these were bright and gleaming. What was the secret? 'There's only one way to brighten up a still', said Drew. 'Steel wool, plenty of sweat ... and a coat of linseed oil.' That sweat came

from the men of Dalmore, and I was struck by their skill and dedication, by the major part *they* played in the character of the spirit. Dalmore Distillery was a close-knit community, almost a family, and I left there feeling I had been embraced by that family.

As I drove south again I vividly remember stopping my car at the top of the hill outside Inverness and gazing over the Moray Firth, the Black Isle and beyond. It is indeed a captivating landscape. I could not help thinking that the 'Spirit of the Northern Highlands', and especially Dalmore, was very much part of me now. Mashman Dod Anderson wrote a poem following an abortive Customs & Excise raid on the distillery. It could easily have been about events in the early 19th century, but was actually written about events that took place on 29th June 1978!

It was on a Thursday morning
The Excise were feeling frisky
They made a raid upon Dalmore
To search for missing whisky.
They searched the barns
They searched the stills
They searched the mash tun too
They even searched the mill room
But never got a clue.
They climbed upstairs and then climbed
    down
And crawled along the wall
The boys looked up in wonder
To see if they would fall.
They searched the burn
And poked the sand
And then they searched the dam
But went home disappointed
For they never got a dram.

My visit to Dalmore had left me with a burning ambition to visit more Highland distilleries when the opportunity arose, and with the recent acquisition of Fettercairn and Tomintoul, two more distilleries in the north were already waiting for me. Their purchase was a major step for Whyte & Mackay, but a vital one. If we wanted to compete in the bulk export market, especially to America and the Far East, then a considerable stock inventory was essential.

However, this new era for Whyte & Mackay was one I look back on with a sense of insecurity. There were many changes going on in the company and jobs were under the microscope. There was no room for complacency. However, this merely reflected society in general. The days of 'a job for life' were coming to an end. It was quite a relief, then, to be able to escape from the uncertainties of the Glasgow office to the apparently timeless surroundings of Fettercairn.

Fettercairn is situated some 25 miles south-west of Aberdeen, set in beautiful farming country – known as the Mearns – immortalised in Lewis Grassic Gibbon's classic trilogy A Scots Quair. The village name derives from the Gaelic for 'wooded slope.' The day of my first visit remains fresh in my memory. It was May 1974, and I had been sent north to Fettercairn to review our stocks for future single malt bottlings. After a two-hour drive I approached the small village. It was almost as though I was entering a different world. An early morning mist hung over the red sandstone houses. As I turned right at the Ramsay Arms I was suddenly confronted by an enormous Gothic-style stone arch flanked by two massive octagonal towers

which framed the sleepy, picturesque village. I turned onto Distillery Road and the white-painted warehouses of Fettercairn Distillery with their contrasting black roofs stood out majestically against the backdrop of the Grampian foothills. To my mind this was the epitome of a classic Highland distillery. Unlike Glen Scotia, this one truly welcomed me. Even today I would be surprised if the visiting whisky lover was not seduced by its charm.

Like any old distillery in Scotland Fettercairn has its history and legends, and the foothills of the Grampians were once a hive of smuggling activity, swarming with illicit distillers. After visiting the establishment during the mid-1880s Alfred Barnard wrote, 'The Fettercairn Distillery … is situated at the foot of the Grampians, where "our fathers fed their flocks" and smugglers made the Whisky. It was the head-quarters of these latter gentlemen, and many a racy tale is told by the villagers of their daring and boldness.'

Tarfside and the Cairn o'Mount in particular were great centres for illicit distilling and the wild and remote Cairn o'Mount route from Banchory to Brechin and Dundee was also extensively used by Speyside's unlicensed distillers, keen to get their illegal liquor to market. Many landowners such as Sir Alexander Ramsay of Balmain, owner of the Fasque Estate, were prepared to turn a blind eye to this illegal activity, as many of their tenants needed to sell barley to the illicit distillers in order to pay their rents.

However, by 1823 illicit distilling was rife, and it was estimated in Scotland there were something like 14,000 illicit distilleries in operation. Action was required. And quickly. In my opinion, the 1823 Excise Act (Friday

As the celebrations began for the new millennium, Dalmore was filling its first cask. Left to right: Valerie Tait, Morag Swanson, Steve Tulewicz, Bert Stewart, Scott Horner, Doug Fraser, Brian Dunnett, Donald Dunnett, Drew Sinclair, Reg Tait, John Peter MacDonald. *Courtesy of Andrew Allan.*

18th July 1823), which was designed to curb the illegal trade, opened the doors to the modern Scotch whisky industry as we know it today. It also, perhaps, helped to reduce alcohol abuse as cheap and often crude spirit became much more difficult to obtain.

Ramsay may have been happy to turn a blind eye to illicit distilling in the past, but now legislation was in place that made legal distilling so much more attractive, he was keen to develop a more professional enterprise operating on the right side of the law. Accordingly, he set about converting a former corn mill at Nethermill, on the outskirts of Fettercairn village, into a distillery in 1824.

This was a good location, with fresh water supplies from the Grampians, and abundant locally grown bere, or bigg, a primitive barley, known as 'the drink crop'. The existing tenant at Nethermill was James Stewart, who had a reputation as a former illicit distiller, supposedly producing high-quality spirit in the remote country between Fettercairn and Clattering Bridge, at the foot of Cairn o' Mount. He must surely have possessed some of the vision and commitment of George Smith of Glenlivet, regarded as the first distiller to take out a licence under the provisions of the new act.

On 15th June 1824 James Stewart wrote

Fettercairn village circa 1890.

to Sir Alexander Ramsay regarding 'the mill, kiln and miller's houses of Nethermill ... It is also understood that I am to convert the premises into a distillery, part of which is already erected with your approbation and your promise to allow me to build additional houses for carrying on that work, conform to a plan thereof produced and to be subscribed by us as satisfactory ... I am to have the liberty to take in partners to the distillery.'

Sir Alexander Ramsay accepted Stewart's proposal, and an annual rent of £21 was agreed. It seems the new distillery was working early the following year. It was not long, however, before Stewart was complaining to the Board of Excise about the activities of illicit distillers in the county of Kincardineshire. This seems somewhat ironic considering his own previous occupation. Old habits seem to have died hard for Stewart, as

he was fined the large sum of £21 in the spring of 1828 for distilling with worts stronger than permitted by law.

Clearly he was not the only one facing financial difficulties, as Sir Alexander Ramsay was forced to sell the Fasque Estate during 1829 for less than £80,000. The new owner was John Gladstone, who had made a fortune as a merchant in Liverpool, but wished to retire to his native land. He took up residence at Fasque in January 1830. Shortly after the Gladstones arrived, James Stewart died, and James Durie took on the Nethermill lease in November 1833. The boom times that initially followed the 1823 Excise Act were to be followed by much more subdued trading, and from 329 distilleries in 1825 the figure fell to just 128 by 1858. However, James Durie was clearly one of the more astute distillers, and not only did Fettercairn survive, but when he

Fettercairn village today.

died on 6th December 1854 Durie left the impressive sum of £16,500.

Three years previously, Durie had handed over management of the distillery to his 22-year-old son, David. In the same year Sir John Gladstone died, being succeeded at Fasque by his eldest son Sir Thomas. Thomas Gladstone was a staunch Tory, in contrast with his younger brother William Ewart (1809-98), a Liberal who was already making his mark in the political arena. Durie remained at Fettercairn until 1888, and shortly after his departure a serious fire destroyed half of the distillery buildings. It must have been a spectacular sight, visible for miles around, as employees and villagers worked to extinguish the flames, fuelled by thousands of gallons of fine whisky. As a result Fettercairn remained silent for the next two years, and on 12th October 1889 the Fasque factor wrote, 'The

farmers feel the loss of the ready and convenient market afforded by the distillery for the barley grown in the district ... the proprietor is anxious to see it again at work on something like the same scale as it was carried on by the late tenant Mr Durie.'

The following year Fettercairn reopened, now trading as the Fettercairn Distillery Co, with Sir John Gladstone as chairman. During that year William Gladstone, now a highly respected elder statesman, visited his nephew's distillery, touring the reconstructed premises and taking away some samples of its spirit. This must have been a momentous occasion for the villagers and distillery staff, and a particularly proud moment for Sir John Gladstone. I would like to think that perhaps some crucial cabinet decisions in London were taken over a glass or two of Fettercairn.

According to Archibald Cowie Cameron

Fettercairn distillery lies at the foot of the Cairn o'Mount.

in his *History of Fettercairn* (1899), the 'Grand Old Man', as Gladstone was affectionately known in his later life, ' ... when at Fasque ... spent much of his spare time in visiting the poor and the aged on his father's estates.' In view of Gladstone's great political career, serving an unprecedented four terms as Prime Minister and his family's long-term generosity to the parish of Fettercairn it seems surprising that there is no tangible monument to 'The People's William.' Hopefully, one day in the future this may be rectified. Gladstone, of course, was not the first Victorian icon to visit the village. Back on Friday 20th September 1861 Queen Victoria and Prince Albert slipped quietly into the Ramsay Arms at 7.15 in the evening. Her Majesty subsequently described

Fettercairn as ' ... a small quiet town, or rather village' with ' ... not a creature stirring.' Three years later that landmark arch was constructed in the centre of the village to commemorate the queen's visit.

During the boom years for blended whisky in the late 19th and early 20th centuries Fettercairn was popular as a malt component in many well known blends, including those of John Walker & Sons, Buchanan's and James Munro & Sons of Leith. However, the distillery's economic situation was always precarious, and in 1926, at the height of the industrial depression, Fettercairn, like so many other Scottish distilleries, finally succumbed. The distillery was silent for 13 years from 1926, and was on the verge of being demolished as no buyer could be found. But in October 1936 James Mann, the Fasque Estate factor, was approached by the colourful distillery entrepreneur Joseph W. Hobbs with a view to purchasing the distillery. Hobbs was a Canadian Scot who had prospered by 'bootlegging' during America's prohibition era, and had recently acquired Glenury Royal Distillery in Stonehaven. He informed Mann that he wished to buy 'another one in this vicinity.' The purchase of Glenury had been undertaken in association with the Glasgow firm of Train & McIntyre, which was part of National Distillers of America.

Negotiations dragged on, but on 27th January 1938 James Mann optimistically wrote to Hobbs offering him Fettercairn Distillery for £5,000. The price was accepted, and when yet another Fettercairn Distillery Co was formed, more than one hundred years of Gladstone family ownership came to an end. Not many Scottish distilleries can boast such an illustrious association with a great British dynasty. Hobbs' empire now included not only Fettercairn and Glenury, but also Bruichladdich, Benromach, Glenlochy and Hillside distilleries, along with the silent Aberdeen distillery of Strathdee. In 1938 all these distilling interests were amalgamated into Associated Scottish Distillers Ltd.

After the Second World War, while the whisky industry in general prospered, ASD performed disappointingly and in 1953 Train & McIntyre and four of the ASD distilleries were acquired by the Distillers Company Ltd. Fettercairn, meanwhile, was the subject of a separate deal which saw it sold to Aberdeen businessman Tom Scott Sutherland. The

1960s were a great boom time for Scottish distilling, with 11 new distilleries opening during the decade, including Tamnavulin and Tomintoul. Many other distilleries were 'doubled up' in capacity, and Fettercairn was no exception, with a second pair of stills being installed in 1966. Five years later Fettercairn was sold to the Tomintoul-Glenlivet Distillery Co Ltd and this firm was then acquired by Scottish and Universal Investment Trust in 1973, bringing it into the Whyte & Mackay fold.

Single malts were still very much in their infancy, with a few notable exceptions such as Glenfiddich, and one glance at our Fettercairn labels clearly showed that we were really just playing at it, along with many others. It was off-white, with a garish red tartan border. What a disaster! One of our Fettercairn Distillery brochures dating from 1967 declares, ' … although not generally realised, after being matured for 6–8 years, Fettercairn makes a most excellent single malt, a taste which is now becoming more popular with whisky connoisseurs.'

Fettercairn had shown a degree of innovation the following year by introducing 'Fettercairn 875', an eight-year-old single malt bottled at 75° proof. It proved notably popular in North and South America, the Middle East, Spain and France. Aged whiskies for that period were generally available at around the age of eight, but as the market has matured, palates have demanded softer, more mellow characteristics. This is one reason why I feel today single malts between 12 and 18 years old are preferable to younger expressions.

The standard Fettercairn single malt being marketed then was an eight-year-old, but

The staff of Fettercairn Distillery, 1990. Standing, left to right: Gordon Fraser, Gordon Paton, Stewart Walker, Andrew Brandie, David Doig, Gordon Low, Dick Dargie. Seated, left to right: J McGuigan, Phyllis Ewen, Steve Tulewicz, Alexander Watson, Duncan Pirie.

when I visited the distillery for the first time, in 1974, I was keen to see what older casks were available in the distillery warehouses. Waiting to welcome me when I arrived was the assistant manager, Douglas Cooper. His boss was John Livie, who had been managing Fettercairn since 1954 and was now nearing retirement. John was perhaps best summed up by Harry Diamond in an article published in *Drinks International* in November 1969. 'People who don't really know what makes him tick say that beneath that rather uncom-

promising exterior beats an uncompromising interior.'

That day John was down south on business, so it was left to Douglas to show me around. My initial warm impression of the distillery was reinforced when I entered the stillhouse. Practically everything was in front of me in that one room. The two pairs of stills were bright and burnished. They possessed character and charm. An open mash tun stood to the left, and the cereal smell from it filled my nostrils. A range of larchwood washbacks was visible in the tun room to the right. Douglas grinned at me and said, 'I can see you've not seen a distillery like this before, Richard.'

'You can say that again!' I replied, 'especially with that water running down the outside of the stills. I guess it must help contribute to the character of Fettercairn?'

Douglas explained that the low wines stills were fitted with water jackets, and that as soon as the foreshots were running, the flow of cooling water was switched on. This forces a lot of the congeners to the bottom of the still, rather than allowing them to pass over the lye arm and through the condensers. Fettercairn is already a full-bodied malt, but this idiosyncratic process tends to add complexity to the final spirit. In order to nurture the spirit, good wood management is essential.

'Come on and I'll show you some casks which I know will interest you', said Douglas. On the way to the warehouses he told me something about himself and his time at Fettercairn.

'I was just 18 years old when I started work at Fettercairn', he recalled. 'My father had a small dairy farm about four miles from the village. It was the start of January 1940, and the brewer had just been called up to join the Royal Navy. The manager was George Hampton, very old school, with a heavy moustache, but a lovely man.

'I started as a driver, as the manager didn't drive and so he had a chauffeur. He lived in Laurencekirk, and his driver had been called up. At that time Fettercairn belonged to Associated Scottish Distillers, who also had a number of other distilleries, and Mr Hampton looked after those too. We would often go to Glenury, as well as Strathdee in Aberdeen,

which was closed, but they still used the bonds, and to Hillside at Montrose.

'As well as driving, I also helped out with tapping the casks and taking samples in the warehouses, as a lot of the young men who worked at the distillery were being called up. At that time most of the whisky from Fettercairn went out by rail from Laurencekirk. Because of food rationing, distilleries were not allowed grain, but around 1945 every distillery got a quota of grain so it could distil again, but it wasn't usually that much.

'I served in the Royal Marines when it was my time to be called up, and I came back to Fettercairn in May 1946. Alistair Menzies, a former major in the Highland Light Infantry, was in charge then, and I went into the maltings, situated where the cooperage is now. Alistair Menzies wanted me to go over onto the distilling side, and so I did. There was a little bit more money, because you were working shifts. I earned £2 15/- a week when I first joined, and I suppose after the war we were getting about £3.

'In the maltings we allowed ten or eleven days for germination, with everything being turned by hand, with wooden shiels, of course. Golden Promise barley was starting to become popular in the late forties and fifties. Our peat came from New Pitsligo in Aberdeenshire, and the men would cut it during the silent season. Sad to say, in those days a lot of the men were laid off in the "silent season", when the distillery closed for several weeks for annual maintenance, and then were taken back on again when distilling started up.

'In the stillhouse you had a fair bit of work. You had the old wooden balls on the stills, just wooden balls with string right through them. You heard the different noises when you hit them against the still. If the neck of the still had filled up you didn't get the usual "dong" sound so you knew you had to be careful the wash didn't come over the top of the still and flood the spirit safe. The stills were always run on oil in my time. We ran the spirits very low key. I think they distil too quickly today. With slow distilling it would mature earlier because you'd get some of the oils off. There's only a light spirit going over if you run it gently.

'We were getting good wood, lots of sherry casks, and lots of nice fresh casks were coming back to us. They hadn't been sitting about drying out. I think concrete warehouses are too dry. Ash-floored warehouses gave you a nice moisture.

' "Billing the cask" still went on in my time. You'd see folk rolling an empty cask up and down Distillery Road here to get out a bottle or two of whisky for Christmas or whatever. Sometimes they'd to pour water in and roll it around to get the billings out. Glencadam in Brechin was the last place they would do that. Being in the town people would see the empty casks and maybe manage to get hold of one.'

Douglas' stories fascinated me, and over the next few years he would be of great support. I could always count on his good advice and distilling knowledge which he passed on to many people, including Alec Watson and Dave Doig. To his credit, they too went on to manage Fettercairn. Both these great custodians of Fettercairn's heritage would play an important part later in my career. But for now, back in Glasgow, amidst all the upheavals at Whyte & Mackay, one new figure was about to dominate my life.

Chapter Six
THE MASTER BLENDER

'Scotch whisky ... born in the purity of Scottish winters and nurtured to perfection by the skills of Master Distillers and Master Blenders, for worldwide enjoyment.'

KENNETH GRAHAM,
FORMER MD, WHYTE & MACKAY

There was a deadly silence in the blending department.

Everyone was on tenterhooks. 'He' was in the building. I was finding it difficult to concentrate on my work. I heard voices and heavy footsteps approaching along the corridor. Surely this must be him. The door swung open and Jack Ligertwood walked in. 'Well Kenneth, this is where it all happens', he said. 'Good morning everybody', Kenneth Graham replied, 'I'm delighted to meet you all.' He walked forward and shook hands with Alistair Hart. I watched as they talked. It was immediately obvious to me this was someone who commanded respect. He was tall, well built and sharply dressed, with a deep, sermonic voice.

This was a man on a serious mission.

Abruptly he turned to me and shook my hand. The handshake was firm and confident. 'I'll be talking to all of you very soon', he said, and with that he was gone, closely followed by Jack. Alistair and I looked at each other. We were both momentarily stunned. 'Shit!' said Alistair. 'He means business.'

And he did.

Kenneth Graham was our new chief executive, appointed by SUITS (Scottish & Universal Investments Trust Ltd) to bring together all the various elements of the recently-enlarged company. His key role was to raise the profile of Whyte & Mackay and make the brand even more competitive. This was the 1970s and the buzzword was 'marketing', but Jack Ligertwood had been with the firm for almost 30 years. I can well imagine him thinking to himself, 'It might be dressed up differently, but I've heard all this before.'

Kenneth Graham had come to us from the role of export director for Arthur Bell & Sons Ltd of Perth. There he had worked under the legendary figure of Raymond Miquel, who had become managing director of the company at the age of just 37. He, more than anybody, had revolutionised Bells, turning it from a gentlemanly, slightly sleepy company into a modern, predatory organisation. In his own words, 'I'm not ruthless or aggressive, but I'm competitive: I always have been. I learnt early on that winning beats losing.' When Miquel was at Bells there were no such word as 'recession' – only 'opportunity'. He had ceaseless drive, and in my opinion was one of the 'greats' of the Scotch whisky industry. I wish we had more like him today.

Although he was his own man, Kenneth Graham had clearly been strongly influenced by the 'Miquel Way', and brought some of that energy and dedication from Perth to Glasgow. In an increasingly competitive commercial environment, these qualities were vital. He soon made a number of new senior appointments in the sales, marketing and finance departments to help build our brand business. He also recognised there were weaknesses in many areas of our operation. I remember him walking into the sample room when I was working late one evening. He seemed agitated. 'Glad to see you're still here, Richard', he said. 'It was pure mayhem out there in the corridor at five o'clock tonight. I nearly got mowed down by a stampede of our staff eager to get home. The worst thing of all – it was the bloody managers who were leading them!'

Our old ways and our Victorian offices in Baltic Chambers epitomised the whole ethos of the company. Old, traditional and a little tired. It was time for a change. Kenneth Graham saw this immediately and decided a statement needed to be made. Whyte & Mackay had to be seen to be modern and dynamic, and one clear way to reflect this was to move to new premises. Accordingly, we took over part of a recently-completed office block on St Vincent Street, in the heart of Glasgow's commercial district. It was slick and chic, open-plan instead of a warren of small offices, and best of all you didn't have to share a toilet with Alcoholics Anonymous! There was a real buzz about the place, a sense that Whyte & Mackay was a serious contender amongst the premium blends, particularly in the Scottish market, where our main rivals were Bells, Grants and Teachers.

As the company was moving ahead in a new and exciting way, so was my personal life. On 10th April 1974 I married the lovely girl I had met at The Rock in Hyndland Road. Susie Prosser was a member of the illustrious Glasgow Rover dealer, H. Prosser & Son, who had been in the motor trade since the early 1900s. Rather like Whyte & Mackay, it was a Glasgow institution. These two institutions were brought together on our wedding day, and in recognition of this I ended my speech with the flippant warning, 'Please don't drink and drive, but if you must, make sure you're drinking a Whyte & Mackay and driving a Prosser's car.'

Our honeymoon was spent on the lovely island of Ibiza, in the days before it was taken over by youthful, drunken clubbers. I'm not sure just what Susie was expecting on our first night together, but she did seem slightly surprised when I got out my Hugh Johnson's *Wine Atlas* and began to study the great

chateaux of Bordeaux. I may not have come across as the last of the great romantics, but I did have my Wine & Spirit Education Trust diploma course to finish!

Back in Glasgow we settled down to married life in Rutherglen, and at work Kenneth Graham's new regime was ringing in further changes. Towards the end of 1975 I was offered a golden opportunity. One day in December Kenneth Graham summoned me to his office, the inner sanctum. This usually only happened if something had gone seriously wrong. He gestured to a chair and I sat down, feeling apprehensive. However, his warm smile soon reassured me this time I was not in trouble.

'Well Richard, how do you feel about becoming our chief blender? Do you think you could handle the extra responsibility?' This was the moment I had been waiting for throughout my career, so obviously I replied positively.

'Right, then', he said, 'that's settled. But remember, I'm looking for a long-term commitment from you. By the way, as of now you'll be reporting to Bobby McCall, not Alistair Hart. Well done, Richard.' He shook my hand firmly. The interview was over. I came out of the office with mixed emotions. I was happy finally to be in this position, at last following in the footsteps of my father and grandfather. But unfortunately it meant the end of the good old days and the late, boozy nights with Big Al. I would even miss his curried breath. It was the end of an era.

The changes at Whyte & Mackay were exciting, but they did have a human cost, and I could not help being saddened that some of the informality and fun of work had gone forever. The acquisition of W&S Strong and Hay & Macleod, which had brought us Fettercairn and Tomintoul distilleries, also brought Bobby McCall onto the Whyte & Mackay payroll. Bobby was a complex, likeable character, almost eccentric. Funny, witty, something of a showman, yet also someone who demanded respect and could be a hard taskmaster.

For the majority of his working life Bobby had been a whisky broker, and was known in the trade as a real wheeler-dealer. He was also a distiller, as he had been one of the founders of Tomintoul Distillery in the mid-1960s, and was a major shareholder in W&S Strong and Hay & Macleod. When SUITS purchased this company in 1973 Bobby became a very wealthy man. Many people in his position would have been tempted to sit back and enjoy their wealth, but Bobby was a restless character filled with nervous energy. He always needed fresh excitement. No wonder he was so thin.

Bobby had no intention of taking early retirement, and wanted to be part of Kenneth Graham's new regime. There was clearly not room for two brokers within Whyte & Mackay, as Alistair Hart soon recognised. Freed from the routines of nine-to-five office life, which had never appealed to him, Alistair joined forces with his brother Donald and bought a pub in Shettleston, before they ultimately became successful independent bottlers. With the ever-growing interest in specialist limited edition single malts, continuing success seems assured for the Hart brothers.

As 1976 unfolded I had new challenges ahead of me as chief blender and a new sample room in the offices in St Vincent Street. It was small but adequate, and gave me a sense of independence. On the domestic front, I had new challenges, too, as my first child, Sally, was born on 18th September. Sally was not the greatest of sleepers, but a combination of milk and Whyte & Mackay usually did the trick.

From an early age I started to teach her about wines, and whilst she had difficulty remembering the 61 chateaux of the 1855 Bordeaux classifications, she did, however, manage to learn certain grape varieties. At the age of four, her party piece was to take a glass of Burgundy from me when we had friends in for dinner and with the bat of an eyelid identify it as Pinot Noir. Now, almost 30 years on, she still amazes me with her energy, enthusiasm and her adventurous nature. No father could be more proud.

As chief blender my primary responsibility was maintaining the quality and consistency of all the company's products, bulk and bottled. Working with Bobby McCall formed part of that process, particularly as he was responsible for our new fillings and bulk stock acquisitions. In other words, he was supplying the paint, and I was producing the pictures. Our close professional relationship was a rewarding one. Today, Whyte & Mackay and the aged blends are what I would consider our finest creations.

While I was engrossed with the Whyte & Mackay whiskies there were, of course, many other blenders employed in the industry. I was not alone, but it sometimes felt like it. Blending still remained a bit of a mystery and there was very little inter-company communication, whereas today there is much more openness.

So just who were the other blenders at that time?

Established and respected figures with whom I came into contact included Jimmy Lang of Chivas Brothers, Ian Grieve from Bells, Paul Ricards, Alan Reid and Stan Hutchison of Highland Distilleries, Billy Walker of Inver House and Jack Gowdie of Hiram Walker. However, back in 1976, two of the highest-profile blenders were Donald Mackinlay and Trevor Cowan of Mackinlay-McPherson Ltd. In a sense, they were two of my mentors. They were the first blenders to be exposed to the public gaze when featured in the SWA film *Time Was The Beginning*. This is one film I will never forget because I used it frequently while lecturing on behalf of the SWA. These two gentlemen were largely instrumental in lifting the veil of secrecy that surrounded the art of blending.

Since then, whisky festivals, tastings and publications have increasingly exposed the blenders' art to the public gaze. Many of today's blenders have become personal friends, including the 'quiet man' David Stewart, chief blender for William Grant & Sons, for whom he has worked since 1962. Another long-serving blender is 'Gentleman John' Ramsay, who I knew in his William Lawson Distillers days. He is now firmly established with Edrington, while Colin Scott has taken on Jimmy Lang's role with Chivas Regal. The inimitable Robert Hicks, formerly of Ballantine's, is another blender for whom I have always had great respect. The same applies to Billy Walker, one time blender for the Albyn Bond and Inver House Distillers, and now successfully established as Managing Director of the revived Benriach Distillery on Speyside.

Meanwhile, on the other side of the world, in Japan, two other famous blenders with whom I was to become closely associated were also practising their art. They were Ken Sato of Suntory and Shigeo Sato of Nikka. I came to work with them as a result of our bulk malt

Left to right: Jim Cryle, master blender Shigeo Sato, Jens Tholstrup and myself at the Nikka Distillery, Japan.

Shigeo at work in his blending room.

Above. Master blender, Ken Sato, of Suntory with
Bobby McCall and myself in 1975.

Right. Presentation of a certificate and cooper's
shield to Nikka's cooper of Hokkaido Cooperage on
behalf of The Incorporation of Coopers of Glasgow.

sales to Japan and I began a long love affair
with this ever fascinating, intriguing country.

Back home, a new generation of would-be
blenders was growing up, and it featured an
increasing number of women, including
Maureen Robinson of Diageo. Jim Beveridge,
also of Diageo, and Bill Lumsden of
Glenmorangie were still at university when I
became chief blender, but are now key,
dynamic figures in the whisky industry. Each
of these custodians of the art of whisky
blending, young and old, has made his own
inimitable mark. They, and many others, have
greatly enhanced the reputation of the Scotch
whisky industry by their willingness to share
with the world their passion and devotion for
this great spirit. Let us never forget: skilled
blenders make the Scotch whisky industry
what it is today.

As I settled into my new role of chief
blender, the rest of Kenneth Graham's team
was also developing under the chairmanship
of Sir Hugh Fraser. Jack Ligertwood became
UK Sales Director, driving forward our
ambitious brand development. He held this
prestigious position until his retirement in
1990, having loyally served the company for
40 years. At the same time, Hector 'HAC'
Mackenzie of Dalmore Distillery took on the
role of Divisional Director for distilling.

Meanwhile, Tom Frize had been brought
in to review our accounting practices, and he
certainly had an accountant's outlook.
Everything came down to figures, as I was to
discover many years later when he became my
boss. A classic Frize response was, 'If it was
your money, would you make the same
decision?' I recall one occasion when I

received a new company car and had the audacity to ask for mudflaps to be fitted. 'An unnecessary expense. You're not on, sport', was his terse reply. That was the end of the matter. Attempts at negotiation would have been pointless.

One significant appointment still to be made was that of Marketing Director, and in December 1978 Michael Lunn took up that position. This shy but determined and clearly talented figure was set for higher things. Another determined, talented figure who was anything but shy was Margaret Thatcher. She came to power as Britain's first female Prime Minister in the spring of 1979, in the wake of the notorious 'Winter of Discontent.' It seemed to be a time of perpetual conflict between unions and management, culminating in 150,000 people being laid off due to a road haulage strike. But when it came to rubbish piling up in the streets and bodies lying unburied, the public had had enough. Thatcher gained a 70-seat majority over the Labour Party in the House of Commons and set about a programme of union reform.

Meanwhile, on a personal level, a wind of change was also blowing at Whyte & Mackay. On 12th June 1979 SUITS was bought by Lonrho for £29.7 million. Lonrho had started out as the London & Rhodesia Mining & Land Company, and was taken over in 1961 by the buccaneering entrepreneur 'Tiny' Rowland. Rowland had been born Rowland Walter Fuhrhop in an internment camp in India. However, his father was a wealthy German adventurer and his mother was Anglo-Dutch. During the 1930s 'Tiny' Rowland served in the Hitler Youth Movement, and, along with his father, was interned on the Isle of Man during the Second World War. It is rumoured that he spied for the British Government. After the war Rowland emigrated to Southern Rhodesia and set about making his fortune. As Jean Shaoul wrote in his obituary in 1998, 'Rowland's goal was to make money, and lots of it. He let nothing and no one stand in his way. He did not seek the approval of the establishment, nor honours from it. Politicians and governments existed for no other purpose than to enable him to make a killing.' British Prime Minister Edward Heath famously described Rowland as 'the unpleasant and unacceptable face of capitalism.'

Love him or loathe him, you could not fail to admit that Rowland was extremely talented at making money. Lonrho announced a profit of £158,000 in 1961, but just over quarter of a century later that figure had risen to over £272 million. Not surprisingly, he was a hero to his shareholders. However, we at Whyte & Mackay looked on Lonrho's acquisition of the company with some trepidation. But Lonrho adopted a largely hands-off approach, allowing Kenneth Graham to continue running the business much as he had always done. To many of us, the change of ownership seemed to make very little difference. Provided our profits were healthy, 'Tiny' was happy.

Nonetheless, as Michael Lunn says, 'Lonrho maintained its short-term culture, with only an occasional extra pocket money allowance.' Lonrho bought into the Scotch whisky industry at an opportune moment, as 1978–9 saw some of the highest ever levels of output up to that point, with 176,882 proof gallons (459,009 litres) of malt and grain spirit being produced in 1979. Such high volumes would not be achieved again for the best part of 20 years. It was not just a case of high levels of production, as sales figures at Whyte & Mackay were going through the roof. In February 1979 sales for Scotland alone rose by 83% compared to the same month the previous year. This was largely thanks to the business of Haddow's, Allied and Bass.

Nonetheless, there were rumblings of disquiet in the industry, a feeling that overall sales could not increase in the optimistic way projected by sales managers. Surely they must accept some of the blame. Tastes were changing, and younger drinkers associated blended whisky with their boring parents. There was no genuine innovation. The pinstriped executives in the Scotch whisky industry were complacent and underactive. White spirits, particularly vodka, coupled with white wine were becoming fashionable at the expense of whisky, brandy and rum. Over-production appeared to be the order of the day. The EEC was already facing 'butter mountains' and 'wine lakes' and now the 'whisky lochs' were starting to overflow.

It was to take several years, however, before the gravity of the situation was fully understood, but when it finally hit home the consequences were serious. Distillery closures were inevitable. In 1983, DCL shut down eleven of its 45 operational malt distilleries, in order to 'attain the requisite balance between maturing stocks of whisky and the anticipated level of future sales' and a further ten DCL casualties followed two years later. Newspaper stories seemed to be predicting the end of the Scotch whisky industry as we knew it. One headline said it all. 'Scotch on the rocks.'

New markets had to be found for Scotch whisky. Bulk exports were one answer, but the prime target was within the UK. That target was the supermarkets. Jack Ligertwood had long recognised the vital importance of getting our whisky into off-licence chains such as Agnews and Haddows, but he was also well aware of the significance of supermarkets, and had already achieved some success there. But general attitudes towards the likes of Tesco, Finefare and Liptons within the whisky industry were still naïve and rather conde-scending, despite their increasing importance to us. I well remember one senior executive from a major distilling company saying to me 'Supermarkets! You'll never see our brands in a supermarket.' How wrong he was.

Imagine how he would feel today, not only to see his company's brands adorning their shelves, but also the number of 'own label' whiskies specially blended for supermarkets. And who were the customers? Were they men? No! They were women. They were having their say at long last. And leading them was the inimitable figure of Margaret Thatcher, who was known to take a dram herself.

Whatever happened, the whisky lochs were not going to be drained overnight and consistent long-term marketing strategies were clearly essential if they were to avoid refilling in the future. Michael Lunn was a shrewd operator who was well aware of the situation. Accordingly he appointed Charles Shaw as marketing manager. He may have looked as though he had just left school, but one conver-sation with him was enough to make you aware that his deceptively youthful appearance hid a very smart and calculating brain. There would be no whisky loch if

Michael Lunn and Charles Shaw had anything to do with it.

Marketing was becoming an evermore important part of our business, and presentation of the product was key. Over the years our dump-shaped Whyte & Mackay bottle had been subject to a number of cosmetic changes, but something more dramatic had to be done if we were to stimulate future sales. The answer was a new D-shaped bottle. It was more compact, slicker, and was designed to be easier for women to handle, but it still retained the signature gold plastic measure cap. The new bottle was a bold move, but it was evolution, not revolution, and therefore the market readily accepted it.

One reason for this change was to help stimulate the UK market and also assist in our penetration of North America for the first time. The USA was still the world's largest importer of Scotch whisky, and quite naturally, Whyte & Mackay wanted a share of that business. However, to make a success in this huge, diverse market took years, as we were to discover to our cost. Under Kenneth Graham's direction K&M Imports Inc New Jersey was formed to facilitate our penetration of the USA. A large sales force was employed and the aim was to have Whyte & Mackay on sale in every state in the country. It was soon realised, however, that our aims were over-ambitious. The market was a voracious beast: nothing could satisfy its hunger for finance. A company like Whyte & Mackay simply could not afford this commitment in a long-term context, with no guarantees of profitability. The venture was abandoned after only a short period.

In addition to introducing the D-shaped bottle, Michael Lunn and Charles Shaw were also keen to upgrade the presentation of our aged products such as Whyte & Mackay Supreme and our 21-year-old, along with our single malts such as Dalmore, Tomintoul and Fettercairn. It should not be forgotten that despite the initial scepticism expressed by most of the industry in the mid-1960s when William Grant started to aggressively promote Glenfiddich, single malts were now beginning to have greater significance for all of us, and yet had been with us for the best part of five centuries.

The first surviving reference to malt whisky is in a document dating from 1494, apparently relating to 24th August. 'Eight bolls of malt to Friar John Cor wherewith to make aqua vitae.' By happy coincidence our second child, Graeme, was born on that momentous anniversary. Unlike his sister, however, he has steered well clear of the 'demon drink'. Obviously, there is no chance of him following in my chosen career, but he seems to have inherited some of my drive and enthusiasm for things about which he feels truly passionate.

As the 1980s opened, the Scotch whisky industry faced many problems, including over-production and a general recession, which had left more than two million people unemployed for the first time since 1935. Companies could not deal with these problems in isolation. The industry had to react as one body. Firms were also now no longer solely dealing just with whiskies, they were investing in other spirit brands and wines. Training of staff and inter-company contact were high on the agenda, and the 49 Wine & Spirits Club of Scotland and the Institute of Wine & Spirits of Scotland came into their own at this formative time. Both were already highly regarded within the industry, and were well represented at the top tables of official dinners. If you were young and ambitious these bodies represented almost the only way of obtaining fresh, up-to-date information on the world of drinks. Remember that specialist wine and spirits publications were few and far between in those days.

I had been a member of both these prestigious organisations for many years, slowly working my way through the ranks, and in 1980 it was my privilege to be elected president of the '49 Club.' We met for lunch approximately every month, and these were always convivial, well-attended occasions, which consisted of a short address by a guest speaker, the meal itself, and plenty of good conversation. There was never any shortage of drink, and sometimes the lunches drifted on well into the afternoon. The good old days my father had enjoyed were not quite over after all! Nonetheless, it was a great chance to meet people, make contacts and keep up with old friends.

The role of president included ensuring that members were offered an exciting and informative programme of events throughout the year, with the opportunity to taste the finest wines. Accordingly, I managed to persuade Moet et Chandon's managing director Nancy Jarret and the export sales director of Chateau Mouton Rothschild, Hervé Berland to visit Scotland and address our eager audience at the RAC Club in the heart of Glasgow. We were presenting some of the world's great Champagnes and fine wines, so not surprisingly both events were sell-outs.

One guest I remember with much admiration was Jim Watt, who was Scotland's reigning World Lightweight boxing champion and sponsored by Whyte & Mackay, along with World Junior Middleweight champion Maurice Hope. Watt is one of Scotland's true sporting heroes, and was rewarded with an MBE and the Freedom of Glasgow. However, winning the world championship had certainly not given him an inflated ego. Apart from delivering a witty speech, he found time to talk to many of our members when he was guest of honour at our annual awards luncheon. He still remains an outstanding ambassador for Scotland today.

After almost half a century of informing and entertaining, the '49ers' remain in good spirits today. Over the years, many people have put in a great deal of their personal time to ensure its success, and it is a part of my life I will always remember with great affection and satisfaction.

When it came to more formalised tasting and education, however, the Institute of Wine & Spirits of Scotland could not be surpassed. Their meetings, both in Edinburgh and Glasgow, boasted a wide variety of subjects, from the vineyards of England to the Barossa Valley of Australia.

My presidency of the '49 Club' in 1980-1 stood me in good stead when I was subsequently invited to become president of the institute. Because so much information is now available in books, magazine and via the Internet, the institute remains the only official association which actively promotes further education in both wines and spirits. It is therefore an organisation that will always have my support and respect. Those three years of presidency were significant for me. Although I found speaking in public a daunting task, and still sometimes felt physically sick, I did begin to develop a sense of confidence and a degree of professionalism.

This experience proved invaluable as I found myself undertaking more and more presentations on behalf of Whyte & Mackay. This gave me the opportunity to convey to my audiences the burning passion I had for whisky and its heritage. Unfortunately, Susie did not always share my passion. This was not surprising, however, as I would often come home late to find her exhausted after a long day with our two boisterous, young children. It sometimes reminded me of what my mother had to go through with my father and she certainly did not have an easy time of it, either. Just like blending, it was sometimes difficult to get the balance between work and home life right.

Demand for presentations steadily increased, and their apparent effectiveness made them the perfect tool to drive forward our marketing. Charles Shaw devised the brilliant idea of a 'road show', taking the brand to the people for the first time. We had a specially-hired 'Whyte & Mackay Road Show' double-decker bus which we took to all the major cities of England, hosting state-of-the-art slideshow presentations for clients and potential clients in leading hotels. It was slick, professional and imaginative, but technically it was a nightmare. Nine slide projectors were synchronised in order to fade images in and out, accompanied by rousing music. The whole effect depended on precise timing. Unfortunately, our second presentation in London turned into a complete disaster when the supply of electricity was cut for a split second. This was enough to throw the whole mechanism into chaos, with random images of bottles, casks and Highland rivers appearing all over the screen. It was like a bad dream, but we had to sit and suffer. Although it only lasted a few minutes, it seemed like hours to us. Despite this technical hitch, overall the road show was an enormous success, and would be repeated four years later.

The road show was one positive way of moving the company forward, and the increasing importance of marketing, along with expanding sales and accounts teams, soon necessitated another change of office. We transferred the short distance to a brand new building at 296/8 St Vincent Street, officially opened by Michael Kelly, Glasgow's Lord Provost and one of the driving forces behind the famous 'Glasgow smiles better' campaign.

This certainly reflected the company's growing success, and in 1984 Whyte & Mackay became Scotland's top-selling blended Scotch whisky in the off-trade sector. This was a notable achievement, but Lunn and Shaw were never content to rest on their laurels, particularly in the English market, where there was still much work to be done. We may have been one of Scotland's most popular blends, but when it came to England we were virtually unknown. It was more like 'Whyte & Who?'

One way of increasing our brand awareness south of the Border was by sponsoring a major English sporting event. We had already supported a number of localised activities, such as junior level football, show jumping and golf. But now a deal was struck to take on the PGA Golf Championship at Wentworth in Surrey, and to demonstrate our serious intent, we invested in excess of £3 million in the venture over a three-year period. This was serious money when you think that in 1951 our total advertising budget amounted to just £296.

However, sponsorship never carries any guarantees. For one thing, you are dependent on the weather attracting the right players and large crowds, and during our first year of sponsorship the event was almost rained off. You also need sympathetic and consistent media coverage, and this may take three years and more to develop. Was it really value for money?

It is not just sponsorship that carries no guarantees, but also packaging innovations. Our last bottle change had been in 1980, when we switched from the 'dump' to the 'D-shape.' Then, in 1985, Charles Shaw carried out market research which revealed that compared to our principal competitors – Bells, Teachers, Grant's Standfast and Famous Grouse – our bottle looked short and rather insignificant on the shelves. Consumers felt they were being short-changed. As a result of this market research a new, taller 'D-shape' Whyte & Mackay bottle was introduced, bringing us into line with our main rivals. In order to publicise the fact, Charles Shaw's advertising spend was increased to over £1 million

From a blender's perspective, packaging changes inevitably cause concern. It seems, no matter how much reassurance you give, consumers still believe that you must also have changed the blend itself. In this instance, they actually thought we had improved the quality of the product, which just goes to show the significance presentation can have. Clearly we were going in the right direction with our packaging, as at the Cannes Symposium in 1985 we were awarded the prestigious trophy for 'Duty-free Product Range of the Year.'

Those buying our whiskies in the duty-free market were fortunate compared to our domestic customers. Following chancellor Nigel Lawson's budget of 19th March the average price of a bottle of blended whisky rose to £7.50. Of this the government took no less than £4.73 in duty. To those of us in the Scotch whisky industry, and many of our customers, this seemed an outrageously large amount. Duty had risen with unimaginative predictability in every budget I could remember. It truly felt as though successive governments were bleeding us dry. Such high levels of duty prevented the industry from investing in its future, so it was hardly a smart long-term move. It was said that they were killing the goose that laid the golden egg and I had to agree.

Staying on the domestic front, the day after the 1985 budget I was in a meeting with the spirits buyer of Marks & Spencer when I got an urgent phone call from Susie. I was to drop everything and immediately go to Rotten Row maternity hospital as soon as possible, even if Marks & Spencer was an important customer! I managed to make it to the hospital with half an hour to spare before our third child, was born. I suggested calling him Michael, after the patron saint who gave his name to the Marks & Spencer brand, but Susie put her foot down. We finally agreed on Tom.

The Paterson household was now complete, and deep down I had hopes that one of our children might become the fourth generation to be involved in whisky blending. I certainly was not going to push any of them, however. As far as I was concerned, provided they were happy and explored their passions with determination and integrity I did not really mind what they did.

My own family may have been complete, but the same was not true of the Whyte & Mackay family. Early in 1986 the apparently invulnerable DCL had fallen prey to an audacious takeover bid from Guinness, led by Ernest Saunders. The unthinkable had happened. DCL were whisky royalty, surely not vulnerable to such vulgar commercial ploys. The 'gentlemen' of the DCL had been caught napping, and the Scotch whisky industry was never to be the same again.

When I first heard the news of the Guinness takeover, I could not help but wonder whether that arrogant DCL figure who had so brusquely dealt with my request for samples back in my days with Gillies & Co was feeling quite so comfortable now. Some of the 'mighty' may have fallen, but my thoughts were principally with the several thousand DCL workers who surely now faced an uncertain future. Cutbacks would have to be made if Guinness was to achieve its financial expectations.

But it was not only the workforce that faced rationalisation. As a condition of purchase, Guinness was legally required to dispose of a significant number of Scotch whisky brands and Michael Lunn was quick to see their potential for Whyte & Mackay. A series of frantic meetings between Lunn and DCL representatives led to a successful agreement. Lunn recalls, 'Over one weekend Whyte & Mackay had doubled the size of the company and profitability ... 'Tiny' was abroad and apparently out of contact, so he

came back to find a "done deal". Living dangerously!' Suddenly Whyte & Mackay had a much larger family to contend with.

This exciting new deal gave us the UK rights to Crawford's 3 Star, Crawford's 5 Star, Haig Fine Old, The Buchanan Blend and Real Mackenzie, along with the world rights to John Barr, Claymore, Old Mull, Stewart's Finest Old and Jamie Stuart. The real commercial gems within this range were Haig, Crawford's and Claymore, though to my mind the Buchanan Blend was in a class of its own.

Suddenly these historic whiskies were part of my portfolio, and I felt privileged to be their custodian. Our contract stipulated we must rigorously maintain the formulation for these blends that had been established by DCL, and it was up to me to ensure that happened. I was particularly proud to be involved with the legendary Haig brand, a Scottish icon with roots going back to at least 1665, when on 4th January one Robert 'Hage' was rebuked by the elders of St Ninian's Parish Church in Stirlingshire for distilling on the Sabbath.

For many years Haig was the bestselling blended Scotch in Britain, well known for its catchphrase – 'Don't be Vague – Ask for Haig.' Through the 1970s competition from other brands saw it decline to a shadow of its former self, however, but we were determined to reverse that decline. To assist in this, Don Whitford, formerly of DCL, was brought in to deal exclusively with sales of this brand and Charles Shaw's team completely repackaged it, changing it from its traditional brown dump bottle to a clear tall bottle.

Additional sales and marketing staff were recruited to handle the business generated by our new acquisitions, and naturally bottling, too, was a serious issue which had to be addressed. William Muir (Bond 9) Ltd had been our bottlers for many years. They were a highly respected independent blending and bottling company, who had invested in modern machinery and put in place stringent quality control procedures.

They had always worked hard to retain Whyte & Mackay's business, and one obvious solution to our need for bottling capacity was to purchase the company. We did this in December 1988, and part of the deal included a 49% share of the Scotch Whisky Heritage Centre, close to Edinburgh Castle, which had opened earlier that year. It never ceases to amaze me that while the earliest reference to Scotch whisky occurred in 1494, it took another 494 years for the industry to open its first heritage centre. Why was it so slow to react? Was it conservative commercial rivalry? Today this thriving enterprise, now re-branded as the Scotch Whisky Experience, is one of Edinburgh's leading tourist attractions, bringing in more than 100,000 people per annum.

It provides the perfect platform for the inquisitive visitor who wants to learn more about Scotch whisky, and I would heartily recommend a trip there before setting off to tour Scotland's distilleries. Surely one day there must be a Scotch Whisky Experience in the heart of London, or even China. I wonder how many years we will have to wait for that!

I have always been a great supporter of this institution, and still conduct many presentations on its behalf. I was therefore very proud when I was subsequently made a director. Similarly I have been very much involved with the Scotch Whisky Association

for the same number of years, becoming one of their lecturers in the autumn of 1988.

The SWA is also based in Edinburgh and does a sterling job protecting the integrity and reputation of Scotch whisky. It had its origins in the Whisky Association of 1917, but this was dissolved in 1942, when the SWA was formed. It is the industry's watchdog, and one of its great achievements has been to influence the lowering of extremely discriminatory tariffs around the world. It has helped to make a more level playing field on which Scotch can compete with locally produced spirits. During my time in the industry, SWA stalwarts have included Colonel 'Bill' Bewsher, Richard Grindal, Tony Tucker, Hugh Morison and the long-serving Campbell Evans, now Director of Government and Consumer Affairs.

With Scotch whisky now being exported to more than 200 different countries the SWA plays a vital role in upholding the image and integrity of our national drink. Fresh challenges inevitably lie ahead, but current chairman Gavin Hewitt and his team will face up to them with the same resolve as his predecessors. Whatever these challenges may be, it is essential we act in unity as one body in support of the SWA. Inevitably, there will always be dissenters, the moaners and groaners who have their own agendas, but we simply must work together.

Michael Lunn had succeeded Kenneth Graham as managing director of Whyte & Mackay in May 1988 and he was soon facing major challenges in the shape of yet another takeover. We had enjoyed a happy association with the boxer Jim Watt, and in 1989 another ex-boxer appeared on the scene. His name was George Walker and in business he was a street fighter. His brother, Billy, was known in boxing circles as the 'Blond Bomber'. George Walker headed the Brent Walker Group, which purchased Whyte & Mackay from Lonrho for £180m in February 1989.

Brent Walker only owned the company for 12 months, but it felt like a 12-round bout. You just never knew where the punches were coming from. For me at the ringside it was a time of uncertainty. Michael Lunn's hands appeared to be tied, as he was not being given the resources and direction necessary to take the company forward. It was a frustrating and bruising period. Lunn recalls that 'George was a likeable character and very colourful, but could be extremely blunt. When exasperated this was mixed with conviction and attitude. Occasionally one felt there was a physical element lurking just below the surface. Perhaps it was the way he held his hands!'

The possibility of a management buy-out raised its head, and even a potential merger with rival company Burn Stewart Distillers was discussed. For Michael Lunn and Eric Riddell these were rollercoaster times. Neither of these possibilities came to anything, however, but thankfully, the next bout was going to be one of stability and growth. In February 1990 Brent Walker sold Whyte & Mackay to Gallaher Ltd, a subsidiary of American Brands Inc. formerly the American Tobacco Company.

American Brands was responsible for the iconic bourbon Jim Beam with roots going back to 1795. Jim Beam remains one of the world's best-selling bourbons, but in 1989 the company, recognising the extraordinary global growth in single malt Scotch whiskies, had pioneered 'small-batch' bourbon. This was hand-crafted, aged bourbon, personally selected by the legendary distiller Booker Noe, the true father of this innovation. Small-batch bourbon was the American response to single malts, and has subsequently been adopted by virtually every other bourbon producer.

Once American Brands acquired Whyte & Mackay they became agents for Dalmore in the USA. Our warm relationship continues to this day, and Booker Noe's son, Freddie, is a personal friend and a whiskey-maker for whom I have enormous respect. Jim Beam had a great heritage, but so to did Gallaher Ltd, founded in Belfast during the early 1860s, and today the Gallaher Group is the largest manufacturer of tobacco products for the UK market. This was clearly a prosperous company which saw the way the smoke was blowing with regard to the health lobby. Accordingly, it decided to diversify, and the drinks industry was one of its new interests.

Within a matter of weeks of taking over Whyte & Mackay, Gallaher, unlike George Walker, was pulling no punches, when the vast sum of £33 million was paid to Greenall Whitley for Vladivar vodka. At the time, £33 million may have appeared generous, but, as I always say, never underestimate the value of a brand.

Gallaher's acquisition of the Vladivar vodka brand was a sign of things to come. In August 1991 a bid was mounted for the Invergordon Distillers Group, but this proved initially unsuccessful, being fiercely contested by Invergordon's managing director Chris Greig. It is recorded that Invergordon spent some £4 million resisting the bid. Invergordon Distillers Ltd had been established in 1959 to create a new grain distillery at Invergordon, on the Cromarty Firth, just a few miles from Dalmore. Production began in July 1961, and today the distillery is at the heart of Whyte & Mackay's whisky-making operations. It provides grain spirit for our blends and for reciprocal trading with other companies.

Invergordon may be more like a factory than the traditional image of a picturesque Scottish distillery, but the scale on which it operates is most impressive. A few statistics will illustrate the point. The distillery employs a total of 135 staff, and uses 2,000 tonnes of wheat per week. There are no fewer than 23 washbacks, serving Invergordon's two vast column stills. Together they turn out some 36.5 million litres of pure alcohol (mlpa) per year, compared to the 3.5 million made at Dalmore, and there are no fewer than 46 warehouses on the site, each holding between 25,000 and 40,000 casks. The angels certainly get their share around Invergordon. In addition to the Invergordon plant, at the time of the Whyte & Mackay takeover Invergordon Distillers owned four malt distilleries, namely Bruichladdich on Islay, Jura, Tullibardine in Perthshire and Tamnavulin on Speyside, which the company had constructed in 1965–6.

The principal reasons Whyte & Mackay were prepared to fight so hard for control of Invergordon Distillers included Invergordon's highly successful 'own-label' Scotch whisky business and, of course, their grain distillery. This facility would allow the company to become self-sufficient in terms of grain whisky, the backbone of many blends.

While the fierce battle to take over Invergordon was being fought, Whyte & Mackay was not standing still. Indeed, we were very active. Complacency was the last thing on our minds. By early 1992 we were preparing to fully integrate the United Distillers brands which we had acquired six years earlier, including Claymore, Haig and Crawford's.[13] They had previously been bottled by United Distillers at Leven and Shieldhall near Paisley but we were now planning to bottle them 'in house' at William Muir's newly upgraded Leith plant. We had already invested in new labelling for several of these brands, as well as for our own Whyte & Mackay bottling.

Later the same year, we moved from 296 St Vincent Street to a brand new building at 310 St Vincent Street. By this time the company employed 672 staff, and with the likelihood that we would eventually secure Invergordon, extra space was clearly needed. Whether Michael Lunn and financial director Eric Riddell could really justify having an entire floor of the building to themselves remains a matter for conjecture. The press dubbed it their 'ivory tower' and the name stuck with our staff. This was a major move, but the biggest move of all came in November 1993, when Invergordon was finally captured. The Invergordon Group was valued at £382 million, which was extremely impressive, considering the company had been valued at just £2 million back in 1967. Had they been phenomenally successful, or had we paid over the odds? The argument is still debated today.

Just one look at the state of Invergordon's neglected distilleries showed very little of the large profits they were making had been

13 The Guinness takeover of DCL created United Distillers (UD) as its spirits' arm.

ploughed back into the infrastructure.

Our total workforce now numbered 1,206, almost double the pre-takeover figure, we owned seven malt distilleries and a grain distillery, as well as three bottling plants. We also had Invergordon's head office building in Leith in addition to our Glasgow offices. Clearly, rationalisation was high on the agenda. To my mind, it was as though battle lines had been drawn up, with Edinburgh on one side and Glasgow on the other. There was open aggression and inherent resentment. It was by no means clear who would win. However, many from the 'Edinburgh' or Invergordon side who held shares in the company had prospered beyond their wildest expectations, and some were not prepared to stay on under the new regime. Integration was clearly going to be prolonged and painful.

Early in 1994 this was brought home to me in a very personal way. Tuesday 8th February was a day I will never forget. Not only was it the anniversary of the execution of Mary, Queen of Scots, in 1587, but it was also the day my self-esteem got the chop. I had been a director of William Muir since 1989, and the board was now being restructured, along with many other parts of the company. I was informed by Tom Frize on that day that my directorship was being removed and instead of reporting to him, I would be answering to Brian Megson. He had been shadowing Bobby McCall and was to become our new bulk sales director. Brian was 'Mr Nice Guy' which made him great to work with and his tireless, hands-on approach to the business was appreciated by his colleagues.

My ego had received a serious blow, but as my wounded pride began to recover, I realised it wasn't the end of the world. Some of the grit and determination I had inherited from my father began to resurface. However, all of this paled into insignificance compared to what my father had been going through. He needed not just resilience but courage too, as he had been diagnosed with cancer and had undergone a major operation at Canniesburn Hospital in Bearsden several years previously. The operation was a success but he was forced to spend many weeks recovering in hospital. This caused him a great deal of frustration, as he was an active man and accustomed to numerous daily 'snifters'. During his convalescent period I received a phone call from his surgeon, Mr Jackson, who was rather abrupt and straight to the point.

'Does your father drink, Mr Paterson?'

I hesitated, wondering what the relevance of this was, before replying, 'He's a whisky blender, Mr Jackson. Of course he does! He likes his dram, but he's not an alcoholic. Sorry, but why are you asking me this?'

'Well, as you know, your father has been on a drip for several days now, and from my observations, he appears to be showing definite withdrawal symptoms.'

'What!' I exclaimed. 'Are you sure?'

'Well, there's only one way we're going to find out', replied the surgeon. 'When you're visiting tonight will you please bring a bottle of his favourite whisky?'

This seemed a very unusual request, but I duly arrived at the ward with a bottle of Paterson's Best blended Scotch whisky. I thought perhaps Mr Jackson and I were going to share a dram as we discussed the old man's condition, but what happened was altogether more bizarre.

He summoned a nurse and asked her to set up another drip. Soon 'Paterson's Best' was circulating through my father's system. I'd shared many a dram with him in the past, but never before a nip in a drip. Happily, before my visit was over, a warm smile of contentment had spread across his face.

Mr Jackson's diagnosis had clearly been correct.

My father had actually been given just two years to live at the time of the operation, but he survived for the best part of a decade. I like to think his indomitable spirit carried him through some hard times in his later years. He had always been there to encourage me, offering advice and taking a keen interest in my career. As I'm sure most people feel in these situations, I only wished I had listened and learnt more from him.

Like any son, I wanted him to be proud of me, particularly as I was following in his footsteps. One of my biggest regrets was that he was not alive to see me receive the 'Spirit of Scotland Trophy' at London's Guildhall in October 1994, as he had passed away earlier that year.

This prestigious award had been organised by the International Wine & Spirit Competition to celebrate the first reference to Scotch whisky 500 years previously in 1494. All of the major whisky companies had been invited to submit an aged blended whisky, of which no more than 500 bottles had been produced. This was, indeed, putting the blender to the test, and my colleagues and I took it extremely seriously. We all wanted to win this prestigious and unique accolade.

Accordingly, I searched our inventories for the most appropriate makes. For years I had been in the habit of keeping back casks of exceptional character which I just could not bring myself to use in our blends. Most of them were now in excess of 21 years old. I was looking for a blend with weight and body, but with a rich, velvety finish. Although grains such as Cameronbridge, Caledonian, Port Dundas and Invergordon were included, because I had decided the blend would be a minimum of 21 years old, the grains would only play a minor part. The true backbone of the blend would be single malts from the Highland region.

In order to give it finesse and elegance I included Longmorn, Glenrothes, Macallan and Glenfarclas. A subtle whisper of Islay was provided by Bruichladdich.

A total of 16 component parts were included. However, the key to it all, once more, was the perfect marriage. Once again, as in the case of Dalmore sherry finishes I called on Gonzalez Byass to provide the most perfect Apostoles Oloroso sherry butts.

At the launch of the 500th Anniversary competition at the Scotch Whisky Heritage Centre in Edinburgh during April, I was able to sample William Grant's entry, blended by David Stewart, and UD's whisky, produced by Gordon Nielson. Both were seriously impressive, and I knew I was up against some stiff opposition. Even at this stage I was not entirely satisfied with my own blend, and as the deadline for judging approached, I found myself sampling it every week, hoping it would reach its peak in time.

This had not been the best of years for me professionally or personally, and so as the competition date neared I became more and more tense. I really needed to win this to boost my morale and confidence. That night in the packed Guildhall was one I will never forget. All the nominated blenders assembled on stage to the accompaniment of trumpets and bagpipes. When the golden envelope was opened and my name read out I was numb. It was one of those rare occasions when I was speechless. It was a momentous evening, and I wanted to share my emotions with those people I really cared about. In particular, I wanted to share them with my father, though sadly, of course, he was not there. After all, he had done so much for me, and as is so often the case with father and son, I had never really thanked him.

With Whyte & Mackay commemorating its 150th anniversary that same year, this really was a time of celebration for the company. However, nothing good lasts for ever, and the corporate knives were already being sharpened for Michael Lunn. American Brands only seemed to be interested in short-term strategies with high returns, and clearly, despite his loyalty to Whyte & Mackay over a 17-year period, Michael Lunn was not meeting the financial returns expected by our US friends. Nonetheless, as Lunn himself says, 'We achieved Whyte & Mackay "Special" sales of 650,000 cases per annum, which was no mean feat given where we all started from'. That figure has still never been surpassed, and his successor Ken Hitchcock was certainly not able to do any better.

Hitchcock was a brash, larger-than-life Australian who had been highly successful for American Brands back in his homeland. His approach to business could be summed up by the stuffed cockerel that stood in his office. A meat cleaver was stuck in the mounting block

alongside the bird itself, together with the prominent inscription, 'Your cock is on the block.' During the next ten years the company lacked focus and direction. There was no definitive and *consistent* policy regarding investment or marketing. It reminded me of the dark days of George Walker and his associates.

By September 1995 I had served 25 years with Whyte & Mackay, and I was duly presented with a carriage clock. Looking at the photograph taken that day, several of the eight directors present were to leave the company in less than five years. Their departure did nothing to promote continuity and stability.

Cost cutting was on everybody's lips, and even before Hitchcock's arrival, Bruich-laddich, Tullibardine and Tamnavulin distill-eries had all been mothballed. To be fair to American Brands, each of these distilleries had suffered from a lack of investment on the part of Invergordon Distillers, and would now have needed significant sums spending on them. With hindsight, seeing the extraordinary growth of interest in single malts, particularly those from Islay, perhaps we ought to have kept Bruichladdich open. But hindsight is a wonderful thing.

Growth was the order of the day. In December 1996 American Brands amalga-mated all its drinks interests under the control of Jim Beam Brands Worldwide and Whyte & Mackay subsequently became known as JBB (Greater Europe) plc. At one stroke of a pen in an office in Chicago, over 150 years of heritage disappeared. JBB (Greater Europe) plc! James Whyte and Charles Mackay would not have been amused, and neither were our customers. They were confused. And who could blame them. Some of our customers now thought we were selling sportswear. Our distinctive 'Scottishness', which had been such a selling point, was now a thing of the past. Where exactly was 'Greater Europe' anyway?

And it got worse. From 1st March 1998 we were really singing the blues. On that date our new Whyte & Mackay label was introduced. Previously there had been an almost unconscious policy of evolution rather than revolution, but this was a radical departure. Gone was the distinctive cream label and double lions motif, and in its place was something uncompromisingly blue. Would our consumers accept this dramatic change, and just as importantly, would our sales team give it their wholehearted commitment?

At our Glasgow sales conference in March Ken Hitchcock did not mince his words. 'My cock may be on the block, boys, but so is yours', he exclaimed. 'I want to see at least one thousand new accounts.' This seemed a totally unrealistic target, as one look at the faces of our sales team confirmed. This was a mountain to climb, and they knew it. Ironically, however, one of our chief rivals gave us the perfect opportunity to achieve Hitchcock's aims.

Four days after our blue label launch the *Scottish Licensed Trade News* front page headline announced, 'Perth thumped in early Diageo review.' The story below it read, 'The one-time major whisky town of Perth is reeling from the announcement that newly formed drinks mega firm UDV, the wine and spirits arm of drinks, bakery and burger conglomerate Diageo, is to shut the Cherrybank office in the town – which was

formerly the home of Arthur Bell and until now the site of the UK sales and marketing HQ of United Distillers.'

According to the report, some 120 jobs were likely to be lost, and the sales and marketing operation was to be relocated to Harlow in Essex. Not surprisingly, this caused outrage in Scotland. Many hotel patrons were 'disgusted' and a significant number of landlords stripped Bells bottles from their gantries in protest. As the *SLTN* noted, 'It appears some independent traders in particular are increasingly considering a switch to a competitor blend – Whyte & Mackay, for example, is the main beneficiary.'

Thanks to UD, Ken Hitchcock's formidable challenge was not only met but surpassed. The sales teams had a field day, but not everyone was receptive to our new blue label. This was borne out when our Glasgow rep called on one of his accounts in the Parkhead area of Glasgow. No sooner was he through the door than he was back out again. The colour blue had not gone down well in this pub frequented by Celtic supporters. Green was the only colour tolerated. Even in this day and age, religious bigotry lives on in many parts of the industrial west of Scotland, and the blue of Rangers and the green of Celtic represent the public face of this Protestant/Catholic rivalry. You would have thought that at least Scotch whisky might have helped to unite the factions. Nae chance!

Despite the great efforts of our sales team, their triumph was to be short-lived. In August 1999 Maxxium was formed, with its headquarters in Amsterdam. This was a joint sales and marketing venture with Jim Beam, Remy-Cointreau and Highland Distillers.

When this major reorganisation was taking place, a Jim Beam spokesman announced, 'We expect that Maxxium will allow greater professional development opportunities for all our staff going forward.'

One group of people clearly not going forward was our own loyal sales force. More than 50 dedicated people with invaluable local knowledge and contacts became surplus to requirements. Many were replaced by Highland Distillers' Famous Grouse reps. We were no longer masters of our own brands, particularly Whyte & Mackay. As Brian Megson recalled, 'It was an unmitigated disaster to have no Whyte & Mackay people in the team.' This was borne out when eager new reps from Maxxium, confident of immediate sales, descended on the market for the first time. In one classic instance an Ayrshire publican made his feelings very clear. 'Even though you're from this new Maxxium outfit I know you used to be just a Grouse rep. Thanks to you the Whyte & Mackay guys got the short shift. Get to fuck out of my pub!'

Although Ken Hitchcock had enjoyed some successes, they were not good enough for Jim Beam. Like that Maxxium rep in the Ayrshire pub, the company seemed to be going nowhere. It needed a fresh approach, and Brian Megson was seen as the ideal person to replace Hitchcock as Chief Executive.

It had long been one of Brian's cherished ambitions to lead Whyte & Mackay back into control of its own destiny, and this opportunity arose in 2001, when he put together Scotland's largest management buy out, at a cost of £209 million. At the time, the whole company was excited and enthusiastic about gaining its independence once more. It was a huge undertaking, requiring vast borrowing from the German bank West LB, whose representative was Robin Saunders, known as the Claudia Schiffer of the financial world. Mezzanine finance was provided by Rotch Property Group, headed by Robert Tchenguiz and Vivian Imerman. Imerman in particular was to play a major part in Whyte & Mackay's future fortunes. The new venture was clearly a gamble, but in the prevailing healthy climate of low interest rates and a general revival in the whisky industry, there was certainly cause for optimism. Or was there?

A feeling prevailed in the Scotch whisky industry that since the acquisition of Invergordon in 1993, Whyte & Mackay was still carrying a significant amount of 'fat.' Success depended on reducing this by severe rationalisation, including a reduction of manpower. One glaring example was operating two bottling halls. Many hours were spent debating this contentious subject, but ultimately nobody on the board was brave enough to take the appropriate action. It was essential that rationalisation was coupled not only to increased volume of sales, particularly in the branded sector, but to sales at a realistic market price. Megson and his buyout team anticipated that prices would rise. In reality over the next few years they continued to fall. The alarm bells were already sounding.

The sale of supermarket 'own-label' brands was healthy and still growing. However, they were spoilt for choice of supplies from the vast 'whisky loch' that still existed. Supermarkets could ruthlessly dictate the price at which they were prepared to buy whisky. And it was never high. Despite this, there were many hungry suppliers waiting in the wings, prepared to take any crumbs that were thrown their way. Business was tough and margins were exceedingly tight.

So long as the whisky loch was overflowing, there was no incentive for the supermarkets to invest in their own long-term stocks. But who could blame them? One must never forget, they were fighting ferociously amongst themselves for market share. It was a dog-eat-dog world out there. As 60% of our business was now with supermarket own-label brands, we had no choice but to play the game by their rules.

One thing I would have ruled out immediately was the name given to our new company. If JBB (Greater Europe) plc had been a significant departure from the Whyte & Mackay heritage, 'Kyndal' certainly took us into the twilight zone. Half the people couldn't pronounce it (*kin-daal*), let alone spell it. And that was just our staff!

Brian Megson had chosen this less than inspiring name from a list of 15 prospective contending titles put forward by a marketing specialist a fortnight before the buy out was due to be concluded. Perhaps we were fortunate, as among the alternatives rejected were Bottle, Splash and Nip. As Megson said at the time, 'Our Japanese customers would have gone nuts!' According to Brian Megson, the definition of Kyndal was to spark or ignite in Old Norse, but sadly it soon burnt itself out, along with Megson and virtually all of his fellow board members.

As Megson says, 'The only people willing to put the money up were in the "high risk" end of the financial markets. The management team was aware that in these circumstances,

like other similar ventures, it was a gamble, but we were willing to give it a shot. However, after 17 months the shareholders were not happy with the way things were progressing. It really wasn't working. So we had to move on.'

What did the future hold for Whyte & Mackay? I really didn't know. It was the lowest point in my 32-year career with the company. We were a rudderless ship, adrift in a storm, without a captain. The crew was confused and tired, and the packaging of our products was in a similar state. Although there were financial constraints, there was really no excuse for this. No matter how good the liquid in the bottle, the importance of presentation cannot be over-emphasised.

This may have been a low point for Kyndal, but from a personal perspective 2002 was probably the highest point of my career. We had just won the International Wine & Spirit Competition 'Distiller of the Year' award, and now *Whisky Magazine* honoured me with its 'Blender of the Year' accolade. The respected US publication *Malt Advocate* voted me 'Industry Leader of the Year', and the crowning glory came when Diageo awarded me its 'Outstanding Achievement in the Scotch Whisky Industry' trophy.

I was genuinely honoured to receive these accolades, particularly the Diageo award, as it came from a highly respected rival company. However, I am always aware that in reality these awards are not just for me. They are for the many people who support me and help make my job possible, from the distillery mashmen to the bottling hall operators. It is indeed a genuine team effort.

Inevitably, the team consists of many contrasting characters possessing a diversity of abilities and strengths. Although Whyte & Mackay had gone through several changes in ownership and management, one constant factor was the commitment and loyalty of our staff. Working together in harmony the overall team was stronger than its individual members, and I could not help thinking that in a way we were like a well-crafted, blended whisky. The whole was stronger than the sum of the parts, and we had certainly needed to be strong during those difficult years.

Despite all the uncertainties and changes of that period, my passion for whisky and for blending remained undiminished. One thing I had learnt as master blender was that, no matter what was happening within the company, I must never allow circumstances to affect the blend. I must always remain focused on my key role, which is to maintain the quality and consistency of our products. After all, the blend and its integrity are everything.

It is what my grandfather and father had strived to instil in me with the hope that perhaps one day I too would pass on the knowledge of whisky blending to the next generation. Now, after 40 years, my love of whisky blending and its many hidden secrets are deeply locked inside of me.

It is time to reveal some of these secrets.

Chapter Seven

THE ART OF
WHISKY BLENDING

*'In a symphony orchestra, each instrument
makes a different sound. In a Scotch whisky
blend, each whisky plays its own note and the
result is greater than the sum of the parts.'* } JAMES BRUXNER, FORMER CHAIRMAN
OF THE SCOTCH WHISKY ASSOCIATION

A blended whisky is a work of art, composed from many inspirational sources. It is created with passion and integrity, in the same way that a true masterpiece is painted. A work of fine art, like a memorable blend, can stir many emotions within the beholder.

When you consider their dazzling use of light and colour, some of the world's greatest impressionist painters, such as Monet, Sisley, Renoir and Cassatt could easily have been master blenders. This parallel was unconsciously captured in 1876 by the eminent French writer Emile Zola when he wrote of Renoir that 'the dominant feature of his work lies in his range of tones and the way in which they are combined in a wonderful harmony.'

The genius of these artists was in perfecting a symphony of colours, each in their own inimitable style. Similarly, the master blender draws from a palette of malt and grain whiskies to create his masterpieces. Harmony is also *his* ultimate aim. No one colour, no one malt, must predominate. Although there have been many distinctive master blenders, one name more than any other stands out for his vision and pioneering spirit. Just as Paul Cezanne was the 'father' of modern art, so Andrew Usher can be considered the 'father' of whisky blending.

Andrew was born on 5th January 1826 into a family of Edinburgh wine and spirit merchants. He was one of 12 children. His father, Andrew Usher Snr, had travelled from his native Scottish borders to set up in business in Edinburgh in 1813, and by the time of Andrew Jnr's birth, the company was a thriving concern.

Andrew Usher Snr was clearly a sound

Andrew Usher (1826–98) considered by many to be the 'founding father' of Scotch whisky blending.

businessman. The Excise Act of 1823 had actively encouraged legal Scotch whisky distilling, and he was keen to become part of the whisky boom. He wanted to represent a Highland distillery, but not just any distillery. He wanted to represent the best. No fewer than 167 distilleries were available to Usher, yet his choice was obvious. It had to be Glenlivet. When King George IV had visited Scotland in August 1822 he was ceremonially served Glenlivet whisky, from the Speyside valley of that name. The area was a hotbed of illicit distilling, so the chances were that the king was actually drinking illicit whisky. Nonetheless, as Elizabeth Grant of Rothiemurchus recorded in her *Memoirs of a Highland Lady,* 'The king drank nothing else.'

The reputation of Usher's company was founded on 'dealing only in articles of first rate quality', and this ethos must have been instilled into his children. Usher took on his new role as agent for Glenlivet with passion and commitment, advertising widely, and by 1844 was so successful that he was even selling significant quantities of Glenlivet in London. However, this success came at a high price for Glenlivet, as Usher was renowned for driving an extremely hard bargain with the distillery.

As the saying goes, 'Behind every successful man there is always a woman', and the Ushers were no exception. Despite the fact that she must have been very busy as a wife and mother to her 12 children, Margaret Usher still found time to be actively involved in the business, having the reputation as a skilful blender of cordials. These flavoured drinks were a concoction made with herbs and spices. Containing little or no alcohol, they had their origins in homeopathic medicine. An *Edinburgh Advertiser* advertisement for Andrew Usher & Co of 22 West Nicholson Street, dated 6th August 1841 lists, 'Rich Raisin and Grape Cordials, Orange & Ginger Cordials, Peppermint and Cinnamon Cordials.' Margaret must have been exceptionally talented, as one of her recipes, reputedly gifted to family friend John Crabbie, became the basis for the renowned Crabbie's Green Ginger, still available to this very day.

Although his father was clearly a major influence as young Andrew grew up, it is said that his blending skills were developed principally by watching his mother preparing these celebrated cordials. Along with his brother John, Andrew must have shown a genuine interest and aptitude for the trade. This was demonstrated in 1845 when their proud father took both eager young men into the family business. Although Glenlivet single malt whisky was a crucial part of the company's prosperity, by this time a new and radical alternative was emerging, which eventually would transform the industry. That spirit was grain whisky.

While Andrew Usher Jnr was in his infancy, Robert Stein of Kilbagie Distillery in Clackmannanshire and the former Irish Inspector General of Excise, Aeneas Coffey, were developing and patenting a revolutionary new type of still. Stein took out two patents in 1827 and 1828, but Coffey's version of the new continuous or 'Patent' still as it later became known was generally considered to be more efficient, and was authorised by the government for use on 10th September 1832.

Coffey's original intention was probably to sell the comparatively pure grain spirit produced by his apparatus for industrial purposes rather than for domestic consumption. He proceeded to manufacture stills to his own design, selling them to several Scottish whisky and London gin distillers, the latter finding the strong neutral spirit of the Coffey still ideal for their product. The basic design of the still remains unchanged today.

The 'Patent' still differed significantly from the traditional copper pot still in that it was capable of producing far greater quantities of spirit and utilised a range of grains which were considerably cheaper than malted barley. The result was a much lighter, less characterful and more consistent whisky, often known as 'neutral' or 'silent' spirit. To many it remained bland and characterless compared to the bold, occasionally harsh 'self' whiskies of the Highland pot stills, but when the two came together something remarkable happened. It was love at first sight. The grains seduced the masculinity of the malt whiskies, and this loving marriage has continued ever since.

Andrew Usher was one of the principal matchmakers, but when he began blending he could surely never have envisaged that this creation would make Scotch whisky a drink for the world. 'Unofficial' blending must surely have been carried out previously by merchants and publicans in order to achieve greater conformity for their customers. But there was also a more disreputable side to blending. It took place in the dark alleys of Scotland's towns and cities where seedy shebeens dispensed elixirs of doubtful provenance. They were blends. But just what was being blended? Who knows what adulterated and mixed spirits were created, and where there was dire poverty, who really cared?

But there was one man who cared, Dr James St Clair Gray, who in 1872 exposed the disgraceful and potentially lethal situation that prevailed in Glasgow. He collected 30 samples of 'whisky' available in the city, and as Edward Burns explains in his groundbreaking book *Bad Whisky* the results were truly shocking.

'Of the 30 samples taken, only two were found to be genuine whisky. Some had nothing more harmful than water as a dilutent, but others contained ingredients like turpentine, methylated spirits, sulphuric acid, and, in the worst cases, were made entirely from a thin varnish. The latter, commonly called "finish", was legitimately used by furniture polishers and manufacturers of hats.

'The rich could pick and choose and afford to avoid goods obviously debased, while the poor did not have that choice and were subjected to the most horrific malpractices imaginable. The ever-spiralling circle of abuse sent many to an early grave.'

Although Dr Gray's work took place in Glasgow, every city throughout the land had its backstreets of despair. However, while there was great poverty there was also undoubtedly great innovation in Britain. Queen Victoria had been on the throne for 15 years. Britain ruled the waves. We had an empire on which the sun never set. These were confident days.

This was also reflected in Scotland, which had been given something of a royal 'seal of approval' by the monarch, who was now regularly visiting the country to stay at her Deeside home of Balmoral. Many illustrious writers such as Daniel Defoe, William and Dorothy Wordsworth, James Boswell, Samuel Johnson and Sir Walter Scott had already popularised Scotland and its hospitable people. More than a century after the infamous battle of Culloden, Scotland was finally being rehabilitated south of the border.

Britain was awash with technological innovation, and Scotland was at the very heart of this industrial revolution. Scotch whisky was about to be revolutionised too. The real wind of change began to blow in 1853 under the Forbes-Mackenzie Act when vatting, or mixing, of malt whiskies from the same distillery while 'under bond' was permitted by law for the first time.

By this date, Andrew Usher's health was beginning to fail, with the result that he allowed his sons a greater degree of control in the family business. Andrew Usher Junior was greatly encouraged by the new legislation, and was quick to use it to his advantage. Within months of the Act being passed, the company launched Usher's old Vatted Glenlivet (OVG), a vatting of Glenlivet malts from different years intended to achieve greater consistency. Ultimately, Old Vatted Glenlivet was to become one of the first, legal, blended whiskies.

The search for consistency reached its apotheosis in 1860, when William Gladstone's Spirits Act went a radical stage further by allowing malts and grains 'under bond' to be blended for the first time. Together, these two pieces of legislation laid the practical and legal foundations of the great blending boom. The floodgates had been opened.

In the wake of the Spirits Act the Ushers were again quick to exploit the potential of the new legislation. In all probability, Andrew would have been quietly arranging the whiskies from his blender's palette in his Edinburgh sample room. Over the months, he must have tried many formulations. His reputation depended on it. Presumably his blend included a high proportion of his beloved Glenlivet, along with other favourite Highland and Campbeltown malts. The grain whiskies would have come from distilleries such as Adelphi, Cameronbridge, Carsebridge, Caledonian, Cambus and Yoker, and their light, fragrant characteristics would have suppressed and mellowed the heavier, rugged malts.

Usher must surely have taken into consideration the 'weight' of his blends. The secret for him was finding the perfect balance between malt and grain. He had to gauge the market and cater to existing tastes. Although blended whisky was in its infancy, he faced serious competition from the mellow style of Irish whiskey which was so popular in Britain at that time. William Ross, Managing Director of the Distillers Company Ltd, later recalled that before blending of Scotch whisky became common, the popularity of Irish whiskey was 'chiefly on account of its uniformity in style' by comparison with Scottish pot still whisky.

To counter this, some Scottish distilleries went so far as to make their own versions of Irish whiskey. One prime example was the Caledonian Distillery in Edinburgh, which, in 1867, installed two large pot stills in order to produce Irish-style whiskey of the 'Dublin' variety, using malted and unmalted barley, along with wheat. The demand for this spirit was principally due to the large numbers of Irish immigrants who had moved to Scotland during the early 1860s to work in the booming construction industry. Irish bricklayers were at a premium.

However, not everybody was a devotee of Irish whiskey. Commenting during the 1870s, one outspoken Glasgow MP declared that 'Every stranger who visited Ireland knew what Irish whiskey was. It was the most dangerous stuff in the world for a stranger to touch. No one but a native could drink it with impunity. It was full of headaches to the brim. He believed a man required to be weaned on it in order to get acclimatised to its use. The coats of the stomach then became indurated – tanned as it were – in time, and it was impossible to get used to it without going through a process of that kind.'

Nonetheless, Usher must have been strongly aware of the 'Irish influence', and would surely have made up a number of different vattings in order to determine the perfect style. His son, Sir Robert noted that comparatively little whisky was sold in England prior to 1860. However, after that date ' ... the trade in Scotch whisky increased by leaps and bounds, the reason being, to my mind, that the blend is lighter and more easily digested, and thus more suited to the public taste. My personal opinion is that the pot still is improved and made more wholesome when blended with patent.'

Clearly, he was following in his father's footsteps. *My* father always maintained that any reputable blend would have at least 50% malt content. Anyone using less was not considered a 'gentleman.' However, it appears that many 'gentlemen' had deviated from that inherent philosophy, including Andrew Usher himself. And why not? Too high a percentage of malt might have led to an unacceptably heavy whisky, and after all, Usher had set out to create something different. But surely Usher must have taken a cautious approach? Altering the characteristics too radically would have alienated his loyal clients, sending ripples of discontent through the gentlemen's clubs of Edinburgh and London. Any change to an existing product is always of concern to a blender. Every brand has its devoted supporters, and they will be the first to air their dissent if the changes do not meet with their approval.

I believe the introduction of grain whisky to Usher's blends would have been a slow, subtle process. He had to be cautious. A damaged reputation could take years to repair. But Usher was an astute gentleman. He knew the public wanted something different, something easier to drink, but more importantly, something consistent, at the right price. As JA Nettleton wrote in his *Manufacture of Whisky and Spirit* (1913), 'In 1870, through the Franco-German War, a boom occurred in the coal and iron trades in the South of Scotland. Miners and workmen were well paid, and the consumption of blends rose enormously, and so continued until 1875 or 1878.'

To cope with this increase in consumption, Usher needed stocks. Ideally his own stocks. Back in 1859 he had already taken steps towards this goal by purchasing Glen Sciennes Lowland malt distillery, renaming it the Edinburgh Distillery. This provided a source of light-style malt, perfect for blending. The company went on to build what was then the world's largest maturation warehouse in nearby St Leonards. In that Aladdin's Cave of casks there would have been many different types of European oak, previously filled with a galaxy of wine, spirits and liqueurs, not to mention beers and ciders. As my father told me on numerous occasions when he was drinking his favourite dram, 'Never forget, son, it's all down to wood, not just any wood, but good wood.'

Andrew Usher must also have been aware of the importance of the cask in order to ensure the consistency and integrity of his house style, and the port of Leith was the perfect place to source the kind of casks he required. After all, Leith then boasted some of Britain's busiest docks, renowned for importing the finest of wines, in particular claret from Bordeaux. In view of the experience Usher already had in vatting his different ages of Glenlivet, prior to the birth of commercial blending, he would surely have allowed the malt and grain whiskies destined for his blends to 'marry' in these chosen casks before determining the final formulation.

During his lifetime, Usher developed many whiskies in his Edinburgh blending room, the principal ones being Old Vatted Glenlivet and Green Stripe. However, he was not alone in his quest for a smoother, more mellow style of Scotch whisky. George Ballantine, William Robertson, William Sanderson and Glasgow whisky broker WP Lowrie were all early blending entrepreneurs, as was Charles Mackinlay, whose company produced Old Vatted Ben Vorlich, and ultimately the famous Mackinlay's blend. Charles Mackinlay's great-great-grandson Donald Mackinlay, himself a prominent former blender, wryly remarks, 'In those years there was much rivalry between the various blending houses. Pride was at stake. We really don't know who was the first blender? What is important is that they created something different. And the public liked it.'

Andrew Usher has always been one of my heroes and mentors, so not surprisingly, I was eager to discover just what these whiskies from a century and a half ago were really like. Ideally, I wanted to be with him in his own sample room, sharing his secrets. Of course, this was impossible, but there was an answer. I chose several bottles from Whyte & Mackay's rare collection of Usher's whiskies, dating back to the late 19th and early 20th centuries. With the aid of a specially adapted syringe we were able to extract small, precious samples of spirit, which were then sent for laboratory analysis. I almost felt like Howard Carter entering the Valley of the Kings in 1922

to discover the tomb of Tutankhamun with its unknown treasures. The results were fascinating.

For one thing, the Old Vatted Glenlivet which we analysed was no longer a vatting of Glenlivet malts, as had originally been the case in 1853. By the time our sample had been bottled around 1890 it had become a blended Scotch whisky with between 30-35% malt content. My tasting notes confirmed this, when I discovered it to be, 'Light, delicate and quite charming. Soft caramel tones. Elegant, good clean wood, hints of vanilla fudge. Soft zest of lemon peel'. We also analysed Usher's Green Stripe, which contained a similar malt content but with a different formulation. I noted: 'Delicate, marzipan, hints of sherry wood, perfumed.' Both of these old blends had one factor in common. Their backbone and structure seemed to me to have been greatly influenced by the Speyside region. Charm and finesse were their hallmarks of distinction.

This appeared to be the Usher 'house style', but analysis of a third whisky, Usher's Antique, offered something altogether different. The laboratory report suggested a very high malt content of up to 70%, and perhaps even higher. This was a blend of distinction. I noted: 'Bold and majestic, rich, honey and marzipan, with hints of almonds and spices. Thick, chunky marmalade orange peel characteristics towards the end complete this magnificent whisky.'

Usher's Antique was not unique in having a high malt content, however, as we discovered while analysing other old blended whiskies. By the late 1880s, Whyte & Mackay Special Blend, for example, had a malt content of 52%, though there was scant information on the bottle label regarding its contents. There was then no legal requirement to state strength or minimum age.

A bottle from this period, with a strength of 45.9% abv, was sampled in the same way as the Usher's whiskies. I noted: 'This was certainly not what I was expecting! Instead of a warm, rich body of Highlands and Speyside to welcome me this presented the complete opposite. A smoky, damp ash nose made its presence felt immediately. I almost wanted to grab a soda siphon to suppress it. There were also hints of furniture polish, pepper and cinnamon. Spent matchsticks and crushed crab apples completed the surprise package. The dominant smoky elements were immediately reflected in the taste. Subtle hints of oak lurked in the background.

'Unlike some of the heavier style of Islay malts such as Laphroaig, Lagavulin and Ardbeg, this was less assertive, suggesting perhaps a prevalence of Campbeltown malts, which I knew from company records we were purchasing around that time. In view of the soft nature of the finish on the palate, there would appear to be a generous helping of aged whiskies in this 'Special' blend. This was nothing like the Whyte & Mackay blend as we know it today. Whether it would appeal to the modern market is extremely doubtful, but it was a wonderful link with the past. It was a great privilege to be back in the era of James Whyte and Charles Mackay, sampling their original creation.'

Despite the comparatively high malt content of these old blends, there was an increasing demand for grain whisky during the 1880s and 1890s. This was reflected in the production figures for 1897, when patent still output stood at 17,300,000 proof gallons (44,893,500 lpa), while pot still whisky output measured 13,979,000 proof gallons (36,275,505 lpa). A century later 277.89 mlpa of grain whisky was being produced, along with 192.98 mlpa of pot still whisky.

Patent still production had been boosted during the 1890s by the existence of the North British Grain Distillery in Edinburgh, which at one time was reputed to be the largest distillery in the world. It had been established in October 1885 as a reaction to a growing DCL monopoly of grain spirit supplies. One of the prime movers in this project was none other than Andrew Usher, who was a natural choice to be the distillery's first chairman due to his vast experience, entrepreneurial flair and the high esteem in which he was held by his fellow distillers and blenders.

By this time, the Usher family had become very wealthy and highly respected. They were among the elite of Edinburgh society, and in characteristic Victorian philanthropic style Andrew Usher wanted to leave a lasting legacy to his native city. According to legend, he was walking along Princes Street one day in 1896, pondering on what he could do with his vast fortune, when he called in at his favourite jeweller's shop, owned by James Aitchison. During conversation it was suggested by Aitchison that he might wish to support one of the arts about which he was truly passionate. Music was one of his great loves, and according to the *Scotsman* newspaper of Thursday 20th July 1911 he was ' ... a cultured musician and loved to take part in amateur musical performances, and to listen to the most talented exponents of music in our own and other lands'. Accordingly, he donated a staggering £100,000 (equivalent to £17.5 million today) to Edinburgh City Council in order to build a hall ' ... that should be a centre of attraction to musical artistes and performers, and to the citizens of Edinburgh and others who may desire to hear good music ... '

Sadly, Usher did not live to see his bequest come to fruition, as on 1st November 1898 he died at his Edinburgh home of Blackford Park, having suffered from bowel cancer for six months. The Usher Hall was not to be opened until 1912, but his widow, Margaret, lived on to see his philanthropy finally bear fruit. On Wednesday 19th July 1911, His Majesty King George V and Queen Mary laid the foundation stone for this great edifice. Usher had retired just weeks before his death, but I would like to think that during those final days he was able to look back with pride on his career and his many achievements. His contribution to the Scotch whisky industry was immense.

However, I feel that this has not always been fully appreciated, and decided to try and rectify the situation. In August 2002 I hosted the inaugural Andrew Usher Memorial Lunch in Whyte & Mackay's Glasgow offices. There was a time when blenders from rival companies rarely communicated with each other, but happily that was no longer the case. I thought an event to honour Usher and bring together as many of them as possible for the first time would set a desirable precedent. Thankfully, the response was outstanding, and on the day no fewer than 24 master blenders assembled at Dalmore House to help create the Andrew Usher Memorial Blend. We are indeed a fortunate industry when passion for

blended whisky can transcend the boundaries of commercial competition. And on that day we came together as one body.

Each of the invited blenders had been asked to bring along a 16-year-old blended sample of their own creation to reflect Andrew Usher's baptism on 16th February 1826. The 24 whiskies were ceremoniously blended together in my sample room and just one bottle was created. This unique bottle is now proudly displayed in the Scotch Whisky Experience in Edinburgh, along with a framed certificate of authenticity signed by all the blenders and Mark Usher, a direct descendant of the great Andrew himself. I would like to think that this special occasion helped preserve Usher's memory for future generations.

Shrewd though he was, Andrew Usher could never have foreseen the phenomenal success blended Scotch whisky would achieve around the world. One major contributory factor in that success was an aphid that measured a mere millimetre in length, but its appetite was insatiable. It may have had an enormous impact on the fortunes of Scotch whisky, but its personal preference was for the grape rather than the grain. It first emerged in Europe in the London district of Hammersmith during June 1863, and from there began its long march around the world. As one French vineyard manager later remarked, 'It is disastrous: it goes forward like an army, laying waste all before it.'

Its name was *phylloxera vastrix* – the dry-leaf devastator – and it made grown vignerons weep with the havoc it wreaked. It was an invincible force. As the great American entomologist CV Riley explained in 1871, 'Small as the animal is, the product of a single

History is made when all the blenders come together for the first time at the Andrew Usher celebration lunch in August 2002. Clockwise from centre, left: John Ramsay, Maureen Robinson, Jim McEwan, David Stewart, Mitchell Sorbie, Graham Taylor, Tom Aitken, Abby Stephen, Andrew Symington, Gilmour Burnet, Donald Mackinlay, Colin Scott, Norman Mathison, Ewen Mackintosh, Eddie Drummond, Terry Hillman, Robert Hicks, Ian Grieve, Stewart Laing, Alan Lundie, Leonard Russell, John Smith, Billy Walker, Richard Paterson, Jim Milne, Gordon Doctor.

year would encircle the earth thirty times in an endless line.'

The phylloxera aphid operated by puncturing the root bark of the vine with its needle-like mouth, withdrawing the essential nutrients. For the vine it was a slow death, but the end was inevitable. The vignerons could only watch as this alien invader destroyed their livelihoods. They were helpless. And so were the distillers of Cognac, when phylloxera finally arrived there in 1872.

Although the French government offered the vast sum of 300,000 francs in an effort to find a solution, it was not until the 1890s that the curse of phylloxera began to be lifted when European vine stock was grafted onto American root stock which proved resistant to its deadly charms. Slowly the crisis came to an end, but phylloxera has by no means been totally eradicated. As the eminent wine writer Dave Hughes notes, ' … thanks to modern grafting methods phylloxera has been kept at bay in the vineyards. But it should never be forgotten it is still there amongst the other plants. Watching. Waiting for that opportunity to strike again. Its thirst for sucking a

The phylloxera aphid – the vine's deadliest enemy which inadvertently helped to open the door for Scotch whisky worldwide.

waiting in the wings. Men like Tommy 'Whisky Tom' Dewar, James Buchanan and 'Restless Peter' Mackie. Along with John Walker & Sons and John Haig and Company, their firms made up the 'big five', when they were finally absorbed into the DCL empire, and they came to dominate the blended Scotch whisky market in the early 20th century. When I think of these pioneers I think of dedicated passion with plenty of 'attitude'. They lived and breathed blended Scotch whisky, fighting for their brands all over the world. Illustrious names such as Johnnie Walker, Dewar's, White Horse and Black & White still remain a major driving force in the industry today.

Vast fortunes were made, but they were also lost. The 1890s were a boom period for blended Scotch whisky, and in 1898 the *Wine Trade Review* confidently reported that ' ... whereas Scotch distilling some twenty years ago was regarded as a very doubtful speculation it is now looked upon as the principal industry in the North, in which it is possible to make money quickly'.

However, 'boom' is invariably followed by 'bust.' Along with the legitimate entrepreneurs there were inevitably some less scrupulous operators. Most notable of these was the Pattison brothers, Robert and Walter, who conducted their business on a lavish and ostentatious scale. They were the 'talk of the trade'. William Ross of the DCL later noted that, 'So large were their transactions and so wide their ramifications that they infused into the Trade a reckless disregard of the most elementary rules of sound business ... Investors and speculators of the worst kind were drawn into the vortex and vied with each other in their race for riches'.

vine dry will never be quenched. One reason why it is never far away from my thoughts.'

Brandy and soda was a staple drink in gentlemen's clubs and bars throughout the British Empire, but thanks to phylloxera, the latter years of the 19th century saw an increasing scarcity of cognac. The gentlemen were not amused. Their favourite tipple was now in short supply. Clearly something had to be done, and the entrepreneurs of blended Scotch whisky were more than happy to oblige.

Men of flair, imagination, and sometimes just old-fashioned dogged persistence were

However, the British Linen, Clydesdale and National banks were almost certainly also guilty of disregarding 'the most elementary rules of sound business' by extending extremely generous credit facilities against over-valued assets. Even as late as 15th October 1898 one prominent distiller arrogantly declared to a reporter from the *Wine & Spirit Gazette*, 'Over-production? Pure humbug!'

Over-confidence and over-production were the order of the day. Did producers not realise the gravity of the situation? Were they just burying their heads in the sand? By the time the Pattison brothers were convicted of fraud and embezzlement in July 1901, the bubble had well and truly burst. There has perhaps been a tendency to make scapegoats of the Pattison brothers and to over-state their influence in bringing to an end a golden era of Scotch whisky distilling. As William Ross declared 26 years later, 'Such was the over-production of Scotch whisky during that period that even until recent years, the results were still felt.'

This is hardly surprising considering that while in 1891 there were 128 distilleries operating in Scotland, by 1899 that figure had risen to a remarkable 161. The last distillery to be built in the 19th century was Glen Elgin, designed by the inimitable Charles Doig. He predicted no new distillery would be built in the Highlands for half a century, and that prediction proved presciently accurate. From a productive peak of 37.1 million proof gallons in 1900, Scotch whisky output fell as low as 285,418 proof gallons in 1932. In line with Doig's prophecy, it was only in 1949 that William Delmé-Evans created Tullibardine

Distillery in the Perthshire village of Blackford. There had previously been a Tullibardine Distillery in the vicinity, but that had ceased to operate by 1837. Interestingly enough, Tullibardine was to become part of the Whyte & Mackay portfolio in 1993, and just to prove that history repeats itself, this was another period in the chronicles of Scotch whisky when over-production and low prices prevailed.

Back in the Pattison era whisky was sold through wine and spirit merchants and small-scale grocers, but by 1993 the supermarket giants were in the ascendancy and provided the perfect outlet for the industry's surplus stocks. During the early 1990s some of the own-label blends being sold by the supermarkets were high in grain content, with as little as ten per cent malt. This was inevitable, given the low prices that they were prepared to pay and the short-term contracts on offer.

This situation had obvious parallels with events during the very early years of the 20th century when the entire future of blended whisky was called into question. Adulteration of food and drink was rampant, and it was in the unlikely setting of Islington in London that the Borough Council raised a court action in 1905 against a number of local retailers for selling as Irish whiskey and as 'Scotch' what turned out to be nearly new spirit, *with 90% grain content*. The 'What is Whisky' case, as it was known, clearly had the potential to prevent blended whisky being sold as 'whisky' at all, and it opened on 6th November 1905, with the blending interests anxious to hear the judgement of magistrate, Snow Fordham. In the event, Fordham ruled that in order to qualify as 'whisky' the spirit, be it malt or grain, had to be produced in a pot still.

This verdict pleased the malt distillers, not least Andrew Mackenzie of Dalmore Distillery, who had been a vociferous opponent of blending. The malt distillers felt threatened by the growing popularity of blends and the power of blenders and grain distillers, but the latter were far from happy with Fordham's judgement, and their influence was great, including as it did the mighty DCL.

In February 1908 a Royal Commission was set up to investigate the situation. The final report of the Commission was delivered in July 1909, and it concluded that the definition of 'whiskey' was 'a spirit obtained by distillation from a mash of cereal grains saccharified by the diastase of malt'. 'Scotch whisky' was defined as ' … whiskey so defined, distilled in Scotland.' In other words, it did not have to be made with malted barley and it did not have to be made in a pot still. The blending interests had won the day, and the future of blended whisky was assured.

Even today, when interest in single malts has never been higher, we must remember that more than 90% of all Scotch whisky sold is still blended whisky. This is largely thanks to the driving spirit of our forefathers, who took the taste of blended Scotch around the world. Nowhere was it more popular than the USA, where even Prohibition could not slake the thirst for it.

The heavier blends remained in demand, but their weight was often doused with large quantities of soda and ice. Not surprisingly, consumers were receptive to easy-drinking, 'lighter' styles of whisky, particularly during the cocktail era of the 'Roaring Twenties'.

Blends such as J&B and Cutty Sark capitalised on this ready market. American fashions rarely take long to cross 'the pond', and easy-drinking blended whiskies were no exception. Indeed, Whyte & Mackay was already being advertised in the UK as 'the lightest Scotch whisky you can buy.'

Nevertheless, 'light' whiskies were not necessarily high in grain content at the expense of malts. The premium brands, such as J&B and Cutty Sark, contained comparatively high quantities of malt, but to give the required light, delicate body, a large number of the component malts were drawn from the Speyside region. The days of bold, rough and ready blends were slowly coming to an end, and as we progress into the 21st century the public preference clearly is for more mellow, medium-bodied blended Scotch whiskies. However, with more than 2,500 brands currently on the market, there is still a style to suit every taste and pocket.

As in my personal blending practice, I tend to classify specific blends within a number of different types. These are 'light', which includes J&B and Cutty Sark, 'medium', which encompasses Grant's, Whyte & Mackay, Famous Grouse and Bell's, and the heavier styles such as Johnnie Walker Red Label, Ballantine's and Teacher's. Remarkably, since the first reference to Scotch whisky in 1494, the basic art of distillation has not radically altered. Similarly, the art of blending remains, in essence, much as it did back in the days of Andrew Usher.

My fellow blenders are constantly striving to do the very best they can with the tools they have at their disposal. These 'tools', in the shape of malt and grain whiskies, have long

Master blenders Donald Mackinlay (right) and Trevor Cowan (centre) with John Russell (left) in Mackinlay's sample room in Leith in 1965.

been categorised, most obviously on a geographical basis, and Scotland's malt whisky distilleries are usually classified within four regional areas.

The 'Highland Line' is a theoretical boundary which separates the Highland and Lowland whisky producing regions, and runs from Greenock on the Firth of Clyde in the west to Dundee on the Firth of Tay in the east. Many commentators consider Speyside to represent a category all of its own, and also sub-divide the Highland region into Northern, Eastern, Western and even Island malts. However, personally speaking, I like to keep things simple, and I know many other blenders share my view. We therefore tend to include them all under the 'Highland' umbrella.

The Campbeltowns and Islays represent the remaining two categories, and I am very pleased to see that the SWA has now reinstated Campbeltown as a region in its own right once more, after many years subsumed within the Highland area. However, it should be borne in mind that these geographical classifications do not necessarily imply stylistic coherence. It could be assumed, for example, that all Islays are heavy, peaty and phenolic in temperament. While judging whiskies in international spirits competitions, I have noticed on some occasions this has meant that 'untypical', lighter Islays such as

Bruichladdich and Bunnahabhain have appeared to suffer unfairly in comparison with the 'heavyweights'.

In today's world we seem to be obsessed by listings and ratings, and this applies to whisky as much as anything else. Classifications and relative merits have never seemed so important to so many people. We live in a competitive age and everyone likes to be seen to back a winner. But this is really not a new phenomenon. Prior to the Great Exhibition in Paris during 1855, Emperor Napoleon III had ordered the classification of Bordeaux wines. As a result, 61 chateaux were divided into five growths or *crus*, and remarkably, since its inception, there has only been one change to this 1855 listing. In June 1973, after many years of intense lobbying by Baron Philippe Rothschild, Chateau Mouton Rothschild was promoted from deuxième cru to premier cru. This was a very public system of rating wines, and even today, everyone in the wine world remains aware of its existence. Whether they accept the continuing validity of these listings, is a different matter entirely.

So much for wine, but when it came to rating Scotch whiskies, distillers and blenders had traditionally judged by personal experience and reputation, though the ultimate arbiter was their relative filling and broking prices. The higher the price, the more desirable the whisky. Going back to the time of Andrew Usher, every blender must have had his secret list of whiskies, ranked in order of personal merit. As the Scotch whisky industry progressed during the first half of the 20th century, however, it became necessary for the larger companies with their vast stocks to compile more formal classifications of whiskies. In the days when much trading was done through whisky brokers, such lists were invaluable to blenders. But they were strictly for internal reference only. Companies operated in isolation and there was no friendly exchange of views and opinions between blenders as there is today.

Despite this cloak of secrecy, it can safely be assumed that rival blenders would generally have similar opinions on the merits of each individual malt. Their opinions would only differ when it came to the actual blending process. What mattered was the character of their 'house style' and its maintenance. Maintaining a house style during these turbulent years of world wars, depressions and subsequent distillery closures called for great blending skill.

The age of whiskies within blends must have altered considerably in accordance with the fluctuating stocks available to blenders. This is not surprising when you consider the varying number of distilleries in operation from year to year. For instance, in 1900 there were 159 working distilleries in Scotland, but by the time the First World War had ended in 1918, that number had fallen to just eight. A mere three years later, however, 134 Scotch whisky distilleries were in production, a number that has never subsequently been surpassed.

Apart from continuity of supply, another factor making the blender's life difficult was the variability in quality of new-make spirit from one week to another, even within the same distillery. But worse still was the unpredictable nature of the casks being used to mature and even marry whiskies for blending. It was a wonder even the most skilful blender

HIGHLANDS. A.
Grant
...and Park
...'s Glenlivet
...aker
...rinnes
...melish
...geenmore
...nfiddich
...allan
...rtisoh
...akwood
...ilune
...en Rothes

CRACK HIGHLANDS. B.
...lendronach
...lenfarclas
...lenlossie
...emintoich
Lochnagar
Balvenie
Balmenach

SECOND CLASS HIGHLANDS. A.
Pulteney
Blair Athol
Glenmorangie
Scapa
Tomiemore
Dalwhinnie
Tomatin
Glenglassaugh

SECOND CLASS HIGHLANDS. B.
Brackla
Glen Mhor
Glenskioch
Inchgower
Ord
Tobermory
Banff
Dalmore
Glentauchers
Millburn
Milton Keith
Coleburn
Glenesawdor

ISLAYS. A.
Ardbeg
Caol Ila
Lagavulin
Laphroaig
Malt Mill

CRACK HIGHLANDS. C.
Tamdhu
Aultmore
Cardow
Craigellachie
Longmorn
Convalmore
Dailuaine Dhu
Glen Elgin
Glen Moray
Knockdhu
Oban
Parkmore
Speyburn
Glendullan

CRACK HIGHLANDS. D.
Dufftown
Glenburgie
Milton Duff
Aberlour
Aberfeldy
Ardmore

SECOND CLASS HIGHLANDS. C.
Perth Isla
Auchinblae
Brechin
Fetteroairn
Glenesadam
Glengarioch
Glenury
Strathage
Strommess
Stronachie
Ballechin
Ben Nevis
Glenoe
Strathisla
Glenlochy
Edradour
Ferintosh

SECOND CLASS HIGHLAND
Benromach
Glencoull
Glenfyne
Glengie
Glenturret

ISLAYS. B.
Bunnahabhain
Lochindaal
Port Ellen

ISLAYS. C.
Bruichladdich.

CAMPELTOWNS. A.
Glenside
Kintyre
Albyn
Scotia

CAMPELTOWNS. B.
Argyle
Benmore
Lochhead
Riechlachan
Springbank
Kinloch

CAMPELTOWNS. C.
Dalaruan
Lochruan
Springside
Hazelburn
Glen Nevis

LOWLANDS. A.
Dean
Edinburgh
Linlitgow
Rosebank
Provanmill
Glenkinchie

LOWLANDS. B.
Auchtertool
Auchtermuchty
Bankier
Gresnook
Littlemill
Grange
Camlachie
Glengoyne

GRAINS. AA.
Cameronbridge

GRAINS. A.
Caledonian
Adelphi
Carsebridge
North British
Yoker
Port Dundas

GRAINS. B.
Avigowan
Gartloch

GRAINS. C.
Bo'ness

The 1924 classification of malts and grains which was probably compiled by George Ballantine & Son. The eagle-eyed will notice the mystery malt Glencoe in the Second Class Highlands 'C' category.

could maintain brand consistency under these circumstances.

But by the 1950s an overall air of confidence was beginning to pervade Britain. In 1953 Elizabeth II was crowned queen, and this beautiful young monarch symbolised an end to the austere aftermath of the war years; Mount Everest had just been conquered by Edmund Hillary and Sherpa Tenzing, and in May 1954 Roger Bannister ran the first sub-four-minute mile.

One month later something else was on the move, and that was whisky. Sir Compton Mackenzie of *Whisky Galore* fame officially opened W&A Gilbey's new Edinburgh bond and bottling store at Haymarket, as well as naming two road tankers *Whisky Galore I* and *II*. These were specially and securely designed to carry blended whisky from Aberdeen to Edinburgh for bottling, collecting malt whiskies from various distilleries on the return journey. By all accounts, this was the first transportation of whisky 'under bond' by road tanker. Considering how difficult and frustrating it was to obtain Customs & Excise approval for any innovative measure, this was a genuine milestone. Its true importance seems to have been strangely neglected and unappreciated by commentators on the Scotch whisky industry.

The ability to move stocks of whisky efficiently and securely by road became more important than ever as distillation doubled between 1950 and 1960. This increase in output gradually gave blenders larger stocks with which to work, and therefore a greater degree of stability.

It is therefore not surprising that this was the era when most of the large distillers began to use formal documentation to classify their stocks. Over the years I have been fortunate enough to assemble a collection of these almost secret documents from a variety of sources, including the Paterson family company archives. Some of the most interesting examples were produced by Chivas Brothers, George Ballantine & Son and DCL's malt whisky distilling subsidiary SMD. The

earliest of these classifications in my possession comes from 1924 and is believed to have come into the possession of Hiram Walker of Dumbarton via their subsidiary George Ballantine & Son.

Perhaps the most informative from the modern perspective is that issued by SMD on 25th August 1954. In common with classifications employed by their competitors, SMD grouped distilleries into 'Scotch Grains' and the traditional geographical distilling areas of Highland, Lowland and Islay then into sub-categories of First, Second or Third Grade. Interestingly, SMD did not record any Campbeltowns at this time. This must have been due to the fact that many of the Campbeltown distilleries had been closed for decades, and the style was no longer of relevance to most blenders.

But clearly they must have once had a great deal of relevance to blenders, as Ballantine's classification from 1924 includes not just a listing, but a grading, of Campbeltowns (see below).

Other companies preferred different terminology. For example, 'Crack', 'Crackerjack', 'Top Notchers' and 'First Class.' Whatever the wording, there was broad agreement within the industry as to which were the most desirable blending malts.

CAMPBELTOWNS. A.	CAMPBELTOWNS. B.	CAMPBELTOWNS. C.
Glenside	Argyle	Dalaruan
Kintyre	Benmore	Lochruan
Albyn	Lochhead	Springside
Scotia	Riechlachan	Hazelburn
	Springbank	Glen Nevis
	Kinloch	

SMD CLASSIFICATION OF SCOTCH WHISKIES, AUGUST 1954

ISLAY MALTS

1st Grade	2nd Grade	3rd Grade
Caol Ila	Ardbeg	Bruichladdich
Lagavulin	Bowmore	Bunnahabhain
Laphroaig		Lochindaal
Malt Mill		Port Ellen
Talisker		

HIGHLAND MALTS

1st Grade		2nd Grade		3rd Grade	
A	B	A	B	A	B
Aultmore	Balmenach	Balvenie	Aberlour	Aberfeldy	Ardmore
Benrinnes	Glenfarclas	Cardow	Coleburn	Ballechin	Auchinblae
Cragganmore	Glenlivet	Convalmore	Dallas Dhu	Banff	Benromach
Glenfiddich	Highland Park	Craigellachie	Glendullan	Ben Nevis	Blair Athol
Glen Grant	Lochnagar	Dailuaine	Glen Elgin	Brackla	Brechin
Glenlossie	Miltonduff	Glenburgie	Glentauchers	Dalmore	Dufftown
Glenrothes		Glendronach	Glenury	Glen Albyn	Edradour
Linkwood		Glenspey	Imperial	Glencawder	Ferintosh
Macallan		Longmorn	Knockando	Glengarioch	Fettercairn
Mortlach		Speyburn	Knockdhu	Glen Mhor	Glencadam
		Teaninich	Milton-	Glenmorangie	Glen Coull
		Clynelish	Strathisla	Glen Moray	Glenfyne
			Ord	Millburn	Glenglassaugh
			Parkmore	Oban	Glenlochy
			Strathmill	Pulteney	Glenskiath
			Tamdhu	Scapa	Glenturret
			Dalwhinnie	Tobermory	Glenugie
				Tomatin	Inchgower
				Towiemore	Strathdee
					Stromness
					Stronachie
					Tay

LOWLAND MALTS

1st Grade	2nd Grade	3rd Grade
Glenkinchie	Grange	Auchentoshan
Rosebank	Linlithgow	Auchtermuchty
	Inverleven	Auchtertool
		Bankier
		Bladnoch
		Camlachie
		Dean
		Edinburgh
		Glengoyne
		Greenock
		Littlemill
		Provanmill

SCOTCH GRAINS

1st Grade	2nd Grade	3rd Grade
Caledonian	Adelphi	Ardgowan
Cambus	Carsebridge	Bo'ness
	North British	Gartloch
	Dumbarton	Glenochil
		Port Dundas
		Strathclyde
		Montrose

The SMD classification of August 1954. Note many of our lost distilleries.

However, given enough age and the appropriate cask, a 'Second' or even 'Third Class' malt could easily be the equal of a moderate example of a 'Top Notcher' in the eyes of the blender. It was, after all, just a guideline.

As a blender working today, I view classifications from a slightly different perspective. In the first instance, I consider the character of blended whisky required by the customer, and to help me attain the desired 'body' I draw on my stocks of component malt whiskies, which I initially categorise as 'light', 'medium' or 'heavy.' The principal objective of the blender has to be consistency. I cannot stress this strongly enough. It is no use creating the finest blended whisky today if you cannot reproduce it tomorrow. This central tenet of blending is always with you, and is echoed by many of my fellow blenders, as it was by my father. I recall him saying, 'If you want respect in this world be consistent in your character and be consistent in your blend.'

Jim Beveridge is one of Diageo's most respected master blenders, and closely associated with the Johnnie Walker brand. According to Jim, 'If whisky blending was simply just coming up with a recipe which then has to be adhered to forever, there is no need for a blender in those circumstances. Blending is about ensuring consistency in a world of changes. When stocks are changing, the blending job is to manage that in a way so that the change is accommodated to maintain consistency of character.'

The various conditions of the casks and the manner in which they are stored are always subject to change. Inconsistencies will naturally occur. Every blender is aware of this

criteria and he will take these two points into consideration when formulating his blend. This is one reason why I like to be amongst all the casks in the blending warehouse, nosing each one prior to blending. As my father frequently told me, before the casks are even blended you must firstly 'see and feel' the spirit. Only then will you sense the blend's likely personality.

The blender must forever be thinking ahead. He has to have a clear view of stock availability and be in a position to introduce substitute whiskies from the same stylistic 'family' when necessary. One major factor in our calculations is the necessity of operating in line with sales predictions. At times this can be a complete nightmare. For example, if a 21-year-old blend suddenly began to exceed all market expectations in the Far East, this could, given its age, present us with some difficulties. In view of the overall growth of single malt sales in recent years, it is inevitable that the range of 20-year-old plus malts available to blenders will be severely restricted. This is just another challenge the blender has to face and overcome.

I would be the first to admit that nobody becomes a master blender overnight. It takes years, and I am still discovering new nuances that continue to excite and motivate me. From that first moment when I was eight years old and my father introduced me to the sensations of nosing whisky, I have been fascinated by the very soul of the spirit. Every time I encounter a whisky, I am still aroused by its personality and by what it has to offer me. I ask what contribution can this make to the blend I am creating? And in its silent way, the whisky always gives me an answer, though it may not be the answer the accountants want to hear.

I remember my father once saying to me, 'You won't discover much about Scotch whisky sitting on your backside, boy. Get out there and learn. Feel it.' So that is just what I did. There is only so much you can be taught about the mysteries of blending. Beyond that it is up to you to develop your own abilities by a process of trial and error. And there will be many errors, but the key to any success is learning from them. Essentially, this elusive success comes from nosing cask after cask after cask. Watching, waiting, nosing. And more nosing.

Whiskies are like people. Each has its own personality and particular 'weight.' Each will be dressed differently, and will change through time. Just as we inevitably judge people and group them into types, so I categorise whiskies in a similar manner. Based on personal experience, I have, over the years, collated my own 'family tree' of whiskies.

Since the vast majority of blends on the market will be aged for between four and six years, I have created a system of evaluation focusing on whiskies of approximately that age. While I use 'Light', 'Medium' and 'Heavy' as my principal categories. I also take into consideration the complexity and individuality of each whisky, and the way it will interact with the others for optimum harmony. The 'rogues' and 'agitators' must be kept at bay.

Unlike the earlier 'class systems', where the winners and losers have been individually segregated, within my classification I am looking for union rather than separation. To my mind, every single malt and grain whisky will have a part to play, and when properly selected and housed within the appropriate family, their genetic compatibility can be maximised.

The role of the blender may be likened to that of a marriage guidance counsellor. Not all of the whiskies will instantly fall in love with each other. Indeed, some may be totally incompatible. The boisterous, younger malts might simply flirt, only to go their separate ways. The chosen whiskies must be given time to court, time to sort out their differences, and to make necessary compromises before a perfect partnership is achieved. Never push or rush them. Let them glow in their own time. Just because a blend contains a high percentage of malt, this does not mean it is necessarily going to glow. It is all down to selecting the ideal available malts at the optimum ages but, more importantly, pairing them with their ideal partners. Only then will the relationship blossom.

Every time I create a new blend or a different single malt expression the adrenalin immediately starts pumping through my veins and my stomach begins to ache with excitement at the challenge ahead. However, so many questions need to be answered.

Will the various malt and grain whiskies be compatible? Are they sufficiently matured? How long will it take for them to consummate their marriage? Will it be a long, loving partnership? Then there is the ultimate question: will the consumer even like the style when it is finally tasted? Only time will tell. However, before we get to that point, the blender must take on yet another role. He must demonstrate that he truly is 'the perfect host' at a whisky dinner party.

This analogy is a good example of what faces any reputable master blender. His

The 2008 Paterson Classification of malt and grain, based on 4–6-year-old whiskies

HEAVY	MEDIUM	LIGHT	ISLAY	GRAIN
FIRST PREFERENCE	FIRST PREFERENCE	FIRST PREFERENCE	FIRST PREFERENCE (HEAVY)	FIRST PREFERENCE
Aberfeldy	Aberlour	Glenfiddich	Ardbeg	Cameronbridge
Balmenach	Alt-a'Bhainne	Glen Grant	Caol Ila	Dumbarton
Gragganmore	Auchroisk	Glenmorangie	Lagavulin	North British
Dailuaine	Balblair	Glen Ord	Laphroaig	Port Dundas
Glendronach	Balvenie	Kininvie		
Glen Keith	Benriach	Knockando	SECOND PREFERENCE (MEDIUM)	SECOND PREFERENCE
Glentauchers	Benrinnes	Royal Lochnagar		
Pulteney	Braeval	Strathisla	Bowmore	Girvan
Talisker	Dalmore		Bruichladdich	Invergordon
	Dalwhinnie	SECOND PREFERENCE	Bunnahabhain	Loch Lomond
SECOND PREFERENCE	Glendullan			Strathclyde
	Glen Elgin	Deanston		
Ardmore	Glenfarclas	Glengoyne		**LOWLAND**
Aultmore	Glenlossie	Glen Moray		(LIGHT)
Ben Nevis	Glenlivet	Glen Spey		Auchentoshan
Clynelish	Glenrothes	Glenturret		Bladnoch
Fettercairn	Glen Scotia	Inchmurrin		Glenkinchie
Glencadam	Imperial	Isle of Arran		
Glen Garioch	Isle of Jura	Loch Lomond		
Highland Park	Linkwood	Speyburn		
Inchgower	Longmorn	Speyside		
Macduff	Macallan	Strathmill		
Miltonduff	Mannochmore	Tamnavulin		
Tobermory	Mortlach	Tomatin		
	Scapa	Tomintoul		
	Springbank			
	Tamdhu			
	Teaninich			
	SECOND PREFERENCE			
	Benromach			
	Blair Athol			
	Caperdonich			
	Cardhu			
	Craigellachie			
	Cardhu			
	Dufftown			
	Edradour			
	Glenallachie			
	Glenburgie			
	Knockdhu			
	Oban			
	Royal Brackla			
	Tormore			
	Tullibardine			

selection remains paramount. One wrong malt, one wrong guest, could ruin the blend and his party. His reputation and skill could be brought into question.

One party which I love to organise is for our rare 22-year-old Supreme blended whisky which I affectionately call our 'pensioners' party'. The component whiskies are old, but their great age has brought out the best in them. It is all down to careful selection. My guest list includes some distinguished gentlemen who demand respect and careful preparation. Many are set in their ways. The secret is to give them all time.

Who are my principal guests, and have I made the right choices?

Top of the list are none other than the Highland Chieftains from the straths of Speyside. Their heritage and reputation will never cease to arouse passion in an aged blend of this quality. Glenfarclas, Longmorn, Glenlivet, Glenrothes, Mannochmore, Macallan, Aberlour, Mortlach and Benriach are just a few favoured guests who are always welcome. I love them all.

And why do I love them? Because, to my mind, with age nothing can beat their noble characteristics. They are elegant and sophisticated, bold and majestic. On their own they shine, but when combined with their counterparts they radiate like a beacon in a dark sea. These great Casanovas know the true art of seduction. No other malts can resist their enticing charms. But our principal guests must share their talents. They must have support. A 22-year-old blend such as this requires backbone, structure and warmth, but the key

is finesse.

Behind these great Highland Chieftains, as behind all great men, there are usually women. Their part is equally important. When you find them, hold on to them and cherish them. Then carefully blend them. The line-up reads like a Miss World contest: Balblair, Balvenie, Auchroisk, Tamdhu, Glenfiddich, Benrinnes, Linkwood, Glenmorangie, Dalmore, Strathisla, Ord, Springbank, Speyburn and Edradour. If you are looking for refinement and culture at your dinner table these beauties will not disappoint you. Their silky smooth countenance will sensually make their presence felt as they slowly slide under the covers with our top table guests.

But like any party, the playboys, the smooth talkers, are never far away. They generally prowl on their own but when working in a pack they are a formidable force. Any great blend must have excitement, complexity, muscle and authority. Their ranks include Clynelish, Glentauchers, Pulteney, Cragganmore, Ben Nevis, Ardmore, Glendronach, Tobermory, Glen Keith, Aultmore, Macduff, Glencadam and Glen Garioch. Although in the first instance they will flirt and tease with their gutsy attitude, given sufficient time their distinguished qualities will emerge. Never underestimate the talents of these single malts. These are the Vikings of the North. They possess grit and brashness, and their greatness is only truly recognised when they work as part of a team.

Any premium blend of distinction needs muscle and an extra 'lift' and they will contribute that. Then, when they are in their twenties and they become old and grey and a little tired and grumpy, give them space. Give

Opposite. My own classification.

them time to circulate among the other guests. They will rise to the occasion. But like any dinner party, a great blend needs an outstanding malt whisky, an eloquent speaker with a magnetic personality. A true professional who will entertain his audience. Someone who knows where the boundaries are, and is prepared to push them.

The blender faces the same daunting task as that speaker when it comes to our next guest. She is raunchy. She is beautiful. She lives alone on an island, and that island is Islay. She breathes fire and brimstone, but when taken and tamed at the right age she reigns supreme. Others remain impotent by comparison.

Know your audience. Know your blend.

Islay single malts are boisterous and assertive when young. Gently lead and ease them into the blend. You must never push or underestimate their distinctive peat smoke characteristics. These are born leaders and they will leave their mark too strongly if you ignore their authority.

During their 'probationary' period of around three to 11 years, in my opinion, three per cent in a young blend is the maximum amount you should allow, unless you are allocating Islay's two gentle giants – Bruichladdich and Bunnahabhain, whose levels of peatiness are usually considerably lower than all the other Islays. In many instances they could be mistaken for Highland malts with their salted bananas, tang of cinnamon and other spicy attributes.

However, when it comes to our 'pensioners' party' the fearsome Islay storm troopers of Ardbeg, Laphroaig and Lagavulin lead the first assault with their barrage of bonfire smoke, sea spray, tar and fresh spearmint. Caol Ila and Bowmore quickly support them with their attractive spicy, smoky notes, along with whispers of tar rope and sea salt. What a bonfire of delight! But never forget these peaty aromas are not just confined to Islay. Talisker, from the beautiful island of Skye, stands proudly like Landseer's Monarch of the Glen, except this is an island malt with its own individual breeding. Thick, spicy, pine wood with hints of briny sea spray and peat smoke, along with a final, distinctive kick of pepper.

Our blend, like our dinner party, needs to be served by efficient staff. Regrettably, they are often overlooked. They too have an invaluable contribution to make, and to me, the 'Lowland ladies', like the waitresses, can make the evening flow smoothly. Sometimes they are unfairly dismissed for their light, feminine charms. They may be light in body, but lightness should not be confused with blandness. Auchentoshan, Rosebank, Glenkinchie and Bladnoch all possess attractive tones of freshly cut flowers, crushed grape pulp and pear. And although Glengoyne is now classified as a Highland malt, to me it shares similar characteristics. If you want peace and harmony in your blend, then these light beauties will ease in nicely every time.

Highland, Lowland, Campbeltown and Islay – each area will have an invaluable contribution to make in the final blend. It is all down to 'setting the style' and then maintaining it.

Selecting the right single malts from these regions helps towards this taste profile. But ultimately it is down to our final guest, who frequently remains hidden in the background. That guest is, of course, grain whisky. So often

Whyte & Mackay's Invergordon grain distillery and blend production centre. *Courtesy of Gavin D. Smith.*

overshadowed by the noble single malts, grain whisky is frequently the key to a great blend. Like the Lowland malts, grains also bring a certain calmness and warmth to the blend.

Grain spirit from each of the remaining seven Scottish grain distilleries will allow the malts to shine through when all the component whiskies are mixed together. Cameronbridge, North British and Port Dundas provide an elegant soft structure and gentleness. With age, these great diehards are at times almost undistinguishable from some of the single malt whiskies. This is one reason why so many bottled, aged, grain limited editions are appearing on the market at the present time.

However, when it comes to wanting more awareness of your malts, coupled with a generally light character, Girvan, Strathclyde and Invergordon grain whiskies are the perfect tools to assist in this exercise. Their grassy, floral, apple flavours, along with their magnetic personalities, will bring together the whole family, hopefully making it a thoroughly contented one.

I may use as many as five different grain whiskies in a blend, however, while I like to select as many as 25 to 30 malts for my younger blends, when it comes to our 22-year-old Supreme blend I do not have the same luxury. At this great age stocks are naturally limited, therefore the figure may be as low as 15 various single malts.

No matter the number of malts and grains that I use, my foremost concern is always to maintain consistency of character. I am often asked whether it poses a problem for me when a distillery closes or stocks become exhausted. The simple answer is 'no', because blending requires long-term strategies, and the blender must always be thinking years ahead. Accordingly, when a substitution is required, to avoid the risk of any character change I will usually replace the whisky in question with two or more malts of a similar style. It is often impossible to find an identical substitute, so 'mixing and matching' several malts is the best way of achieving the same effect.

The days of 'large' vattings, comprising up to 40 malts are virtually over, due principally to stock rationalisation within the industry. Nevertheless, big is not necessarily beautiful. It is about setting the style which fulfils your needs and those of your customers.

It is much the same with the malt content in a blend. In most cases this information is still known only by the blender. Not surprisingly, it remains a matter of confidentiality. Tastes are changing to light, easy-drinking whiskies, but additionally, financial constraints are frequently placed on the blender by customers, with the result that many of the non-premium blends will now often have a malt content of less than 25%.

Despite the financial implications in tying up spirit for a longer period, like my father and grandfather before me, I remain a strong advocate of traditional 'marrying', allowing the whiskies to come together and settle down with each other before their final commitment. If you have the money, the necessary storage capacity and the time, then marry them; the longer the better.

However, there are a number of marrying options open to the blender. The first,

generally the most popular in the whisky industry, is a 'fleeting romance', since it hardly qualifies as a marriage. This simply means the malts and grain whiskies have been amalgamated together in a vat, roused and then bottled as required. What I would call a 'traditional' marriage is when the malts and grains are blended together then transferred back into their original wood or specially selected casks and left to marry for many months before finally being bottled. But at Whyte & Mackay we take our blend a stage further. Our 35 malts, aged between four and eight years, are vatted together and run off into in-situ sherry butts to allow them to commence their 'first marriage', which lasts for almost four months. Normally, six different grains are then selected at the same age as the malts. These are then combined with our mix of malts to complete the blend. Instead of bottling at this stage we want to fully consummate the union by allowing a second or 'double marriage' to take place. This is carried out in another set of in-situ sherry butts for a minimum period of two months.

I believe this important double marriage gives the blend the key to its success – time. Time to harmonise and time to form a perfect union; an ideal partnership. Not everyone would necessarily concur with this practice, but every blender will have his own modus operandi that works along similar lines.

In the instance of our 22-year-old blend, I believe marrying to be essential. At this age many of the component malts need time to adjust to their new situation, to become familiar with their new surroundings and their fellow whiskies. I advocate a marrying period of at least a year for my distinguished 'pensioners'. Only then are they eligible for the full status of a 22-year-old Supreme blend for the connoisseurs' delight. Sometimes good things really do come to those who wait.

In my opinion, *any* blend of this age and quality should be given due reverence. Classic aged blends can reveal so many enticing, hidden complexities. Yet many people who taste them fail to take a realistic time to explore their true meaning. I find this quite frustrating, because I know what they are missing. There is often a problem of perception. After all, to many they are simply blends. To return to our opening analogy with the world of art, I believe that fine old blends are comparable to great masterpieces, except the palate, not the eye, is the receptor of their pleasure. The same artistic temperament of an 'inner world', as the great American artist Jackson Pollock aptly described his work, lies within the *soul* of the blend, waiting to be discovered and enjoyed. But ultimately, any picture is most effective when given the context of a harmonious and complementary frame. The same applies to Scotch whisky, which needs to be nurtured in oak casks to bring out its 'inner self'.

Over the years, with an efficient wood management programme in place I have generally found that young single malt and grain whiskies are in most instances consistent and reliable in quality. It is only with whiskies of 20 to 40 years of age that their backgrounds come into question. The importance of using reliable casks of known provenance has only been fully appreciated during the last two decades, and therefore, the older the whiskies, the more patient you must be with them. Some of them had deprived childhoods

and many different homes. In order to reintegrate them into society we need to give them a fresh start, with fresh wood.

The ideal way to do this is to fill them into the whisky distiller's best friend, American white oak *(quercus alba)* from the Ozark Mountains of Missouri which has previously held bourbon. This wood, often sourced from great American distillers such as Brown-Forman, Heaven Hill and Jim Beam, is the bedrock of the modern Scotch whisky industry, and was first imported into Britain in large quantities during the late 1940s. Julian P. Van Winkle III of Old Rip Van Winkle Distillery in Kentucky explains that from 1st March 1938 it was a legal requirement ' … that any whiskey made on or after this date had to be placed in new charred barrels to be called *straight*, with the exception of corn whiskey'.

Seventy years on this situation still prevails. It keeps the American coopers happy, and with ex-bourbon casks in high demand in Scotland, we are not complaining either. It is universally acknowledged that no wood other than oak provides the ideal characteristics for optimum whisky maturation. American white oak soothes the hot, fiery temperament of the young spirit, and encourages the development of its essential character over the years. This character will change many times, in just the same way that people change as they grow older.

While American white oak is now the blending industry favourite in terms of wood, historically, particularly during the 19th century, most Scotch whisky was matured in European oak *(quercus patraea* and *robur)* casks that had previously held sherry. And today, sherry wood still plays a vital part in the art of blending, particularly in terms of aged blended whiskies. Where it really shines, however, is for single malt maturation. In order to maintain the silky smooth character of my aged whiskies, it is vital to ensure *consistent* supplies of good wood. This is one reason why I, in common with most of my colleagues, make an annual trip to Jerez. During those visits I purchase sherry butts from the highly prestigious bodega of Gonzalez Byass, with whom Whyte & Mackay have been doing business since the 19th century.

Jerez, like Scotland, is steeped in history, and sherry is an ancient and noble drink with a remarkable heritage. Entering one of Gonzalez Byass' renowned bodegas, such as La Concha, always sends a shiver of anticipation down my spine. The first thing you are aware of is a dramatic contrast between the baking heat of the Andalucian sun and the cool, peaceful bodega, filled with black silhouettes of monstrous, slumbering casks. The damp air is filled with a musty aroma of heavy wines. What treasures lie within these casks? I respect them in the same way as I do my grain whiskies, and if carefully selected they can successfully seduce even the most tempestuous single malts.

When I visit the bodegas I have the style of our various single malts set clearly in my mind, and my main task is to search for those sherry casks which will not only be compatible but will also enhance their flavour and character. sherry is not just sherry, as people often mistakenly believe. There is a vast stylistic range from which to choose: fino, oloroso, amontillado, manzanilla, for example, but not every sherry will be compatible with a single malt. Selecting the right cask is the key to a perfectly matured whisky.

But it is also a matter of *waiting* ... and watching. The sherry wood will nurture the whisky, but this cannot be hurried. However, the blender instinctively knows when it is ready. Leave it too long and it becomes tannic and bitter. But when it is captured at the perfect moment, wonderful hedonistic aromas of crushed almonds, marzipan, liquorice and hints of citrus will emerge, and the effect of the sherry wood will also provide an almost intangible inner warmth. Then, of course, there is that lovely rich, dark inviting colour. When the balance is right, nothing can beat good sherry wood.

Once my final cask selection has been made, the chosen casks will remain in the cool bodegas, their contents maturing as time passes. They contain noble sherries with wonderfully evocative names such as Apostoles, Amoroso and Matusalem. The rare and distinguished Matusalem sherry has a minimum age of 30 years, and is the perfect partner for some of our most exclusive 'Rare and Prestige' Dalmore bottlings. These are the largest casks used for Scotch whisky maturation, with a capacity of just over 600 litres. They are coopered from Spanish oak, which has greater porosity than their American counterparts, with the result that they refine the whisky during maturation, but more importantly add a warm, nutty complexity.

When I require these casks for finishing and developing our single malts, a shipping schedule is put in place. In view of their great age and potential fragility, particular care must be taken when these butts are being removed from their stows in the bodega in preparation for shipment. The casks are almost emptied of sherry, but five litres are kept back in each one to prevent the wood from drying out during their lengthy journey to our warehouses in Scotland.

On arrival, these Spanish giants are gently removed from their container and transferred to a warehouse, awaiting my vatting instructions. We ensure they are used within one week of arrival to prevent the old staves from drying out, but before use any sherry remaining in the casks must be emptied out to conform with the strict definition of 'Scotch whisky.' However, during my early years in the industry, the use of *pajarete* was permitted. *Pajarete* is a sweetened wine from Spain and until 1982 quantities of it could be added to whisky in order to give additional flavour and colour.

One of the principal uses of the butts for Whyte & Mackay is to mature or 'finish' Dalmore single malt. A small number of these butts are retained for the maturation of new spirit, but the vast majority are used to give a secondary period of ageing to ten-year-old Dalmore that has previously been stored in American oak. It will spend at least two years in these sherry butts, and that whisky will then be vatted with Dalmore that has been matured entirely in American oak. Between 30% and 60% could be added, depending on the ultimate style I am seeking. People often refer to the process as a 'finish', but I prefer not to use the term. I see it as a 'transformer', a process that motivates the spirit into a new dimension.

It is like buying a brand new suit or dress. You feel good when wearing it; specially if it costs a lot of money. I must ensure I buy the right 'clothes', the right wood, for my whiskies, and Gonzalez Byass is the equivalent of a Savile Row tailor. Believe me, these butts are not cheap. As I write this, a good butt could cost as much as £500, whereas an ex-bourbon cask sells for around £45. If you think of the scale on which distillers operate, this represents significant extra expenditure, but to my mind it is well worth it.

Having dressed our whisky in its expensive new outfit, it must be placed in the wardrobe, in other words, the warehouse. This may sound like a straightforward matter of storage, but in reality, the type of warehouse and its location can have a significant effect on the spirit as it matures. Traditional 'dunnage' warehouses are constructed from stone or brick, with ash or earth floors, and concrete access walkways. Casks are stowed three high on wooden runners, and for many experts the damp, cool conditions with good air circulation provide the idea situation for maturing whisky.

However, problems of access, constraints of space, finance and health and safety issues mean that dunnage warehouses are now in a minority. Most whisky is held in racked facilities, where casks may be stored twelve-high, or in 'palletised' warehouses with four or six casks being stored upright on wooden pallets. Given the choice between the three types of warehouse, I would always opt for dunnage, and most of my fellow blenders concur. David Stewart of William Grant & Sons Ltd says, 'We've got a couple of warehouses in Dufftown that are palletised, but the malt from there will be used in our blends rather than for single malts. You always feel that the old traditional warehouses are the best, and probably we all know that, but it's no longer economic. Next best will be a racked warehouse, because there will probably be more air circulating, and logically, therefore, it is better. Dunnage warehouses are smaller and damper, with earth in the floors, so we still think that these are the best warehouses for maturing whisky. If you compare the same age whisky out of a palletised warehouse, a racked warehouse and a dunnage warehouse, that out of dunnage will always look more mature.'

Regardless of which type of warehouse it is stored in, each cask will have a specific lifespan, and this lifespan is divided into 'fillings'. The usual practice for both malt and grain whisky 'first filling' would be between three to eight years, and after this period the cask will be used for as many as three more fillings. In total, a cask might have an active life of 25 years or longer. A cask that has been used to its limits is often described as 'exhausted' at which point it may be sold to a garden centre to resurface as a planting tub or piece of furniture. Rather a sad end after years of devoted service. However, there is an alternative. The cask may be given a new lease of life by a process known as 'de-char, re-char'. This involves scouring a few millimetres of the surface wood from the inside of the cask with something like a mechanised Brillo pad, before it is 'fired' with a device not dissimilar to a flame thrower. Within a few minutes the surface is burnt to the desired level, leaving a new layer of char. In effect, this charring process reopens the pores of the wood, allowing it to interact in a more positive

manner with the next filling of new spirit.

From my point of view, such casks are like sad old men who have been fitted with pacemakers. One is simply postponing the inevitable. Give me fresh wood every time. Dr Bill Lumsden is master distiller for Glenmorangie Ltd and he says, 'We will sometimes use de-char, re-char casks, though my personal preference is to use more first fill ex-bourbon casks, because I like the 'butteriness' you get from them. Fresh re-charred casks tend to give a burnt wood-shaving note to the spirit, therefore I keep them in the minority.'

The maturation process is one of several key factors that influence the ultimate quality of the whisky we drink, along with new malt and grain spirit. Diageo's Jim Beveridge makes the point that, 'In my opinion, it's a three-legged stool. There's no hierarchy, you need the three legs to make it work, and you couldn't say one factor is more important than the others. If you've great wood but poor new make spirit, that's no good. And if you've got wonderful new make but poor wood, then that's no good either. If you've got terrific malts and terrific wood, but terrible grain, then the blend will be just as bad'

Bill Lumsden says, 'I agree that the three-legged stool, as Jim calls it, is important, but some of the elements to me are more significant than others. For blends, I would personally say that the malt and the wood are almost equally important, whereas the grain to me is slightly less so.'

Whatever the minutiae of maturation, the whisky in the casks is, of course, ultimately destined for drinking. In order to persuade the discerning consumer to purchase your brand, its style and quality must appeal. Quality is everything, but when it comes down to controlling and setting the desired standard, there is only one place in which to carry out this mission. It is not just any place. It is the blender's second home ... his sample room. It has been mine for almost 40 years.

The copper curves of a pot still, the aromatic silence of a warehouse, the sheer elegance of an old whisky never cease to arouse passion in me, but they all pale into insignificance when compared to the strong emotions I have for my sample room. It is a place of peace and reflection where wonderful whiskies arrive from their cradles for their first baptism, their first assessment. It will be many years before I see them again. Some of the single malts will immediately be released for blending or bottling. Others will be allowed to sleep on – only to be woken before they are finally married, checked and divorced from my care. The spirit is ready and waiting to be comforted by the warmth of the consumers' palate before it slips over into oblivion. Every beat of a whisky's life can be found in my sample room. It is like opening up a family album: every picture, like every bottle, will have a story to tell; sometimes disappointing, sometimes exhilarating, but always fascinating.

My theatre of magic with a cast of a thousand different characters is located on the top floor of Whyte & Mackay's Glasgow head office. As you enter the 'lion's den', as it is unofficially known, a pride of the company's rampant lions roars at you. The Double Lions' motif is our founding fathers' trade mark and has been prominently, and rightly, restored on the current bottle label. Before entering the sample room you must make your way along a short corridor which is lined with brightly lit glass cabinets displaying the company's glittering achievements over the years. Many also contain old bottles both from the 19th and 20th centuries. Every inch of space on the walls is taken up with pictures of my heroes: Usher, Barnard and Doig, as well as our founders James Whyte and Charles Mackay and their descendants. They are all here to welcome me as I enter my hallowed domain.

The first person to greet me is always John.

John has been with me since 1994. He is over six feet tall, with a drawn, sallow complexion supported by a long, grey beard. Sadly, over the years he has fallen on some hard times, having had both his head and hands completely replaced. Yet he never complains. He stiffly stands in the corner, minding his own business and watching over his small pot still. As you may have surmised, he is a model rather than a real person, but a very special one. He represents Friar John Cor of Lindores Abbey in Fife, who has gone down in history as the first recorded Scottish distiller, featuring in the Exchequer Rolls of 1494.

Five hundred years later, we replicated his still as a timely reminder of how we have progressed since that historic date. Yet the basic concept of distillation remains practically the same today. I am not embarrassed to admit that when I am working with my samples I frequently talk and swear at him. I find his presence and spiritual silence somewhat comforting. Yet on several occasions he has been threatened with redundancy by members of the board, but I have always managed to keep him on. He is very much part of my team.

However, the real spiritual presence is my collection of samples. Every cupboard is filled to capacity with single malts from the Highlands, Lowlands, Campbeltown and Islay, not to mention a wide range of grain and blended whiskies on the many shelves. There are over a thousand samples of every description. These are the tools of my trade; the beginnings of a new blend. Apart from my vast library of reference samples, daily blend and bottling samples arrive from our various distilleries and our Grangemouth bottling plant for evaluation and approval.

Whether I am nosing in the sample room, the warehouse or during a master class presentation, my approach remains the same. I always take a generous measure of the whisky in a crystal copita glass, holding the base tightly between my thumb and forefinger. I consider the colour. Is it young, is it old, is it from a sherry cask or American white oak? But before I consider it too carefully I've thrown it on the floor. Not the glass, of course, just the contents. With this almost sacrilegious act I might have lost some whisky, but I have ensured that any 'foreign' notes that may have been lingering on the rim of the glass have been totally removed. If I am conducting a public tasting, it is also a great way of getting everyone's attention. Especially if you are sitting in the front row!

Before I pour a replacement dram I warn my audience with mock aggression, 'If I ever see you holding a glass with your hand wrapped around it and sniffing it six inches away from your nose – I'll kill you!' You need to keep your hand away from the bowl of the glass as you do not want to warm it. The aromas of the whisky must be allowed to develop naturally, at natural room temperature. Swirling the whisky is enough to awaken its soul. The nose must be almost embedded into the glass, so there is no room for the aromas to escape, except up your nose.

In order to appreciate whisky properly, you should approach it in the same way that professional blenders do. I assess a whisky in just the same manner I would assess a person. I need to get to know them, to communicate with them. And how do I do that? The natural way. I must be patient and in the right frame of mind. I pick up the glass, take a deep breath and close my eyes. I gently raise the glass to my nose and say, 'Hello.' I open my eyes and welcome it. Now I'm looking at the whisky. 'How are you?', I enquire. I swirl the whisky around in the glass and allow the aromas to arise. First to my left nostril, then to my right. At varying times of day one's sensory evaluation will alter in sensitivity from nostril to nostril. The whisky begins to open up. 'Tell me about yourself', I say. Its inner character begins to reveal itself. 'Quite well, thank you very much', replies the whisky. But inevitably it doesn't give away its full identity immediately. After all, you wouldn't expect a new acquaintance to tell you their life story in the first five seconds.

When I am nosing any sample it has to have my full attention. Nothing must distract me from this task. Behind the closed doors of my sample room, I become oblivious to everything except the whisky in front of me. I approach it in the same manner as a tea blender or master perfumer. A woman's perfume is reputed to have at least 26 different nuances, and I expect to find as many in my whisky. There will be top notes, middle notes and base notes, and these will only emerge as I gently swirl the whisky within its copita glass. They will range from metallic, acidic notes right through to fresh fruits and floral nuances.

As Patrick Guedj, creative director of Kenzo Parfums explains, 'One entire year is generally devoted to the perfecting of the scent alone, but it of course depends on the project'. And how does he know when he has got it right? 'When I feel it perfectly matches what I have in mind. But I can only know whether I was right or not once the fragrance is made'. Blenders and perfumers share that moment of reference and excitement when they nose their creation for the first time. Both approach this 'exploration' in the way they feel most comfortable

Unlike many other blenders, I prefer to nose my whisky at its natural strength. Only when I want to get 'deeper' into the whisky's personality will I add a small quantity of still water to tease out any remaining hidden characteristics. Sometimes, particularly with older whiskies, I will even leave the sample in its glass for several hours, or even days, after my initial evaluation as such whiskies may eventually reveal unacceptably musty, stale, off notes. Ultimately, there can be no secrets. I need to know everything about it in order to maximise its potential. By looking at the sample and nosing it I reckon to learn at least 96% of what I need to know about the whisky. Only when I am unsure of its personality will I actually taste it. Before doing this I will reduce it in strength to around 30% abv. Otherwise, a full strength whisky at 65% abv will completely anaesthetise the taste buds.

Unlike wine, Scotch whisky, in most instances, will reflect its aromas on the palate. As far as I am concerned, I expect my palate to confirm my initial olfactory assessment. Like the nose, the tongue is a complex organ, sensitive to a wide variety of tastes. I fill my mouth with whisky, immersing my tongue. I then form a bowl in the centre of my tongue and hold the spirit there for a few seconds to concentrate it, then by raising my tongue to the roof of my mouth the whisky passes over the sides of my tongue and flows beneath it; then by lowering my tongue and forming a bowl again, I bring the whisky back into the centre of the top of my tongue. I always tell an audience that if a whisky has matured for 12 years, the least they can do is give it 12 seconds in their mouth before swallowing. However, when I am working, I usually spit the whisky into a spittoon rather than swallow it. Sometimes, though, a whisky is just too good to waste, and it ends up in my stomach rather than the bucket.

The warmth of the tongue and the act of drawing in some air will help me to fully appreciate the whisky. Regardless of whether it is a well-matured single malt or a young blend, I always ask the same questions. Is the balance right? Is it lacking something and can I help to influence it by allowing it to mature or marry for longer, or by introducing it to other whiskies? It may take up to 40 years to mature a whisky, but it will only take a matter of seconds to recognise and appreciate its qualities. However, for any blender, those few seconds are a distillation of a lifetime's experience and familiarity with whiskies that have become old friends.

Therefore, before I physically create a blend, I will have in mind a reasonable idea of what each component whisky can be expected to bring to it. Nonetheless, in practice what I must do is to combine as many as 25 different whiskies, measuring varying quantities of them one by one into a graduated glass cylinder. Inevitably, adjustments will have to be made. It is a process of trial and error, no matter how experienced the blender may be. It is not just a question of combining different whiskies, but also taking cognisance of cask variations. After all, I am only using whisky from a small range of samples in my 'model' blend. In practice, depending on the size of the actual blend, I may use as many as 50 casks of one component whisky, and within those 50 casks there can a wide range of maturation variants.

Based on the work done with the 'model' blend in my sample room, I arrive at a definitive formulation for the blend. From a handwritten specification, this is officially processed and costed by my colleague Margaret Nicol, the blend controller. Margaret has bravely put up with me for almost 30 years, and brings a wealth of dedication, experience and responsibility to her vital role. Just as importantly, her warm personality and Glaswegian humour help to keep us all sane in times of pressure and stress.

Ultimately, from a one-litre measuring jar, we arrive at a situation where theory is put into full-scale practice, with a 125,000-litre-blend being assembled at our Invergordon blend centre, where the annual throughput is in excess of 30 million litres. However, this is far from being the end of my involvement with the whisky. Many evaluations will be carried out before it is finally bottled.

Blending and what leads up to it is a lengthy, meticulous process, and sometimes I will be asked how long it has taken me to create a particular blend. In the case of something like our 40-year-old, I can honestly say it has taken me 40 years. After all, I have lived with the whiskies which make up this blend since the day they were born. It gives me great satisfaction to watch them develop, come together, marry, be bottled and finally released. But what gives me most satisfaction is the knowledge that they are being appreciated by the consumer. I love to see someone who is deep in conversation raise a glass of blended whisky to their lips, take a mouthful and suddenly become oblivious to everything around them. Their total focus is on the whisky. Nothing else matters. An expression of genuine pleasure then spreads across their face as they savour it. To my mind, this is what the 'art of blending' is really all about.

Chapter Eight
THE SPIRIT OF
THE ISLANDS – JURA

'Scotch whisky has always been at the heart of my life;
from my first visit to the Isle of Jura as a young boy,
opening my first cask as an 18-year-old and receiving
my first copy of Whisky Magazine as an adult.'

} DAMIAN RILEY-SMITH, FOUNDER
AND PUBLISHER, *WHISKY MAGAZINE*

To create a great blended whisky you need many outstanding single malts. It is therefore not surprising that I am often asked which are my favourites. Inevitably, I have fallen in love with many. The list is lengthy, but one malt consistently stimulates and excites me and is truly as individual as they come. I have grown to know it as an old friend as I have had the pleasure of its company through much of my working life. That malt is Isle of Jura.

Although I have never lived on Jura, I have, over the years, visited it on many occasions. It encompasses all of the things I love most. Stunning Scottish scenery, exciting walks, birds of prey, history, wonderful people and, of course, a fabulous distillery. There is something magical about Jura. Whenever I am travelling to the island and catch a glimpse of the three mighty, breast-like 'Paps' looming in the distance, a great warmth comes over me. I am lured by their feminine charms. It is as though I am coming home. Like the Cuillins of Skye, the Paps of Jura are one of the most distinctive features of the Hebridean landscape.

However, this delightful place is sometimes overshadowed by the reputation of its nextdoor neighbour, the 'whisky island' of Islay. It is only a five-minute trip by ferry from Port Askaig on Islay to Feolin on Jura, yet it never ceases to surprise me that comparatively few visitors make the extra short journey to explore the island. Those who do are never disappointed.

The name 'Jura' is said to be derived from the Norse for 'deer island.' However, another version considers it to be linked to the brothers Din and Rah, who came to the island from Denmark, after being exiled for committing a string of violent robberies. The story goes that the brothers fought and killed each other in the village of Knockrome, and two seven-foot-high standing stones were subsequently erected, reputedly with the ashes of the brothers buried beneath. Certainly, this version of the name's origins was current at the time when Martin Martin wrote his *A Description of the Western Islands* in the 1690s. A third version states that the name derives from the large number of yew trees on the island as yew is 'juar' in Gaelic. Whatever the true origin, today Jura certainly remains a sanctuary for deer. According to Gordon Muir of the Astor Estate, there are currently 6,800 deer on the island, and in the rutting season at the end of summer you can hear their great lovelorn bellowings echoing eerily around the hills. Remarkably, deer outnumber the human population by more than 25 to one, and in much of the island you are far more likely to see a deer than a person.

You cannot help but sense the past on Jura. It is everywhere you look. Eight sites of standing stones remain dotted around the island as testament to an ancient and still not fully understood way of life. Archaeological excavations have revealed that the island was occupied from around 8,000 BC. Dr Gary McKay of the Feolin Study Centre declares that, 'Jura is the second holiest island in Scotland after Iona. According to legend its waters were blessed by Columba.'

St Columba was the Irish-born monk who became abbot of Iona in 563 and spread Christianity across much of Scotland. Legend also claims that the people of Jura were very long-lived, which may be attributed to

The Paps of Jura as seen from Kilmory Bay, Knapdale, Argyll. *Courtesy of Allan Wright.*

drinking water from the well of Tobar Leac nam Fiana – which translates as 'the Holy Well with the Stone Monument of Finn'. Presumably Gillour McCraine drank from the Holy Well, as he is reputed to have, 'kept 180 christmasses in his own home and died in the reign of Charles 1.' If this was really the case, the Holy Water must have contained something remarkably special.

Gary McKay obtained a sample of the Tobar Leac nam Fiana water and had it analysed, discovering that it contained the trace mineral selenium, which is considered to have age-defying properties, so maybe there is another 'water of life.'

Those seeking the real *uisge beatha* leave the ferry at Feolin, and head along Jura's 'long road', its one public highway, which runs east and then north for more than 30 miles. This feat of engineering was undertaken by no less a figure than the great Thomas Telford between 1809 and 1812. The first time I visited Jura I foolishly thought I had this bleak and lonely road to myself, and with no policeman on the island I certainly was not worrying about speed limits. However, Jura has its own form of 'sleeping policemen.' I was soon stopped in my tracks by several sheep and cattle which lay on the road, chewing contentedly with no intention of moving for anyone. After all, this was their land.

After avoiding livestock for eight miles the village of Craighouse appears at the foot of the hill, with the Small Isles Bay opening up to the east. Craighouse may be just a small place, but it is the island capital, 'the house of the rock', and the hub of Jura activity. Central to the village is the Jura Hotel, which stands opposite the distillery and looks out across Small Isles Bay. It was in use by 1742 as one of several 'change houses' on the 'long road.' These were inns used by travellers, especially the drovers, who took herds of cattle to market on the mainland. The inns were introduced by royal statute because the old Highland tradition of giving passing travellers food and shelter caused hardship for very poor families. The drovers were hardy characters, used to every hostile environment, but the thought of a dry, warm bed at the end of a long day must have given them some small comfort.

Today, if you want gossip, music, great stories and the hearty company of native *Diurachs*, this is the only place to go. I have spent many a happy evening in the hotel's public bar, chatting to the locals and the many visitors who are attracted to the island. It is also not uncommon to find members of the distillery staff enjoying an off-duty dram there and in days gone by it was surely somewhere that the island's many illicit distillers would meet to barter and sell their raw spirit.

As Peter Youngson writes in *Jura: Island of Deer*, 'Copper stills of 10-gallon capacity could be bought complete with worm, arm and head for under £5 from Campbeltown. Since distilling took nearly a month and co-operative work, largely left to women, was needed among the families of a township,

many widows and spinsters distilled for themselves, or gave their service to local men, which encouraged early marriage.' One hundred and nineteen distilling sites have been identified on Jura by Dr Gary McKay, which is an extraordinarily large number for a comparatively small island. Gordon Wright notes in *Jura's Heritage* (1989), 'One elderly islander remembers being told of one such still being worked by the Ardmenish burn when he was a boy.'

Distilling is said to have been carried on in caves close to Craighouse, and may have been taking place as far back as the 1600s. Accurate information is hard to come by, but the site of the present distillery, owned by the Campbell lairds, was probably first used for whisky making around 1810. However, we have to wait until 1831 for legal confirmation of its existence, when the distillery was officially licensed to William Abercrombie, having been substantially rebuilt by a far-sighted Archibald Campbell. His entrepreneurial spirit and faith in the ongoing prosperity of the whisky industry was clearly justified as there were no fewer than 240 legal Scottish distilleries in operation around that year and on the Hebridean island of Skye, Talisker Distillery had been established between 1830–3.

Nevertheless, Jura Distillery seems to have suffered more than its fair share of financial problems and it was only when James Ferguson & Sons of Glasgow took over the lease in 1876 that relative prosperity was established for what was now known as the Small Isles Distillery and no less than £25,000 was subsequently spent upgrading the plant, giving it a theoretical capacity of 180,000 gallons per year. When Alfred Barnard visited

Jura in the mid-1880s the Fergusons were actually producing 60,000 gallons of spirit per year, only slightly less than Dalmore and Fettercairn were making around the same date. Barnard described the distillery as ' ... one of the handsomest we have seen, and from the bay looks more like a castle than a distillery.'

This apparently idyllic situation was actually far removed from what was going on behind the scenes, with the Fergusons embroiled in a series of lengthy disputes with their Campbell landlords. This all came to a head in 1901, when the Fergusons ceased distilling and proceeded to strip the distillery of its plant. However, this may have had more to do with the prevailing dramatic downturn in the Scotch whisky industry than with squabbles between landlord and tenant.

Maturing stocks of whisky remained in the Jura warehouses for some years, with the last being removed to the mainland in 1913, though the Fergusons continued to pay rent until their lease expired five years later. Legal arguments over the upkeep of the Craighouse pier and various other matters went on for some time afterwards, and in 1920 the laird, Colin Campbell, had the roof of the silent distillery removed in order to avoid paying rates.

The closure of the distillery was a bitter blow for the fragile island economy, with its consequent loss of jobs and much needed income. Visitors staying at the Jura Hotel must have wondered at the bleak scene of devastation before them. Distilling on Jura was at an end, and with the world's economies in turmoil after the First World War there was nothing to suggest whisky making was ever likely to return to the island. It was indeed a sad time for the people of Jura.

Every family on the island must have been affected to some extent, and the Campbells were not immune to this. The inter-war year saw their fortunes failing, and in 1938 Charles Campbell, the last of the Campbell lairds, was forced to sell up and leave the island after 300 years of family residency. Legend has it that an old woman with the second sight once prophesised that the last Campbell on Jura would be a one-eyed man and that when he left all his possessions would be transported away in a single cart pulled by a white horse. Charles Campbell had a glass eye and when he left the island in 1938, everything he took with him did, indeed, fit into one cart. So the prophecy was eerily fulfilled.

One part of the Campbell's Jura estates was sold to the Riley-Smith family, who had made their fortune in the Yorkshire brewing industry. Their purchase comprised 10,000 acres of the Ardfin Estate, in the south of the island, which included the Campbell's former residence of Jura House and a modest inn, which was subsequently developed into the Jura Hotel.

I have had the pleasure of staying in Jura House on several occasions as a guest of Damian Riley-Smith whose great-grandfather acquired the estate before the Second World War. Among his varied business interests Damian numbers the publication of *Whisky Magazine*, the world's leading periodical on the subject. When I first visited Jura House, my immediate impression was that things seemed to have changed very little since the days of the Campbells. Mahogany furniture, stags' heads and old Highland paintings dominated, and when we adjourned to the billiards' room after dinner to smoke cigars and drink whisky, it was like going back to another era. I almost expected an ancient, penguin-suited butler to appear with crystal glasses on a silver tray.

Stepping outside this imposing house there is an immediate sense of tranquillity. This is one of the things I value most about spending time on Jura. Mobile phone reception is virtually non-existent, and the mainland is two ferry journeys away. You feel a true sense of remoteness. Often, when I am sitting in a noisy, bustling airport terminal waiting for a flight to Tokyo, Sydney or San Francisco, I long to feel the fresh, clean air of Small Isles Bay blowing gently across my face.

The tranquillity of Jura has, however, come at a price. Depopulation has long been a problem, due to the lack of employment prospects on the island, and the roofless distillery at Craighouse must have been a constant reminder of better times. Few islanders could have believed that the derelict distillery would ever work again but three men of vision, spirit and substance were determined to do something to help restore the island's prosperity and reverse its falling population. These three men were Tony Riley-Smith, Lord Astor and Robin Fletcher who were all estate owners on the island. To help develop a viable project, they recruited the distillery designer William Delmé-Evans, who had previously created Tullibardine Distillery in Perthshire. He later explained, 'In 1956 I was contacted by Mr Fletcher and Mr Riley-Smith, who wanted to revitalise the island as

Jura distillery in 1955. Note the roofless maltings to the rear.

Jura Lodge, as it is now known, formerly the manager's house, in September 1961 after the maltings had been razed.

the population had dropped to 150.'

As long ago as 1794 Reverend Francis Stewart had recorded that 'The spirit of emigration is still powerful in the island, and requires considerable alterations to extinguish it.' Nonetheless, an 1841 census showed the population of Jura as 1,158 and just a decade later the Reverend Lachlan MacKenzie, parish minister, noted that 'Any decrease in the population of the Parish of Jura since 1841 is to be attributed to the Emigration of a considerable number of families to the United States of America and Canada, and to the removal of a few families and individuals to Greenock and other towns of Scotland.'

This pattern of emigration and depopulation continued right up to the post-war period and Delmé-Evans says, 'We looked at many ways of bringing some type of industry

back to Jura, but in the end we thought it would be better to rebuild the old distillery. 'During 1958 I started designing a new distillery which just about trebled the production capacity of the old one. I designed the stills to give spirit of a "Highland' character", and we ordered malt which was only lightly peated.'

Delmé-Evans worked in association with the architect Lothian Barclay, son of Chivas Brothers' managing director Jimmy Barclay. The two were later to team up again when Scottish & Newcastle Breweries commissioned Glenallachie Distillery on Speyside, and Delmé-Evans also played a little-known role in the design of Macduff Distillery at Banff on the Moray Firth coast. The Isle of Jura Distillery Company Ltd was formed to undertake the project, with financial backing

A still arrives at Craighouse to be installed in the rejuvenated distillery.

from Scottish & Newcastle Breweries Ltd. However, in 1961, Scottish & Newcastle acquired the long established, Leith-based blending firm of Charles Mackinlay & Co Ltd so bringing invaluable distilling experience to the venture.

The distillery construction project had started in 1960, with around 230 building workers moving on to the island. They must have swamped the community, and some locals inevitably had misgivings about their presence. The tranquillity of Jura was disrupted by the sound of trucks, drills and hammering. Delmé-Evans recalled that 'Eventually there were more than 400 men in total, working on the distillery, building houses and enlarging the nearby hotel. The builders worked seven days a week, but we had some terrible times at the weekends, as most of them were either Celtic or Rangers fans and there were some awful fights on Friday and Saturday nights. Jura was an island with no policemen, and the local doctor had to patch men up after encounters in the hotel bar!'

These events were, however, over-shadowed by the many practical frustrations of building a distillery on an island. All construction materials and equipment had to be shipped in from the mainland by sea, and often deliveries were frustrated by the vagaries of the weather. Keeping the development on

eft to right: Lord Polwarth, Tony Riley-Smith, W. McEwan Younger, William Delmé-Evans.

rack demanded the close personal attention f Delmé-Evans, but this was difficult as he ved in the south of England. It says much of he character of the man that in order to vercome this problem, he went to the xtraordinary trouble of learning to fly a rivate plane and constructing a landing strip t Knockrome, three miles from Jura Distillery.

Drawing on his experience at Tullibar-line, Delmé-Evans designed a pair of similar, all, lamp-shaped stills for Jura, and in my pinion they are one of the distillery's most triking features. I love their curvaceous shape, Il 24ft 4¾ inches of them! They are truly a ight to be seen, but not for Delmé-Evans, who

hid them away from the curious public. When I spoke to him about his recollections of Jura shortly before his death in 2003, he made the point that at the time he was designing the distillery in the late 1950s there was no 'curious public' interested in seeing stills, however curvaceous they may have been. Out of their curves came a light, fragrant, yet complex spirit which would complement any premium blend, but in particular the Mackinlay's blend, which was heavily promoted by Scottish & Newcastle Breweries as their 'house' whisky.

It must have been a proud moment for everyone concerned when on 26th April 1963 the distillery was formerly opened by Lord

One of the miniatures of the Mackinlay blend which were given away on the 26th April, 1963 when Lord Polwarth re-opened Jura Distillery.
Courtesy of Neil Wilson.

Polwarth. This was a very important date in the history of the island of Jura, but other men of energy were to follow in the footsteps of Delmé-Evans and his associates. Alan Rutherford, later head of production for United Distillers, succeeded Delmé-Evans as managing director of the Jura Distillery Co Ltd in 1976, and set about upgrading and expanding the plant. He recalls that 'Delmé-Evans was very much of the "old school", so with me being a young, energetic whipper-snapper it was inevitable that we didn't always

see eye to eye. He usually knew how thing worked, but not always why. With m scientific background I felt the need t challenge that. Nevertheless, he was usuall right, and I learnt a great deal from him. On thing that soon became obvious to me was th need for additional production.'

Accordingly, a second pair of stills wa installed in 1979 along with six new stainles steel washbacks and a Lauter mashtun. I order to cope with the requirements of th enlarged distillery, a dam was constructed a Market Loch, from where the distiller obtained its process water. Initially, attempt were made to get building materials to the sit by Land Rover, but when this failed due to th inhospitable nature of the terrain, a helicopte had to be employed for the task.

Alan Rutherford was not the only ne recruit to Jura Distillery, however. A youn man from Coatbridge in Lanarkshire name Willie Tait also made the long journey to th island. Unlike many of his predecessors, h stayed, going on to become distillery manage 'The prime aim for the distillery project was t increase the population of the island, and n locals were employed at the beginning,' h remembers. 'I was working for Inver Hous Distillers at Airdrie, not far from Glasgow, i the maltings, which was the dirtiest job I'v ever done. I was ready for a change, and I sav an advert in the *Daily Record* which sai 'Distillery worker required, west coast o Scotland', and gave a PO box number. I' always loved the west coast, so I sent in a application, not giving it much more thought and only casually mentioning it to my wife Christine. However, a month later Delmé Evans turned up unexpectedly at my house while I was out at work. It was important for him to see what kind of family he was going to bring to the island and the only way to do this was visit the home. He talked to Christine, who was there with our baby son, Scott, and arranged to come back to interview me the following week.

'He told me that the job was for a tunroom man at Jura Distillery and we decided the best thing to do would be to go and take a look at the place before making a final decision. Delmé met us off the ferry in his old Rover, and I was really excited about the prospect of living and working on an island, but I wasn't sure Christine shared my enthusiasm.

'I'd never even heard of Jura', she recollects. 'One of the first things I did was look it up on a map, and it seemed a very long way away. I was certainly apprehensive. The journey seemed to take forever, and when we eventually got to the island, as Delmé drove us to the distillery the 'long road' certainly lived up to its name. I thought we were never going to get there and I kept wondering where all the houses were. It was all so empty and bleak and all we saw on the journey were deer.'

The magical feeling that attracted me to Jura had already cast its spell on Willie. 'I fitted in almost immediately', he remembers. 'The people were very warm. Airdrie seemed a million miles away and what made life on Jura so different was that there was literally no escape. But then I didn't want to escape. However, I wasn't so sure about Christine!'

'There were many times when I was lonely and homesick and missed the comforts and conveniences of mainland life', she recalls. 'Even things like constant hot water! It was only when Scott started going to nursery school that I really got to meet people and make friends. It certainly wasn't love at first sight, but in the end I did grow to love the island and its people.'

However, not every newcomer felt the same, and many did seek to escape. Willie makes the point that the policy of attracting new blood to the island was not entirely successful. 'It carried on for several years until it became obvious that people were not staying. The average time was about two years. To my mind, most people come to these remote islands hoping to escape from whatever. But island life turns out not always to be to their liking and they leave.'

Today, most of the Jura workforce is made up of native islanders, with the distillery providing significant employment, and with the growth of 'whisky tourism' it has been responsible for bringing many visitors to the island. Attracting people to live and work on Jura remains a constant challenge. One of the difficulties faced by anyone wishing to live there is that 40% of its houses are currently used as holiday homes, lying empty for all but a few weeks of the year. Unfortunately, this creates a shortage of permanent accommodation, leading to inflated property prices.

Even back in the 1970s accommodation was an issue on Jura, and Willie and Christine lived in no fewer than five different houses. By the time they had their fifth house, Willie had graduated through the key roles of mashman and stillman to become assistant manager in 1979. These were heady years for the Scotch whisky industry, with near-record production levels of spirit. Whisky warehouses the length and breadth of Scotland were bulging with whisky. However, difficult times lay ahead.

9th May 1996. The 33rd reunion of the opening of Jura Distillery in 1963. Back row, left to right: David Birrell, Chris Greig, Islay Davie, Tony Riley-Smith, Geoffrey Whittaker, Lothian Barclay, Alex Davie. Front row, left to right: Donald Mackinlay, Willie Tait, Florence Whittaker, Anne Greig, William Delmé-Evans, Jean Mackinlay, Betty Evans, Mary McIver, Sylvia Barclay.

Due to those bulging warehouses, the early 1980s saw major rationalisation of the Scotch whisky industry, and every distillery came under the accountants' microscope. Making whisky is an expensive business in any location, but the costs increase significantly on a remote island such as Jura. Inevitably, if cutbacks were to be made, distilleries like Jura were most vulnerable. Indeed, the distillery did go onto a three-day working week in the early 1980s, and subsequently closed down completely for one year. However, in 1985 Invergordon Distillers transformed the plant's fortunes when it purchased Jura Distillery along with Charles Mackinlay & Co Ltd. In the same year Willie

Tait also became distillery manager, carrying on the good work of his predecessors Murdo McIver, Don Raitt and John Bulman.

According to Invergordon's former group managing director Chris Greig, 'We wanted to buy the Mackinlay company from Scottish & Newcastle for its Mackinlay and Cluny blended brands. Jura and Glenallachie distilleries came with it.

'In common with the rest of the distilling industry, we did go through some hard financial times, but we were in the business for the long term. One of the advantages we had with Jura was that we already owned Bruichladdich on Islay, so we were able to manage overheads more efficiently by

The staff of Jura Distillery 1994. Standing, left to right: Kenneth Cameron, Willie Cochrane (brewer), Courtney Warnock, Davie Miller, Graham Logan, Ian Cameron, Willie Tait, (manager), Duncan Buie. Seated, left to right: Nigel Boardman, Ian Keith, Billy Dundas. Kirsty the dog (works in the cooperage!)

combining a level of dual employment, particularly with warehousing staff.'

Having acquired Jura, Invergordon had no intention of pouring the entire output of its new distillery into the blending vats, and positioned it among the growing ranks of single malts. Certainly from 1985 onwards, Jura was being promoted in a serious way for the very first time, and its distinctive, squat, 'waisted' bottle was an eye-catching feature. Jura's status as the island's only distillery was a marketing godsend, and an outline map of the island duly appeared on the bottle label.

If the bottle was eye-catching, so too was the company and its vast stocks, especially those from Invergordon Grain Distillery. In August 1991 Whyte & Mackay launched a takeover bid for the Invergordon Group. After a prolonged and bitterly contested battle, Invergordon finally fell to Whyte & Mackay in October 1993, with Jura being one of five distilleries included in this purchase. From a personal point of view, I was excited to have a single malt of such individuality at my disposal, but I was also looking to the longer term, where I could see older expressions of Jura being developed for the market, provided I was able to source the most compatible casks which would enhance some of the spirit's rare flavours over time. Inevitably, this meant that I developed a close relationship with the Jura team, initially under Willie Tait. When Willie departed to manage Fettercairn in July 1999 we needed someone who would continue the same level of dedicated commitment, not only to the distillery but to island life as a whole.

We were fortunate to find this in the shape of Mickey Heads, who had worked as mashman, stillman and brewer at Laphroaig from 1979, before crossing the Sound of Islay to join us. One of the advantages of employing a native 'Ileach' in this position was that Mickey was already familiar with the rhythms and routines of island life. Moving to Jura was unlikely to be a great culture shock. Nonetheless, as he recalls, 'On my first Sunday on Jura I thought I'd have a quiet, relaxing time. I didn't know anybody and I walked down into the village and went to the island's only shop for a Sunday newspaper. "There's no Sunday papers", the assistant announced. "Welcome to Jura!" Some of the guys were sitting outside the pub drinking their pints, and they bought me one. So I didn't get a Sunday paper but I did get a pint … '

'Jura Distillery is crucial to the island', he declares. 'It's the focal point. People have an identity with it. The distillery is the island and the island is the distillery. The locals take a real pride in it. It's "their" brand.'

Like his predecessors, Mickey fitted well into Craighouse and understood the interdependency of community life. This extended to the world of distilling rivals, as he explains. 'All the managers of the Islay and Jura distilleries are automatically members of the "Condenser Club", which meets for dinner once a year. If any of us have a problem with a piece of plant or whatever, the others are always very good at helping out, loaning equipment until we get it fixed.'

Mickey was now one of 'the elite', along with the local doctor and the minister. Latterly, he even became involved with the Jura Development Trust, an organisation set up to promote and develop the ongoing viability of the island. One of the highlights of Mickey's time at the helm of Jura was developing the visitor centre. 'It was only really in the 1980s that visitors started coming over to Islay and Jura distilleries in any numbers', he notes. While Mickey was making a success of the visitor centre I was busy preparing new Jura single malt expressions which would be very much part of this venture.

No matter what innovative styles may be created, everything relates back to wood. From my early professional associations with Jura in the mid-1990s, it soon became apparent that a consistent wood management policy would have to be put in place. The casks in which Jura was being matured varied considerably in quality, with the result that much of the spirit was lacking body and charm. But there were exceptions, and when it was good, Jura was very good indeed, especially in the older expressions. I wanted to increase the body, supported by warm, floral, buttery notes, and to do this for whiskies that would be bottled as our standard ten-year-old we began to vat and re-cask quantities of spirit in fresh, bourbon wood.

One of my prime objectives is to maintain the individual style of Jura. Delmé-Evans declared that he set out to produce spirit of a 'Highland character', but to me Jura is more specifically like a malt from the Spey valley. However, many potential consumers jump to the erroneous conclusion that it is going to resemble an Islay in style when they discover how close the distillery's location is to the 'whisky island'. What is not often taken into account is the great height and surface area of Jura's stills. They are some of the tallest in Scotland, which leads to a considerable degree of reflux.[14]

If asked to describe the essential character of our ten-year-old Jura, I would say it has a zest, a tang of excitement about it. There is a freshness of sea spray, pine and gorse, balanced by a buttery, nutty, vanilla character that comes from the use of American white oak casks. But look out, too, for a seductive, flirtatious, floral side to it.

There is also a whisper of peat lurking in the background, which is not surprising considering that the island of Jura boasts significant deposits of peat. This was brought home to me in forceful fashion during my first visit to Jura, many years ago. I was not exactly spoilt for choice when it came to hotels, as there was only one on the entire island. Running a bath on the evening of my arrival I hoped to feel refreshed before dinner. I certainly was not prepared for the sight that greeted me as the water level slowly rose. It was as though I about to step into a bath of treacle. Who knew what might be lurking beneath the surface? Naturally, I thought there was a fault, and reported it to reception. 'Ach, that's just the peaty water here on Jura', I was told. 'It's grand stuff really, and it'll do you no harm!'

14 During distillation some of the heavier flavours with comparatively high boiling points condense from vapour back into liquid form before leaving the still and are redistilled. This is known as reflux, and the greater the degree of reflux the lighter and 'cleaner' the spirit produced. Short, squat stills produce little reflux, compared to tall, slender stills. The angle at which the lyne arm is attached also affects the levels of reflux.

Over a few drams in the bar later, some of the locals laughed at my reaction to the murky bathwater. After all, it had been a feature of island life for as long as anyone could remember, and it did not seem to have done anyone any harm. They told me too, that it was considered unlucky on Jura to cut peats during the month of April, rather than May. This set me thinking. Surely, the old Jura Distillery of the 19th century would have produced heavily peated whiskies much like those of Islay? There was really no reason why we could not distil heavily peated whiskies once again. All we needed was a high phenol level in our malt, and Port Ellen Maltings on Islay were happy to supply this to us.

We have been distilling batches of this heavily peated Jura since 1999, and the locals always know when we are making it, thanks to the heavy aroma that hangs over Craighouse. A number of different bottling have been marketed as single malts, but the majority of this spirit is used to create one of my favourite Jura expressions, Superstition. This has proved one of our most popular Jura bottlings, and takes its name from the notion that cutting peat on Jura during April would bring bad luck. The number 13 has superstitious connotations, and, accordingly, the idea of 'superstition' was further emphasised by using malt whiskies from 13 to 21 years of age, but with the addition of 13% of heavily peated spirit distilled from 1999 onwards. In the spirit of the theme we ensured the first vatting took place on Friday 13th September and was bottled on Friday 13th December. With all the superstitious elements surrounding this whisky's production, everyone involved was keeping their fingers crossed that nothing untoward would happen, and fortunately that proved to be the case.

The Superstition bottle carries the emblem of the Ankh cross, which symbolises the key of life, and dates from Egyptian times. It reputedly gives immortality to those who wear it, and it helps to evoke a sense of mystery in the whisky. What makes Superstition stand out from the rest of the Jura range is the complex phenolic aromas and flavours, which drift attractively in the background on the nose and palate. Additionally, notes of honey and marzipan are contributed by the 21-year-old Jura spirit included in the whisky's overall composition.

People often ask me what is the best way to enjoy whisky, and I always reply that it depends very much on mood and circumstances. But for me, many whiskies are at their very best when drunk in the open air, close to their places of creation. Talisker is a wonderful whisky in any circumstances, but the Skye malt is surely at its best when consumed on the shores of Loch Harport with the dramatic Cuillins as a backdrop. Similarly, Ardbeg from Islay, Ledaig from Mull and Pulteney from Wick are all whiskies that I feel have an intangible extra dimension when drunk out of doors. Perhaps the best example, however, is Jura Superstition. The combination of peaty, spicy whisky which has spent long years in wood and the cold, biting wind and sea spray that so often characterise the Jura landscape make perfect partners.

This was reinforced on an unforgettable occasion a few years ago when I set out to climb one of the Paps of Jura in company with Mickey Heads and my twin brother, Russell. The mist hung low that morning, but when we finally reached the top it was as though the

world had opened up to us. Not only could we see the whole of Jura, and the clear outline of Islay to the south, but even as far as Ireland. It was a breathtaking sight. Standing there, tired but exhilarated, with a cold wind whipping at our faces, there really was only one way to celebrate our shared achievement. Mickey reached into his rucksack and produced a bottle of Superstition. He pulled the cork and we handed the bottle round, each taking a generous mouthful. No whisky ever seemed so appropriate to its landscape. It was the perfect accompaniment to a memorable day.

We were proud of our achievement in reaching the top of the Pap, but we had climbed it at a leisurely pace, taking a couple of hours. However, when it comes to the annual Fell Race, held each May, the pace is altogether hotter. Competitors travel from all over the world to participate in this famous event. We may have climbed one Pap in two hours, but the record time taken to climb all three Paps of Beinn á Chaolais, Beinn an Oir and Beinn Shiantaidh[15] and four other peaks, is a remarkable three hours, six minutes and 59 seconds! This outstanding feat was recorded in 1994 by Mark Rigby. In total the fell race encompasses 16 miles and 7,500 feet of climbing, and was originally staged in the early 1970s, being revitalised in 1983 by Donald Booth, who still attends each running of it. Taking part must be exhilarating and daunting in equal measure, and for the distant spectator there is an element of excitement and awe as the runners spill down the scree-clad slopes like a herd of deer.

15 Peak of the Narrows or Sound, Peak of the Edge/Gold, Peak of Storms.

A fishing boat enters the Gulf of Corryvreckan on the ebb tide as the Atlantic Ocean floods through into the Sound of Jura. *Courtesy of Neil Wilson.*

almost claimed by Corryvreckan was the writer George Orwell, who produced much of his best-known novel *Nineteen Eighty-Four* while living at Barnhill on the island in the late 1940s. In August 1947 Orwell and various family members and friends were caught in the whirlpool when returning from a camping trip by boat. The small vessel overturned, shipwrecking them on the uninhabited island of Eilean Mór, from where they were subsequently rescued by a passing fishing boat. The adventure ended with Orwell and his companions having to make a three-mile barefoot trek back to Barnhill.

Barnhill is located in the far north of the island, some six miles after the 'Long Road' becomes little more than a track. The cottage was not the easiest of places to get to, as I discovered for myself when I visited it some years ago. As I approached, I felt a sense of Orwell's presence, and could almost hear the click-clack of his typewriter, interspersed with the occasional cough and curse. Life in a remote cottage on a frequently damp Scottish island did little for Orwell's health, and he was already suffering from tuberculosis, but he was determined to finish what has become one of the great novels of the 20th century. *Nineteen Eighty-Four* was completed in December 1948, two years before Orwell's untimely death, and it is often erroneously assumed that the title is merely an inversion of the numbers 'four' and 'eight.' However, the title actually derives from the fact that the novel's central character Winston Smith was supposed to be 36 years old when the novel was completed. 48 plus 36 equals 84.

Orwell was known to be fond of a drink, but rather than the produce of the local

I don't suppose the runners have much time to appreciate the views from the top of the Paps, but when I climbed Beinn an Oir with Mickey and Russell we were able to stop and marvel at the natural phenomenon that is the Gulf of Corryvreckan; a giant maelstrom which lies between the north coast of Jura and the island of Scarba. It has the reputation of being one of the most powerful and dangerous whirlpools in Europe and was noted by Martin Martin in *A Description of the Western Islands* around 1695. Martin wrote, 'The sea begins to boil and ferment with the tide of flood, and resembles the boiling of a pot ... This gulf hath its name from Brekan, said to be son to the King of Denmark, who was drowned here, cast ashore in the north of Jura, and buried in a cave, as appears from the stone, tomb, and altar there.'

Another notable figure whose life was

Barnhill, where George Orwell wrote 1984. *Courtesy of Allan Wright.*

distillery, his preferred tipple was Lamb's Navy Rum. When he had been teaching at Southwold in Suffolk he had made not very successful attempts to distil alcohol from treacle, but there is no evidence that he tried anything similar on Jura. With Jura enjoying such a distinguished link with the great novelist, it seemed only fitting that we should produce a commemorative bottling of Jura single malt to celebrate this association.

'Isle of Jura 1984' was intended to reflect the complex character of Orwell and the vividness of his prose. In order to achieve this I used a combination of different cask types, principally ex-sherry butts from the Gonzalez Byass' bodegas in Jerez. Crucial to the style I wanted to create were aged Olorosos, namely Vina 2 and Apostoles casks. The age of the Jura single malts included was linked to Orwell's novel, in that much of the component whisky was distilled in 1984, along with some parcels from 1980 and 1982. This was because alternative titles considered by Orwell were *Nineteen Eighty* and *Nineteen Eighty-Two*. All these individual aged whiskies were vatted and married, finally being reduced to 42% – half of 84! It was bottled on 10th June 2003, in line with the date of the publishing of *Nineteen Eighty-Four* in 1949. The whisky finally being launched in June 2003, exactly one hundred years after Orwell's birth.

The launch took place in the gardens of Jura House on a glorious, sunny day, and I recall the scent of a profusion of different flowers filling the air and complementing the aromas of the whisky as we sampled it. The floral scents of Isle of Jura 1984 were accompanied by rich, nutty, citrus flavours, with subtle hints of Christmas pudding, spicy nutmeg, cinnamon and liquorice. All lingered long on the palate as we toasted a great writer and his contribution to the heritage of the Isle of Jura.

This was one of many tastings of Jura whisky to take place on the island, not least because for more than ten years Jura Distillery has taken part in the annual *Feis Ile*, or Islay Festival of Music & Malt, staged every late May. This has become one of the most important and eagerly anticipated events in the Scotch whisky calendar, with barely a bed to be had on the islands during the week-long event. It is a time when all the rival whisky distillers come together as one to promote the islands and their most famous export. Each distillery has a designated open day, and usually Jura's falls on the Thursday. In common with many of the participating distilleries, Jura tries to offer a new expression every year in order to further stimulate interest in the brand and provide a new experience for regular festival devotees. All members of distillery and visitor centre staff are closely involved in ensuring the success of the occasion, and keep one eye on the weather forecast as the open day approaches. However, such is the enthusiasm and commitment of the festival-goers that even the heaviest of downpours fails to dampen their spirit.

That enthusiasm is often translated into dancing, drinking and the telling of tales in Craighouse Village Hall and in the nearby Jura Hotel. It is a time of great conviviality for both visitors and locals alike and many enduring friendships are formed over several drams. People come not just to taste whisky but to taste island life. And in their few days on the islands, many become captivated by the place, its people and the fascinating stories and legends that are recounted. Some are ancient, others are modern, but all are part of the rich folklore that has helped to form and maintain Jura's identity around the world.

One of the enduring tales of Jura concerns those famous Scottish clans, the Campbells and the McLeans. The Campbells were, for many centuries, the most powerful family on Jura, and traditionally, the McLeans who were based in the north of the island were great enemies of the Campbells in the south. The story goes that in 1647 a group of McLeans at Glen Garrisdale were caught by Campbells while swimming and were therefore without their weapons. All of them were killed, except for one man who swam out into the bay and hid on a rock. A skull, known as McLean's skull, was visible at Glen Garrisdale for many years, sheltered from the weather under an overhanging cliff. The skull, reputedly turned up while ploughing a field, had a cut in it as though made by a sword.

At some stage, the skull was transferred to an Edinburgh museum and placed in a glass case. However, on several occasions when the museum staff entered the gallery first thing in the morning, the skull was found on the floor, and there were even lurid stories of it gnashing its teeth and jumping up and down! Eventually, this restless spirit had to be returned to its native soil, and it remained at Glen Garrisdale until 1976, when it mysteriously disappeared, never to be seen again.

A much more modern Jura tale concerns the occasion when Bill Drummond and Jimmy Cauty of the techno band KLF drew £1 million from a bank in South Croydon on 23rd August 1994 and flew by chartered plane to the island. They proceeded to burn the money in a derelict boathouse at Ardfin, close to Jura House, videoing the event for prosperity. Jura was chosen as the location for this bizarre and controversial event because Jimmy Cauty had been a teenage friend of Francis Riley-Smith, son of local landowner Tony Riley-Smith. As *The Guardian* observed in a feature about Jura published in August 2006, 'The KLF's motivation was to rid themselves of the gains they'd made out of an ugly music industry they'd found it so easy to manipulate. They'd successfully accrued a fortune from releasing records that varied from the sublime (Tammy Wynette singing on 'Justified and Ancient') to the downright charmless ('Doctoring the Tardis' which sampled Gary Glitter and Sweet). Understandably, this was – and still is – a little outside the average Hebridean's comprehension.'

Another intriguing Jura story, but one that was certainly not captured on film, concerns the rumoured visit of Christine Keeler and Mandy Rice-Davies to the Astor estate during the Profumo Scandal of 1963. John Profumo was Secretary of State for War in Harold Macmillan's Conservative government and resigned after admitting lying to the House of Commons about his relationship with the 'showgirl' Christine Keeler. Profumo had first met Keeler at a house party hosted by Lord Astor at his Cliveden estate in Buckinghamshire in 1961. At the height of the 'Scandal' two years later, Christine Keeler and her friend and flatmate Mandy Rice-Davies were supposed to have spent time on Astor's Jura estate to escape the attentions of the media. More than four decades later it seems impossible to establish whether their visit ever really took place. The natives of Jura have always respected people's privacy. The Profumo affair led to the premature resignation of premier Harold Macmillan due to ill-health, and undoubtedly discredited the Conservative government of the day.

The Astor connection with Jura remains significant from a political perspective even today, as Conservative party leader David Cameron and his family regularly holiday at Tarbert Lodge in the remote peninsula of Rubha nan Crann (Rock of the Mast.) The Lodge is owned by Samantha Cameron's stepfather, Viscount Astor. 'I fish and try to catch the odd sea trout or mackerel', says Cameron. 'It's a wonderful place, and I love swimming in the sea off Scotland. I don't mind cold water and there are really beautiful beaches up there. The quality of the peace and quiet you get is fantastic.'

Jura is obviously not immune to the scandals and sensations of the outside world, which generate lurid tabloid headlines and cause money markets to rise and fall, but nevertheless it offers a sanctuary of calmness in an ever more manic world. This is the principal reason why Jura and its people will always be so special to me. Clearly, I am far from alone in my love of the island. For me, former distillery manager Willie Tait sums it up perfectly: 'I missed Jura very much when I left. It still feels like home when I go back now. Everybody knows where they really belong, and for me that is Jura.'

Chapter Nine
FULLY MATURED

'I'm not in business to be popular, I'm in business to be effective. You can't bank popularity, you can only bank cashflow.' } VIVIAN IMERMAN, EARLCROWN LTD

The Paps may dominate the island of Jura, but back in 2003 one individual dominated the Whyte & Mackay landscape. His name was Vivian Imerman. His first involvement with the company had come at the time of the management buyout in October 2001, when the company's name was changed to Kyndal. Along with his brother-in-law Robert Tchenguiz, Imerman had been responsible for providing £20 million of 'mezzanine' finance through the Rotch Property Group.

By 2003, Kyndal was clearly not meeting its financial targets and urgently required new impetus and a fresh direction. Accordingly, with the departure of Brian Megson, Vivian Imerman was appointed chairman and chief executive in February of that year, going on to strengthen his control of the organisation by building up his personal shareholding during the succeeding years. Inevitably this was not a happy time for Whyte & Mackay's staff. I always look back on this particular time as our 'blue period.' To my mind, our blue bottle label was boring and did not convey the right message of quality and heritage. We all recognised the need for change and with Imerman's reputation as a very astute businessmen and his philosophy of 'I fight to win', at least we had a chance.

Imerman had been born in South Africa, the grandson of Russian immigrants and had begun working for his grandfather when only 12 years old. At the age of 20 he started his own business trading in chemicals, no doubt influenced by his father's career as a chemist. His father obviously recognised his ambition at an early age, as Imerman recalls being told, 'With your confidence you can conquer the world.'

He started to study business law, but abandoned the degree due to lack of time, moving into 'insurance salvage' products. This involved buying goods damaged during transportation and selling them for a keen profit after overseeing their repair. From this trade he began to sell pharmaceutical goods, listing his company on the South African stock exchange in 1987. However, the move that propelled him beyond the South African business stage was his acquisition of Del Monte Foods International in 1993. Eight years later he sold the company for an enterprise value of approximately 600m euros. Despite this success, Imerman remained hungry for further business adventures, which led to his major involvement with the management buyout that created Kyndal. 'It's not just about the money', he says, 'it's about playing the game and winning each milestone of that game.'

For him Kyndal was another opportunity, but this time it was a golden opportunity. In the meantime, there were some hard decisions to be made. If the company was to become profitable once more cutbacks were inevitable and overall productivity would have to improve. One obvious anomaly was that the company operated two bottling halls when in reality one modernised plant would have been sufficient. Our failure to address this had been a major logistical weakness for many years. On the other hand, Vivian Imerman not only recognised the problem, but had the courage to do something about it, ultimately closing the former Invergordon Distillers Leith bottling plant, despite the loss of nearly 200 jobs. 'This wasn't an easy decision to make', recalls Imerman, 'but it was one of those milestone decisions that had to be made if the company was to survive and prosper'. The closure of Leith was a long and slow process, with our Grangemouth bottling facility also being totally redeveloped to meet the technological demands of the 21st century.

Imerman may have had his critics, but one measure that did receive almost universal support was his decision to ditch the Kyndal identity in October 2003 and revert to the old name of Whyte & Mackay Ltd. Other welcome changes were in the area of packaging, where it was recognised that if we wanted to increase our market share we would have to raise our profile. The principal problem was our range of whiskies lacked cohesion in terms of presentation. There was no Whyte & Mackay 'family' which reflected the heritage and quality of the product. This applied both to our blends and to our Jura and Dalmore single malts. In my view, a number of rival distillers had already managed to create very positive identities, which carried across every expression they released. Each bottle of Johnnie Walker, for example, was clearly identifiable as such on a retailer's shelf, regardless of whether it was Red, Black, Gold, Green or Blue. The same could be said of Glenfiddich, which retained its distinctive triangular bottle shape and label design with every new presentation they launched. This demonstrates a great degree of confidence in their brand image, which is still effective to this day, despite many changes in the marketplace.

What Johnnie Walker and Glenfiddich had in common was their retention of the original bottle design, whereas Whyte & Mackay had lost much of its heritage and originality along the way. In order to restore key elements of that heritage, we re-examined the very earliest Whyte & Mackay bottles from the 19th century, using James Whyte and Charles Mackay's original design of 'dump-shaped' bottle as our inspiration. The word 'Glasgow' had been proudly embossed on the shoulder of the early bottles, and we reintroduced that feature to emphasise our enduring roots in this great city, along with the letters 'W&M', which would still identify our whisky, even when the bottle was turned upside down in a bar gantry.

But crucial to the re-branding was the famous red, double-lion logo. Since 1998, the lions had been separated and portrayed in gold rather than red, but in our new presentation they reverted to their original form, side by side and facing in the same direction. The significance of the lions relates to the battle of Glen Fruin, which took place in 1603 near Loch Lomond between men of the notorious Clan MacGregor, whose emblem was a *single* lion, and Clan Colquhoun. As many as 200 Colquhouns were slaughtered and King James VI of Scotland was so outraged by this that he outlawed the Clan MacGregor, whose members became known as 'the children of the mist.' Many were forced to change their names in order to survive, and one of the names frequently chosen was 'Whyte.' When James Whyte and Charles Mackay combined in business they chose to use the lion motif on the label of the whisky they created. Indeed they used two lions, one representing the emblem of his ancestral MacGregor clan and the other the 'lion rampant' of Scotland. These symbolised their partnership and the manner in which they 'double-married' their blend (see page 148).

I was strongly in favour of these changes,

GOODNESS NOSE

which helped to restore Whyte & Mackay's historical identity, but the redesign went a stage further. In recognition of another great Glasgow partnership, that of architect and designer Charles Rennie Mackintosh and his wife Margaret Macdonald, the radically redesigned label used symbols and typography in the innovative style made internationally famous by 'Toshie' in the late 19th century. At last we had a new label which we could all be proud of, but more importantly it gained greater consumer appeal.

Mackintosh is renowned for taking design to new heights, but one other Scottish architect practising at the same time, who was equally innovative in a different field, was Charles Chree Doig who was born in Angus in 1855, the son of a Kirriemuir labourer. He had shown early talent as an architect, ultimately setting up his own practice in Elgin and became intimately involved in the design of new distilleries, particularly on Speyside and also worked on the upgrading and extension of many existing ones, most notably Glenlivet, with which his family enjoyed a 65-year association. As the late Graham Nown wrote in *The Keeper* magazine many years ago, 'Throughout his career, Doig designed everything asked of him – kilns, warehouses, cottages, gaugers' houses, tunrooms, still-rooms and entire distilleries, improving and perfecting production methods as he went.'

He also drew up plans for the renowned Craigellachie Hotel in the whisky heartland of Speyside, and in 1902 this most resourceful and versatile of designers even patented a revolutionary fire-extinguishing system which could be fitted throughout distillery buildings. But Doig's greatest contribution to the Scotch

whisky industry was the revolutionary Chinese-style 'pagoda head'. Previously, the roofs of distillery maltings had been equipped with revolving, conical cowls like cardinals' hats which were the norm to be seen atop the oasthouses of Sussex and Kent. These facilitated the removal of smoke from the kiln below, but were aesthetically unappealing.

Doig's new design was a kiln chimney which attracted air from all directions to provide a better 'draw' for the kiln fire beneath. It also had the advantage of being considerably more attractive. Doig's innovation was born at a site meeting at Dailuaine Distillery, a mile from Aberlour, on 3rd May 1889. It subsequently became a trademark of distilleries the length and breadth of Scotland, and remains so to this day. Whenever I am travelling north on the A9 road towards Inverness and drive over Drumochter Pass on a miserable, dull day nothing lifts my spirits more than the distant sight of Dalwhinnie Distillery with its twin, copper-coloured pagoda heads glinting through the gloom.

As with the Andrew Usher lunch I had organised in 2002 to celebrate the achievements of the 'father of blending', I wanted to do something to commemorate the life and work of Charles Doig. By 2003 Doig had largely been forgotten, which seemed to me quite disgraceful. Surely something had to be done. Accordingly, I organised a walk from Fettercairn Distillery to nearby Auchenblae, where the distillery Doig designed in 1896 is now a private house, owned by the Forbes family. The walk was a round trip of some 23 miles, taking in parts of Gladstone's Fasque Estate and Fettercairn House lands. The

Dailuaine Distillery, where Charles Doig created the first 'pagoda head' malting kiln in May 1889.

at McTear's in Glasgow, and fetched a magnificent total of £8,000. That money went towards the creation of a scale model pagoda head, designed by Highland Spirit of Elgin and destined for installation in the Scotch Whisky Experience in Edinburgh. My fervent hope is this will act as a permanent and richly deserved memorial to an unjustly neglected whisky icon.

Just as Doig predicted at the turn of the 20th century, excessive whisky stocks brought to an end the period of distilling prosperity that had provided him with so many opportunities to grace the landscape with examples of his craft. In 2003, surplus stock was once again a cause for concern. This situation had been developing since the late 1970s, and despite swingeing distillery cutbacks and

participants comprised an invited group of distillers, blenders and whisky-lovers, each of whom had been asked to bring a rare, signed bottle of whisky from their own distillery or company. These were subsequently auctioned

The Charles Doig Commemorative Walk from Fettercairn Distillery in 2003, with the Auchenblae Distillery replica pagoda head in the background. From left to right: Dennis Malcolm, Abby Stephen, Russell Paterson, Alistair McIntosh, Maureen Robinson, Dave Doig, John Brydie, Willie Tait, Richard Paterson, Fraser Hughes, John Miller, Scott Traynor, Donald Renwick, Ian Millar, Woody, Neil Cameron.

Auchenblae Distillery staff, 1924–5. *Courtesy of Gavin D. Smith.*

closures, the problem had never entirely gone away. In the industry we talk about fluctuating production cycles as 'seven years up, seven years down', only this one was to last longer. With sluggish exports it was a 'buyer's market', and supermarkets were therefore able to acquire 'own label' stock very cheaply.

But there was a feeling in the industry that at last the tide was about to turn in favour of the producers; the crucial question was 'when?' At the time of the Kyndal management buy-out in 2001, managing director Brian Megson had anticipated an upturn in the market, but unfortunately for us all, his gamble did not pay off. Far from rising, prices continued to fall. One man who read the situation very shrewdly, however, was Vivian Imerman, whose ultimate aim was to take full personal control of the company. 'I shall never forget the day I first visited Invergordon Distillery', he recalls, 'and saw the thousands of casks maturing, which contained millions of litres of spirit. I realised the huge future potential of its worth when the markets began to rise, as I was sure they would. It all goes in cycles. Economic fundamentals drive them.'

With the financial backing of Bank of Scotland Corporate, Imerman was finally able to achieve his ambition in February 2005. This was a huge vote of confidence by the Bank of Scotland in Whyte & Mackay and perhaps in the wider Scotch whisky industry as well

They, too, were sensing better times ahead. One of the sure signs of optimism came through the single malt market, which had shown steady growth since the latter years of the 1990s. Consumers in this sector had money in their pockets and were prepared to pay a premium for quality products.

However, not all were about to part with the same amount of cash as the customer who walked into the Pennyhill Park Hotel, near Bagshot in Surrey, and spent a reputed £32,000 on one bottle of our 62-year-old Dalmore Single Highland Malt. This was a world record amount for a bottle of whisky purchased on licensed premises rather than at auction, and the great thing was that the customer sat down with his friends and proceeded to enjoy drinking the whole bottle. I was delighted that such rare whisky was being drunk and shared rather than gathering dust on a collector's shelf. They were drinking liquid history. The whole episode generated a great deal of positive publicity, and encouraged us to consider creating more rare and prestigious products in future.

One executive who was intimately involved in developing our brands was Bob Brannan, appointed as group managing director in March 2005. Bob joined the company from William Grant & Sons Ltd, and I was very encouraged by this appointment, because for the first time in many years we had someone in this position with a strong and broad-based business background, but who also understood Scotch whisky. He, too, sensed the optimism and excitement that was developing within the industry.

The momentum of change at Whyte &

Mackay carried on with a move to new offices within our existing Glasgow headquarters, while over on the island of Jura the former distillery manager's neglected house was transformed into the vibrant and eclectically furnished Jura Lodge venue, intended for entertaining selected guests and accommodating participants in Jura's 'Whisky School', promoted by former manager Willie Tait. Despite the remoteness of Islay and Jura, more visitors than ever were finding their way to the islands, and we wanted to play our part in encouraging their exploration of the distilleries and their malts.

This was part of an international trend to bring consumers and producers closer together. An ever-growing number of whisky festivals in all parts of the world, from South Africa to Sweden and Tokyo to San Francisco, have helped to foster an increasing passion for whisky, and no fewer than 1.3 million people now visit Scotch whisky distilleries each year. The international interest in Scotch is phenomenal. Never in my time in the Scotch whisky industry have I heard so many people in so many countries talking about Scotch and displaying a huge thirst for knowledge on the subject. They were not just asking for new expressions, but demanding them, and we, like the rest of the industry, were happy to satisfy their desires with limited editions of old and special 'finished' whiskies. This fascination has translated into strong overseas sales, with 2006 seeing the highest ever volume of exports. A remarkable 294 mlpa of Scotch whisky was sold in overseas markets during that year. This was part of a wider sense of pride and self-confidence in 'Scottishness', with films such as *Rob Roy* and *Braveheart* and the existence of a Scottish Government helping to reinforce a sense of national identity.

It was not just within the confines of Scotland, however, that there was a renaissance in anything with Scottish provenance. The whole world wanted something Scottish, and what was more Scottish than whisky? It is no longer a case of 'Scotch on the rocks', as it had been back in the dark days of the 1980s, but, as *The Scotsman* asserted on 18 February 2007, 'Scotch rocks!' This was music to the industry's ears. You could almost hear the collective sigh of relief. At last the whisky was flowing. As leading Scotch whisky industry analyst Alan Gray declared, 'I'm now looking at three to three-and-a-half per cent overall volume growth of sales during the next five years. I think the big boys are aiming for five per cent growth – it's a huge quantum leap.

'For many years the industry has grappled with the problem of surplus stocks. The situation is now much more in balance and that is why we are seeing the growth in distillery building programmes.

'New distilleries are opening on an unprecedented scale. Diageo's Roseisle at Burghead on the Moray Firth will open in 2009 and produce 12 million litres of alcohol, while William Grant's Ailsa Bay at Girvan is up and running and making 5 million litres of alcohol. The new Port Charlotte Distillery on Islay will make 1.2 million litres of alcohol, and the distillery being created by Duncan Taylor & Co in Huntly will turn out 750,000 litres of alcohol of malt and grain spirit and gin. These will not all be on the market at the same time, but in total they will give an extra 17 million litres of alcohol compared to what we had. Existing distilleries are also increasing output by 13 million litres of alcohol, so in total there will be some 30 million litres of alcohol of extra output.'

This additional spirit will inevitably find its way into many future blends, but a high proportion is likely to be retained as aged single and blended malts. It is not unrealistic to think these whiskies may be used as far in the future as 2050. Age is being demanded by discerning palates in many markets. Consumers may be looking for different expressions, but age will always play a major part in their selections.

What the customer does not realise, however, is that these 'rare beauties', as I call them, are not simply created overnight. They take years. A classic example is the 62-year-old Dalmore, as sold at Pennyhill Park Hotel. Through several decades, successive distillery managers had combined the decreasing contents of a number of casks dating from 1868, 1878, 1926 and 1939, not with any considerations for the future, but simply as 'good housekeeping', to free up warehouse space.

When I took control of these precious casks some 20 years ago, I was aware of their true value, not so much in monetary terms but as a living part of the distillery's heritage. In order to preserve this heritage I had to sensitively select a particularly fine sherry butt and re-rack the contents of the casks into it. However, it took me years to source that cask. In the meantime something had to be done to prevent further evaporation of this priceless spirit. The answer was glass. I therefore transferred it into a single 25-litre French glass bonbonne, until I was able to acquire a perfectly compatible Gonzalez Byass Oloroso

Dave Doig, manager of Fettercairn, and Willie Tait, former manager of Fettercairn and Jura, carrying out the final racking of the Dalmore 62 Years Old.

The Dalmore 62 Years Old became the world's most expensive bottle ever to be sold at an official auction in 2004 when it was knocked down for £25,877.50.

sherry cask. The whisky was filled into it for a further period of maturation, but I still felt it needed more body and charm. Like the finest diamond, it had to be flawless. It deserved nothing less.

In order to achieve this, one of our coopers from Invergordon Distillery created a small and unique cask in which the spirit would spend its final days of maturation. Before the cask could be used, I had it filled with aged Dalmore spirit to prepare the wood, then filled it with Gonzalez Byass Matusalem Oloroso 30 year-old sherry. Eventually, when I felt the time was right, the sherry was emptied from the cask, and our Dalmore spirit was filled into it for its final sleep.

I will never forget that momentous occasion when whisky writer Dave Broom came with me to the warehouse to inspect this liquid gold, just prior to bottling. My heart was in my mouth. I knew the quality was excellent, but the additional months in cask since I had last sampled this spirit could have worked against it. It was make or break time. But one look at Dave Broom's toothy smile told me we had hit the jackpot. It was pure nectar.

Ultimately, just 12 bottles were filled, each of which was given a name with a Dalmore association. One was christened Kildermorie, after Dalmore Distillery's water source, and this was the only bottle to be put up for auction. On Friday 4th December 2002 the Kildermorie was sold at McTear's whisky auction in Glasgow for a staggering £25,877.50, making it the most expensive publicly auctioned single malt in the world at the time. Was it really worth £25,877.50? Every single penny! Just ask anyone who has been privileged enough to taste it. Encouraged by the record-breaking sale not only of our 62-year-old Dalmore but also other whiskies such as the 60-year-old Macallan and 64-year-old Glenfiddich, we wanted to invest in a select range of aged, limited edition whiskies which were rare and desirable, yet more accessible to our customers. Accordingly, we came up with the idea of our 'Rare & Prestige' range. Age was central to the concept, and our aim was to offer comparatively small quantities of a variety of complex and intriguing whiskies, luxuriously packaged to reflect the quality of the spirit.

The range was officially launched in 2007, and included a 1966 Jura, of which only 98 bottles were available. When sampling this I was surprised and pleased to find that the wood notes had not dominated the spirit, which still retained its floral, pine and cinnamon spice characteristics. Its final year in a Matusalem sherry butt added a new dimension of marzipan and chocolate. Indeed, it was a rare beauty, never to be seen again. There were two Dalmore representatives in the 'Rare & Prestige' line up. One was a Dalmore Cabernet Sauvignon 1973. Its sensual elegance surpassed my expectations. The 'king of grapes' Cabernet Sauvignon, drawn from casks at Chateau Haut-Marbuzet in Bordeaux, allowed succulent flavours of brambles and ripe plums to reward the palate. Having bottled it at 45% abv it lingers long on the palate.

The second Dalmore was a 40-year-old, finished in Gonzalez Byass Oloroso sherry butts. This 1966 beauty reminds me of many things, in particular my warm memories of 'Mr Dalmore' himself – ex-distillery manager Drew Sinclair who sadly passed away in 2006 after giving 40 loyal years of service to the distillery. He loved Dalmore and he made sure every visitor left with the same feeling. This special edition is therefore dedicated to him. Like Drew it is a one off – once tasted never to be forgotten. Truly one of mother nature's wonders, it was bottled at a natural strength of 40% abv.

The final whisky in the range was my personal favourite, a 40-year-old Whyte & Mackay blend. The oldest whisky in this spectacular blend was a Dumbarton grain which had been distilled on Christmas Day in 1964. I also wanted to dedicate this blend to somebody special, and who better than our first managing director, John McIlraith. He had served the company for 70 years, and in recognition of that fact I used a 70% malt content, with just 30% grain whiskies. To round it off, this blend was married in Amoroso sherry wood. The complex aromas of Christmas cake and chocolate pudding lingered long in the mouth. Unforgettable.

To my mind, these four expressions epitomise what great whiskies should embrace. All good things come to those who are prepared to wait. They should be sipped, savoured and held long in the mouth. And most importantly, they must be drunk in convivial company, in the same way that privileged person drank his Dalmore 62-year-old in the Pennyhill Park Hotel.

Of course, when distillers create enticing

expressions it is vital that consumers are able to discover them. For more than ten years now, two dedicated publications have kept the public informed and entertained on all matters pertaining to whisky. In the USA John Hansell and Amy Westlake pioneered *The Malt Advocate* specialist beer and whisk(e)y magazine, while in the UK entrepreneur Damian Riley-Smith established *Whisky Magazine*. Not content with simply featuring whisky writing, they went a stage further, aiming to bring the spirit right to the people's lips, by providing venues where producers could showcase their products and offer 'master classes' in whisky appreciation. *Malt Advocate* established a series of 'Whisky Fests' in various US cities, while Damian Riley-Smith founded 'Whisky Live' in London. From this modest beginning, he proceeded to roll out the 'Whisky Live' concept to cities throughout the world, including Tokyo, Toronto, Paris and Cape Town, while Delhi and Beijing are destined to join the line up in the near future.

I cannot emphasise too strongly how much wonderful promotional work these two publications and their respective founders have done for the international whisk(e)y community. However, they have also helped to forge a global network of whisky-related events and festivals of many shapes and sizes, all of which help to foster a greater understanding and awareness of whisk(e)y. Bringing 'the spirit right to the people's lips' requires not just an appropriate venue but also the right glass to maximise discovery and enjoyment. While professional blenders have long benefited from the use of tulip-shaped copitas for maximum sensory evaluation, the public has until recently been deprived of such essential aids,

all too often being served whisky in either a small tumbler or a wine glass.

In order for the whisky to 'open up' and display its essential characteristics it is imperative that the correct type of glass is used. It needs to direct aromas precisely to the nostrils, which a straight-sided tumbler inevitably cannot do. One of the first people to recognise the potential of offering the public a tailored glass similar to those used in a blender's sample room was Raymond Davidson of Glasgow-based Glencairn Crystal.

'I always considered the public were getting a raw deal when it came to nosing and tasting whisky', says Raymond. 'Whenever I ordered a single malt whisky in a bar I asked them to serve it in a Champagne flute glass so I could nose and savour it. As a glassmaker I felt it must be possible to come up with something better and I developed a prototype in 1979. However, because I was busy with other projects this was put to one side and largely forgotten.'

Raymond was almost certainly ahead of his time in drinking malt whisky and thinking of it in this way, but by the time his son, Paul, had entered the business and discovered the prototype in 2000, there was a much greater public appreciation of malt whisky and therefore a significant potential market for the product. Raymond and Paul approached a number of master blenders and asked us to evaluate the glass prior to production. The basic 'tulip' shape with a thick, glass base worked well in terms of aroma delivery, but the bulbous 'pot' of the glass needed to be expanded to hold more liquid. This modification was duly undertaken, and the finished article was launched to great acclaim at

Whisky Live, Glasgow in 2001. To date, more than five million Glencairn glasses have been manufactured, and it has been widely adopted by distilleries and visitor attractions as *the* Scotch whisky glass. Like the two whisky magazines, Glencairn has helped to educate the public about whisky, giving people a tool to aid their exploration into its mysteries. I toast their courageous achievements.

The mysteries of Scotch whisky need to be revealed to the public so that they develop a better understanding and appreciation of our national drink. The same also applies to other spirits and to wine. Although I deliver many whisky lectures around the world each year, without doubt those undertaken for the London-based Wine & Spirit Education Trust give me the greatest satisfaction. The audience comprises students both young and old, who want to further their knowledge and enhance their career prospects.

The Wine & Spirit Education Trust is the largest global provider of education and qualifications in the field of wines and spirits and has been in operation since October 1969. During those four decades its contribution to the drinks and hospitality industry has been incalculable and I admire its achievements enormously. At the present time 21,420 students attend its various courses. Managing director Ian Harris says 'Training is an investment, not a cost.'

Whenever there is a recession I usually find that education is one of the first casualties, and if we want Scotch whisky to remain a world-class industry we must strive to ensure that does not happen in future. 'Knowledge is power' may be an old cliché, but like most clichés it carries an essential

truth. Ian Harris adds: 'My goal with the Trust is to demonstrate to the trade that product knowledge is the best thing for the industry, and there is now also an emphasis on social responsibilities connected with alcohol.'

Although there is a greater awareness of Scotch whisky as one of the world's great drinks, there is also an increasingly vociferous anti-drink lobby at large. But this is nothing new. The drinks industry has had to contend with opposition for a very long time. In 1908 Lord Rosebery declared in a speech that 'The Temperance Party … are engaged in a strife to the death … to the trade.'

Inevitably, today's anti-alcohol movement affects all of us in the Scotch whisky industry, and is therefore a prominent issue for the SWA whose Director of Government and Consumer Affairs Campbell Evans goes so far as to say, 'My biggest concern is alcohol and health concerns and their impact on Scotch whisky. Politicians tackling binge-drinking problems don't discriminate against whisky, even though we are clearly not seen as part of the problem. It's all just seen as alcohol.'

From a distiller's perspective we must be aware of these issues but must not allow them to distract us from our principal objective, which is to produce the finest spirit possible. Traditionally, this fine spirit was produced under the watchful eye of one man, the distillery manager. But just as distillery workforces have shrunk dramatically over the years, so the responsibilities of managers have changed too. The days when each distillery was the domain of one man are now largely gone, and this applies to Whyte & Mackay as well as many of our competitors.

One notable example is Pernod Ricard's

The judges of the International Spirits Challenge presenting Raymond Davidson with a cask in recognition of the production of his millionth Glencairn whisky glass. Standing from left to right: Jim Beveridge (Diageo), Shin Natsuyama (Morrison Bowmore), Colin Scott (Chivas Bros), David Stewart (Wm Grant), Billy Leighton (Irish Distillers), Ian Grieve (Diageo), Raymond Davidson (Glencairn Crystal), Colin Bailey-Wood (Drinks International), Robert Hicks (Allied Distillers), Jim Cryle (Glenlivet Distillery), Seiichi Koshimizu (Suntory), Kneeling, left to right: John Ramsay (Highland Distillers), myself and David Doig (Fettercairn Distillery).

Alan Winchester, who previously managed Aberlour Distillery on Speyside but is now responsible for no fewer than 15 distilleries. Despite his widespread workload, he emphasises that, 'We will never compromise on the quality of our spirit. Our future depends on it. However, if we cannot contain the necessary costs to produce this wonderful spirit in the first instance to allow us to compete, then we may not have a future. Talking to our many visitors and showing them around is something I really miss, but there simply isn't the time. It's all about striking the right balance.'

One man who certainly agrees is Billy Walker, managing director of Benriach

Distillery near Elgin. 'Human contact is sacrosanct', insists Billy, who operates one of the handful of surviving independent distilleries outwith the large whisky groupings. 'Unlike some of our competitors we do not have large budgets to promote our distillery. It's all down to selecting the right opportunities at the right cost which will bring realistic benefits to our business. That includes providing a close working "personal" service.'

The demise of individual distillery managers may represent a sad loss of tradition, but it has been balanced by the welcome emergence of an increasing number of women in the Scotch whisky industry. In my earlier days in the distilling business women were largely confined to typewriters and teapots, but they now enjoy a greater freedom to fulfil their potential at all levels. This is particularly true in the sample room where a number of female blenders are making their inimitable mark. In my early days in the whisky industry this would have been unthinkable; blending was a resolutely male occupation. Nobody could seriously argue that women did not have the ability to do the job just as well as men, but they were simply not given the opportunities to prove themselves. Happily, this is no longer the case, with Diageo's Maureen Robinson and Glenmorangie's Rachel Barrie having made high-profile contributions to the art of whisky blending and to the development of innovative single malt expressions. Most recently, Stephanie Macleod has been appointed master blender by John Dewar & Sons Ltd, succeeding Tom Aitken, who worked with the company for 25 years.

Whether male or female, distillery manager or master blender, we are all dependent on one crucial commodity. Wood. If, as many sources suggest, the cask provides up to 75% of the character of the whisky we ultimately drink, it follows that the coopers who nurture those casks play a vitally important and often overlooked role in the Scotch whisky industry.

The art of coopering dates back at least 5,000 years, and the first biblical reference is made to the use of barrels in the *Book of Kings*. Inevitably, the widespread introduction of aluminium kegs for the storage of beer and the decline of the British fishing industry has led to the decimation of the coopering craft. Even in 1980 there were 1,017 working coopers and apprentices in the UK, but that figure has now fallen to around 200. One of my concerns is that with the dramatic increase in Scotch whisky production there may come a time when demand for casks outstrips supply. The whisky industry must monitor the situation very closely and guard against the use of inappropriate wood which could impact negatively on the reputation of Scotch whisky.

The shortage of casks may also be reflected in a shortage of coopers, bearing in mind it takes a four-year apprenticeship to qualify. Additionally, many companies experience difficulty in recruiting apprentices, as the long hours of hard, physical labour are not attractive to today's young people.

From my perspective, the way a cask transforms spirit from harsh, fiery immaturity into soft, mellow liquid gold makes it one of the most crucial components of my job. It follows that I have a great deal of respect for the amazingly skilled men who tend these casks. This led me to become Deacon of the

The Coopers' Walk, 1st August, 2008. Back row, from left to right: Alan Winchester, Andrew Davidson, John Hutton, Keith Cruickshank, Andrew Scott, Eric Stephen, Fred Laing, Willie Tait, Alistair Longwell, Tom McCulloch, Dave Doig and myself. Front row, left to right: Andrew Bell, Euan Shand, Bob Anderson and Ian Millar.

Incorporation of Coopers of Glasgow some years ago, and my involvement with this organisation has helped increase my understanding and respect for the role of the cooper. One way in which we hopefully helped to raise the profile of the craft was by staging a 'Coopers' Walk' from Speyside Cooperage at Craigellachie, taking in many of the local distilleries. This took place on 1st August 2008 and comprised representatives of Scotland's cooperages and distilling companies, each of whom had been asked to bring with them a single barrel stave. While the walk was in progress, Douglas Taylor of the Speyside Cooperage and members of his staff 'raised' three barrels, using the staves collected from the walkers. In total, there were 103 staves, one to represent each producing distillery in Scotland at the time. These three casks are now on display at the entrance to the Cooperage as a permanent commemoration of the vital role played by coopers in the Scotch whisky industry. Furthermore, plans are afoot to develop a coopering museum in Glasgow which will exhibit tools from cooperages all over the world, helping to ensure the heritage of this ancient trade will never be forgotten.

Heritage is a vitally important aspect of the Scotch whisky industry, but so too is innovation. While most blenders work principally on an organoleptic basis all of them acknowledge the importance of chemical analysis as a backup to their daily work. Maureen Robinson says, 'I think the science is a valuable support. It ensures that we are working within legislative parameters. The rest is really based on nose and taste.' I fully concur with what Maureen says, and I feel it is important to achieve the right balance between instinct, experience and scientific analysis. Geoff Palmer, Professor Emeritus at Heriot Watt University in Edinburgh, states the case for science in distilling.

'Science has been important in telling the industry about the malt quality and spirit yield potential', he says. 'We were able to help a lot with processing efficiency. What science does is allow you to make more informed and conscious decisions. Whisky has never been better than it is today. Control is much better. There's no point in having a brand if you think inconsistency is great. Consistency is now very good.'

This is in no small part due to the pioneering work of the Scotch Whisky Research Institute (SWRI) in Edinburgh, which provides distillers with a better understanding of the highly complex liquid that is whisky. Despite the fact that we have a greater scientific knowledge of whisky production than ever before, the spirit has still not revealed all of its secrets and the SWRI is dedicated to continuing exploration of these unsolved mysteries. It is comforting to know the industry can call upon such able allies as the SWRI and the SWA as we move further into the 21st century and worldwide demand for Scotch whisky is higher than ever. One of the SWA's many roles is to prevent counterfeit whisky being passed off as genuine Scotch, and it is now aided in its battles against counterfeiters by the increased sophistication of scientific analysis at its disposal.

The 'feelgood factor' induced by the desirability of Scotch in so many markets is reflected at the highest level. Both Diageo's CEO and SWA chairman Paul Walsh and his counterpart at Pernod Ricard, Christian Porta, are very positive about the direction being taken by the industry.

'In this first decade of the 21st century Scotch whisky is entering what could prove to be one of the most definitive periods in its long and colourful history', declares Paul Walsh. 'Through the 19th and 20th centuries Scotch whisky established itself internationally as the world's premium spirit, gaining an unrivalled reputation for consistent quality and demonstrating what we would now recognise as truly authentic product values. That international reach and reputation was built by people of great vision and purpose, through the disruption of major global events and despite the volatility and uncertainty of markets where trade was, to say the least, informal. Adjusting to world events, the industry endured a continuing series of boom and bust cycles, the most recent of which remains in the memory of many still working in it today.

'The Scotch whisky industry is in a very optimistic mood. Many of the challenges that faced our predecessors have, sadly, not disappeared from the world: and yet that world is such a different place. Global trade flows more freely than it has done at any time in the past and the communications revolution has transformed our ability to speak directly to each other across distance and time zones.

'The great civilisations of China and India are stepping forward to exert unparalleled influence on the global economy and everywhere we look, there is undoubted opportunity. Scotch whisky is poised, I believe, for a new period of growth and success – possibly the most important yet. To ensure that it happens, we need to remember the vision and purpose of those who laid the foundations for this great venture and we need to invest in our future – in our brands, in our Scottish production base and critically, in our people. For Scotch whisky, the future will be very much what we make it.'

Christian Porta echoes Paul Walsh's sense of optimism. 'There is a demand that's never been seen before, a demand from countries that weren't in the market in the 1970s and 80s. We've got a fantastic product, consumers who are demanding quality. Whisky is a now fashionable, modern product which is stylishly packaged. It is an affordable luxury.'

We should celebrate the fact that single malts and aged blends reflect opulence and sophistication. They have become part of the social scene in many countries around the world, where they epitomise an elegant lifestyle. Although single malts have provided an invaluable boost to the Scotch whisky industry, we should never forget that more than 90% of all Scotch whisky sold is in the form of blends.

One result of Scotch whisky's current enviably high profile is that organisations from outwith the industry have been keen to acquire a stake in it. Most significantly these have included French-based Pernod Ricard and LVMH, Bacardi from the Bahamas, US company Beam Global Spirits & Wine Inc and The Campari Group from Italy. By 2007, Vivian Imerman had successfully revived Whyte & Mackay, and it, too, had become attractive to international interests. Having worked for 14 different bosses and witnessed eight takeovers during my time at Whyte & Mackay, it came as no great surprise when our company was itself acquired on 15th May 2007 by an overseas investor.

Only this one was very different. When I first met him I was immediately bedazzled, not only by his gold bracelets, neck chains, and diamond studded earrings but also by his great, genuine charm. Dr Vijay Mallya is a living legend in India. He is their Maharajah extraordinaire. Ranked by the American business bible *Forbes Magazine* as the 664th richest man in the world, and considered the fifth most influential man in *Drinks Business Magazine*, he heads up United Breweries, the world's third-largest volume supplier, selling 66 million cases in 2007, with revenue totalling $1.65 billion. One of his whisky brands, Bagpiper, sells in excess of 13 million cases per year – making it the world's largest selling whisky. United Breweries controls almost 50% of the domestic beer market in India with its Kingfisher brand. This business spawned Dr Mallya's Kingfisher Airways, which began operating in May 2005. Since then, from two aeroplanes a day flying on the Bangalore-Mumbai route, this has developed into a 82-strong fleet, operating almost 500 flights a day throughout the world. When travelling on his valet-service airline you are taken care of by the most beautiful air hostesses, each one hand-picked by Dr Mallya himself. You are no longer a passenger on his airline, you immediately become one of his 'guests'. Despite the dramatic growth in this business to date, his expansion plans for the future are truly extraordinary.

Speed is not just limited to the air, as in

Vivian Imerman (right) sells Whyte & Mackay for £595m to Dr Vijay Mallya's United Breweries in May 2007.

Vijay Mallya with the newly acquired Whyte & Mackay brands portfolio.

March 2008 Force India hit the F1 Grand Prix circuit with typical Mallya panache. As a former amateur motor racing driver he chairs two rival Indian national motor sports organisations and has been asked by the FIA, the world governing authority of motor racing, to unite them prior to launching India's first F1 Grand Prix in 2010. Everyday life in the fast lane is an opportunity for him; he thrives on success. As Dr Mallya declares, 'You need to be gutsy, you need to have fire in your belly, and there is no point in being scared of the system or of people who are against you. There are plenty of them.'

'I became company chairman at 27', says Mallya, 'and until then I was happy in the security that if I needed anything it would always be there.' This changed on 13th October 1983, when his father suffered a heart attack in Mumbai, aged 59. 'One of the biggest things that dawned on me after he died was that the buck stopped at me', recalls Mallya. 'I had no one to turn to. My industry peers were in their 50s. I stuck out like a sore thumb. I was branded a playboy who only liked fast cars, wine, women and song. This weighed heavily on me.'

By 1996 Mallya had proved everyone wrong by having sold the worldwide Berger Paints Group for a profit of $66 million. Today his holding company United Breweries is worth $5 billion. His Kingfisher business has been built on a lifestyle platform for the last 30 years. He has recognised, particularly in India where 50% of the population is under the age of 25, that, as he puts it, 'Youngsters are aspirational, their needs are constantly evolving. They want better quality and superior experience and they have money to spend. It was extremely clear to me that one day the youngsters would start demanding Scotch whisky. And that was a huge gap in my portfolio because being an Indian company we would never produce Scotch. So there was a compelling reason for me to actively make an acquisition of Scotch whisky assets and production capabilities. On the other side, we actually need Scotch whisky to blend our Indian whiskies.' Whyte & Mackay was therefore the perfect fit. After almost a year of prolonged negotiations, the deal finally went through, with Whyte & Mackay being sold to Dr Mallya for the vast sum of £595 million, giving Vivian Imerman and his brother-in-law Robert Tchenguiz a 197.5% return on their original investment. This was just another successful milestone in Imerman's colourful career.

Dr Mallya is widely known as 'The King of Good Times', and may be seen to epitomise today's world of Scotch whisky. Good times and bad times, for over 40 years now Scotch whisky has been central to my life and that of my family. Since my brother and I entered our father's warehouses over 50 years ago, millions of litres of whisky have been despatched from Scotland's shores. During that time, I have seen the whisky industry go through many dramatic changes – overproduction, distillery closures, rationalisation, amalgamations, the rise of the supermarkets, single malts, whisky festivals, anti-alcohol lobbies and much more. The industry has survived. Once again our pot stills are shining with confidence, our cooperages are in full swing and our glass manufacturers' furnaces are glowing. Our future looks bright. Hopefully we have learned from our past

A toast to the future.

mistakes, but we must never become complacent about the competition provided by other spirits. We must continue to educate and enthuse the world at large on the merits of Scotch whisky. There are still many challenges ahead.

Despite the fierce competition that exists in the marketplace there remains a camaraderie between myself and colleagues from other companies. No other industry enjoys such mutual warmth and respect.

Scotch whisky is indeed a close family. This is borne out particularly after festivals in far-flung parts of the world when everybody meets up in the bar to share jokes, exchange views and take part in good-natured banter. Although we work for different distillers and represent different brands, we all have one common bond. That bond is a true love of Scotch whisky.

There's no other spirit like it, Goodness Nose!

BIBLIOGRAPHY

Apsley, Cherry–Garrard, *The Worst Journey In The World,* London, Pimlico, 2003

Barnard, Alfred, *The Whisky Distilleries of the United Kingdom,* London 1887; new edition with introduction by I A Glen, Newton Abbot, 1969

Bowker, Gordon, *George Orwell,* Great Britain, Little, Brown, 2003

Brander, Michael, *The Original Scotch,* London, Hutchison, 1974

Burns, Edward, *Bad Whisky,* Glasgow, Balvag Books, 1995

Cameron, AC, *The History of Fettercairn,* Parlane, June, 1899

Castledon, Rodney, *British History: A Chronological Directory of Date,* London, Parragon, 1994

Cooper, Derek, *Guide to the Whiskies of Scotland,* London, Pitman, 1978

Craig, HC, *The Scotch Whisky Industry Record,* Dumbarton, Index Publishing Ltd, 1994

Daiches, David, *Scotch Whisky: Its Past and Present,* London, André Deutsch, revised edition, 1978

Dewar, Thomas R, *A Ramble Round the Globe,* London, Chatto & Windus, 1894

Distel, Anne, *Renoir A Sensuous Vision,* London, Thames & Hudson, 1995

Gardiner, Leslie, *The NB – The First Hundred Years,* Edinburgh, Forth Studies, 1985

Gordon, Manual M Gonzalez, *Sherry,* London, Cassell, 1972

Grant, Elizabeth, *Memoirs of a Highland Lady: The Autobiography of Elizabeth Grant of Rothiemurchas 1797–1830,* London, John Murray, 1898

Gray, Alan S, *Scotch Whisky Industry Review 2007,* Edinburgh, Moda Media

Grindal, Richard, *Return to The Glen,* Chevy Chase, Md: Alvin Rosenbaum Projects, 1989

Jackson, Michael, *The World Guide to Whisky,* London, Dorling Kindersley, 1987

Kilby, Kenneth, *The Cooper and His Trade,* London, Unicorn Press, 1933

Lamond, John, *The Whisky Connoisseur's Book of Days,* Edinburgh, 1992

Magee, Malachy, *1000 Years of Irish Whiskey,* Dublin, The O'Brien Press, 1980

Mair, Craig, *History of the Incorporation of Coopers of Glasgow,* Glasgow, Neil Wilson Publishing, 2004

MacDonald, Aeneas, *Whisky,* Edinburgh, Porpoise Press, 1930

Mantle, Jonathan, *The Ballantine Story*, London, James & James, 1991

Markam, Dewey, *The History of the Bordeaux Classification*, Canada, John Wiley & Sons, 1998

Martin, Martin, *A Description of the Western Islands of Scotland*, London, 1716

Moss, Michael S and Hume, John R, *The Making of Scotch Whisky*, Edinburgh, James & James, 1981

Munro, Michael, *The Complete Patter*, Edinburgh, Birlinn Ltd, 2003

Nettleton, J A, *The Manufacture of Spirit*, London, Marcus Ward & Co, 1893

Ordish, George, *The Great Wine Blight*, London, J M Dent & Sons, 1972

Scott, A, *The Wee Scottish Facts Book*, Straightline Publishing, 1994

Sillett, S W, *Illicit Scotch*, Aberdeen, Impulse Books, 1970

Smith, Gavin D, *A to Z of Whisky*, Glasgow, Neil Wilson Publishing, 1997

Smith, Gavin D, *Whisky A Brief History*, Surrey, AAPL Artists, 2007

Smith R I (Ron), *The Railway Spirit – Train Life in Whisky Country*, Keith & Dufftown Railway Association, 2002

Townsend, Brian, *Scotch Missed – The Lost Distilleries of Scotland* (3rd ed), Glasgow, Angels' Share, 2000

Udo, Misako, *The Scottish Whisky Distilleries*, Edinburgh, Distillery Cat Publishing, 2005

Weir, B Ronald, *The History of the Malt Distillers Association of Scotland – The North of Scotland Malt Distillers Association (1874–1926)*, Websters Copying Office, Elgin

Wilson, Anne, *Water of Life – A History of Wine, Distilling and Spirits 500BC/AD2000*, Devon, Prospect Books, 2006

Wilson, Neil, *Scotch and Water*, Moffat, Lochar Publishing, 1985

Wilson, Neil, *The Island Whisky Trail*, Glasgow, Angels' Share, 2003

Wilson, Ross, *Scotch : The Formative Years*, London, Constable, 1970

Youngson, Peter, *Jura, Island of Deer*, Edinburgh, Birlinn Ltd, 2001

INDEX

(Page numbers with footnotes are indicated in *italics*)